# SOUNDS NORTHERN

# SOUNDS NORTHERN
## POPULAR MUSIC, CULTURE AND PLACE IN ENGLAND'S NORTH

EDITED BY EWA MAZIERSKA

SHEFFIELD UK   BRISTOL CT

Published by Equinox Publishing Ltd.

UK: Office 415, The Workstation, 15 Paternoster Row, Sheffield, South Yorkshire, S1 2BX
USA: ISD, 70 Enterprise Drive, Bristol, CT 06010

www.equinoxpub.com

First published 2018

© Ewa Mazierska and contributors 2018

All rights reserved. No part of this publication may be reproduced or transmitted in any form or by any means, electronic or mechanical, including photocopying, recording or any information storage or retrieval system, without prior permission in writing from the publishers.

**British Library Cataloguing-in-Publication Data**
A catalogue record for this book is available from the British Library.

**Library of Congress Cataloging-in-Publication Data**
Names: Mazierska, Ewa.
Title: Sounds northern : popular music, culture and place in England's north / edited by Ewa Mazierska.
Description: Sheffield, UK ; Bristol, CT : Equinox Publishing, 2018. | Includes bibliographical references and index. |
Identifiers: LCCN 2017023208 (print) | LCCN 2017023919 (ebook) | ISBN 9781781796139 (ePDF) | ISBN 9781781795705 (hb) | ISBN 9781781795712 (pb)
Subjects: LCSH: Popular music--England, Northern--History and criticism.
Classification: LCC ML3492 (ebook) | LCC ML3492 .S68 2018 (print) | DDC 781.6409427--dc23
LC record available at https://lccn.loc.gov/2017023208

ISBN: 978 1 78179 570 5 (hardback)
       978 1 78179 571 2 (paperback)

eISBN: 978 1 78179 613 9 (PDF)

Typeset by CA Typesetting Ltd, www.publisherservices.co.uk
Printed and bound in the UK by Lightning Source UK Ltd., Milton Keynes and Lightning Source Inc., La Vergne, TN

# Contents

Introduction
Is It Really Grim Up North? Popular Music in the North of England
*Ewa Mazierska*   1

## Part 1
## Northern Music, Regional Politics and Entrepreneurial Culture

1   Manpool, the Musical: Harmony and Counterpoint on the Lancashire Plain
*Richard Witts*   17

2   Another Uniquely Mancunian Offering? Un-Convention and the Intermediation of Music Culture and Place
*Paul Long and Jez Collins*   37

3   'They Say a Town is Just a Town, Full Stop, But What Do They Know?' Architecture, Urbanism and Pop in Sheffield
*Owen Hatherley*   55

## Part 2
## Pop-Rock Soundscapes, Scenes and Artists

4   'I Thought I Heard That Up North Whistle Blow': African American Blues Performance in the North of England
*Tom Attah*   77

5   The Contrasting Soundscapes of Hull and London in David Bowie's *Ziggy Stardust and the Spiders from Mars*
*Peter Atkinson*   96

6   Hard Floors, Harsh Sounds and the Northern Anti-Festival: Futurama 1979–1983
*Ian Trowell*   112

7   Scrap Value: Sleaford Mods, *Invisible Britain* and the Edge of the North
*Brian Baker*   135

## Part 3
## Hip Hop and Grime

8  From Broken Glass to Ruf Diamonds: Manchester Hip Hop
   *Adam de Paor-Evans*                                                155

9  The Missing Star of MC Tunes
   *Les Gillon and Ewa Mazierska*                                      174

10 Hashtag 0161: Did Bugzy Malone Put Manny on the Map?
   *Kamila Rymajdo*                                                    190

   Index                                                               209

# Introduction

Is It Really Grim Up North? Popular Music in the North of England

Ewa Mazierska

It is a widely acknowledged fact that since the end of the industrial revolution the North of England has lagged behind the South economically, politically and culturally (Smith 1989; Shields 1991: 209–10). The South, even though it covers a smaller geographical area, in the existing narratives is regarded as more prominent. This is understandable. London is the capital of England, the place where the royal family is based and which includes the City, throughout the nineteenth century the world's primary business centre and still a major meeting point for businesses. Such domination of the metropolitan area over the whole country is not atypical; it can also be seen, for example, in Paris. However, in Britain's case the contrasts in the economy and political power appear to be greater than elsewhere in Europe. Today, a large chunk of the North, such as Lancashire, constitutes some of the poorest parts of northern Europe, while London and its surrounding areas are its richest part (Rickman 2015).

The domination of the South over the North is also reflected in what can be described as discursive power: the authority to tell stories about this region. Dave Russell begins his seminal work about the North of England, *Looking North*, by listing various mistakes authors from the South make about the North—what he describes as 'northern grit', arguing that they signal a much larger pattern of unequal relationships between the northern periphery and the metropolitan core, as perpetuated by the national media (Russell 2004: 1–2). Other authors also point to the fact that the North functions as the cultural 'other' of the hegemonic southern Englishness (Smith 1989; Featherstone 2009: 85).

One aspect of the 'master narrative' of the North, on which nineteenth- and twentieth-century literature had a particular influence, reflects the rapid industrialization and then postindustrial decline of this region. This narrative, in which the North can be summarized as 'Povertyshire' and literal and cultural 'Darkshire', can be traced back to authors such as Charles Dickens, Elizabeth Gaskell, D. H. Lawrence and George Orwell. It emphasizes the role of the working class, which created the country's wealth, but was barred from consuming it, because it was appropriated by a few northern (and southern) industrialists (Smith 1989: 11–24). Graham Turner mentions a man from Batley who pictured the North as a fat and generous sow lying on her side while the greedy little piglets (the South) fed off her (Turner 1967: 13). Rob Shields continues this line of investigation, claiming

> Disraeli in *Sybil: The Two Nations*, contrasts life of the rich in London with that of the poor in the mines of Mowbray, Lancashire and in the metal-working district of Woodgate (Birmingham). Mrs Gaskell's (1848) *Mary Barton: A Tale of Manchester Life and North and South* (1976) and (1855) *North and South* (1973) emphasises the regional contrast of the North with the South. Her heroine lives an idyllic life in a South England village 'sleeping in the warm light of the pure sun' until her father abruptly resigns from the church and transports his family to Milton (Manchester) in the pseudonymic county of 'Darkshire' to become private tutor to a mill owner. She wonders 'what in the world do manufacturers want with classics, or literature, or the accomplishments of the gentleman?' (Shields 1991: 209–10).

In contemporary times, popular music frequently responded to such a perception of the North. An iconic example is a techno track aptly titled 'It's Grim Up North', recorded in 1991 by the Justified Ancients of Mu Mu. In it, the singer lists various places in the North, beginning with Bolton and finishing with Bramall, adding the chorus 'It's grim up North'. The video uses a typical iconography of the literary North. It is shot in black and white, in what looks like a disused factory or warehouse and on a nondescript road leading towards the North, as the sign pronounces, giving it a spooky feel, which is further accentuated by the lighting and camera positions in the style of German Expressionism. In this song and video the North is thus presented as an object of dark tourism (Lennon and Foley 2010). Its attractiveness lies in rejecting the features that normally appeal to tourists and magnify those that put them off: darkness, danger, desolation, poverty, decay. When re-watching this video for the purpose of writing this introduction I thought about a fragment from *24 Hour Party People* (2002) by Michael Winterbottom, in which Tony Wilson, while walking in a building that is to become his music club, The Haçienda, muses about the way buildings change people, including the way they think. He mentions Renaissance Florence, to which his interlocutor replies 'This is not Renaissance Florence, this is Dark Ages Manchester. It's like a fucking abattoir.' Comparing these two fragments points to the skills with which the northerners were able to extract cultural and even monetary capital from their 'abattoirs'. This point is raised by Ian Trowell in the chapter included in this collection, in which he examines Leeds Festival Futurama in part as an experience in dark tourism.

The domination of the South, which bears similarities to colonial supremacy (Featherstone 2009: 89–92), produced two types of reaction. One was a desire to catch up with the centre or even exceed it on its terms. The symbol of this approach is The Beatles' relocation to London to take advantage of the technological, cultural and economic opportunities offered by the capital. In this context it is worth mentioning that prior to The Beatles, as Ian Inglis argues, the

> popular music industry [in England] was based exclusively and inevitably in London; it was utterly implausible to seek to pursue a musical career from outside the capital. Indeed, one of the reasons why the Decca record label rejected The Beatles in 1962 was that it opted instead for the safety and convenience of signing the London-based Brian Poole and the Tremeloes (Inglis 2010: 13).

The second reaction to London's dominance is defiance. As Tony Wilson, one of the most famous Northerners, used to say, 'We do things differently here'. This attitude is of particular importance in this collection, because when music is concerned, doing things differently does not mean doing them worse than in the metropolitan centre. There are an unprecedented number of musicians from the North of England who gained national and international recognition, with The Beatles from Liverpool still holding the record in this respect. Also bands originating in this region, such as Herman's Hermits, the Animals, Joy Division, New Order, Pulp, Oasis and Arctic Monkeys are amongst the most revered and imitated British artists nationally and internationally. If we also consider popular music in a wider sense, then we should also include here singer and actress Gracie Fields, a native of Rochdale, who 'by 1931 was the highest-paid performer of her time, developing a career of unprecedented mobility that exploited new developments in technology, performance venues and marketing of mass entertainment' (Featherstone 2009: 92–93). Featherstone also observes, confirming the view that musicians in the North can do things their own way and well, that Fields' success depended upon 'her assertion, on stage and off, of the continuity of her fame with her humble origins. Paradoxically, she became England's greatest modern star by appearing to stay provincial and ordinary' (93). The North of England also gave rise to important movements and styles, such as Merseybeat, post-punk and Madchester. As Dave Russell notes, 'Music has provided the region with some of its most potent cultural, symbolic and psychic capital and earned some of the most positive and least grudgingly given external respect' (Russell 2004: 208).

We can list a number of reasons for this success. One of them is, paradoxically, the fact that after the end of the industrial revolution the North economically lagged behind the South, as demonstrated by the unemployment rates there being consistently higher than in the South. For many young northerners music constituted a refuge from the bleakness of their everyday struggles, marked by unemployment or poorly paid and boring work, as Sara Cohen aptly demonstrates in her study of Liverpool in the 1980s (Cohen 1991: 19). In addition, postindustrial spaces, such as abandoned factories and warehouses, proved ideal for the production and consumption of music. It is not an accident that one of the record labels most associated with northern pop-rock was named Factory. In many northern towns, such as Hebden Bridge, musicians could rent studio space for very low prices, eventually transforming whole quarters of towns into areas of artistic creativity and, in due course, music heritage. Music in the North has played a major role in transforming its economy, society and cultural make-up. In the North of England people have not only produced great music and enjoyed it, but also lived in 'musical cities'. As Richard Witts observes in this collection, since 2015 Liverpool has been named a 'City of Music' according to UNESCO, and Manchester the 'Music Capital of Britain' according to a survey jointly commissioned by Trinity Mirror and Ticketmaster. But not only Manchester and Liverpool, but also many smaller cities and towns, such as Sheffield and Hull, have used their musical heritage as a means to attract tourists and business people to visit and invest in various redevelopment schemes. Following the process of decline and de-industrialization, the North had to reinvent itself and find a new identity. Music, which requires relatively little monetary investment, provided a perfect vehicle for such reinvention and regeneration. Of course, this would be impossible without people devoting their energy and intellect to such projects. The most famous of them is Tony Wilson, the music producer and impresario, whose label Factory Records and club Haçienda rendered Manchester in the 1980s and 1990s the coolest city in the UK.

Another factor contributing to the high reputation of music from the North has to do with its perception as 'authentic'. George Orwell, in a widely quoted fragment from *The Road to Wigan Pier*, states that

> there exists in England a curious cult of Northernness, a sort of Northern snobbishness. A Yorkshireman in the South will always take care to let you know that he regards you as an inferior. If you

ask why, he will explain that it is only in the North that life is 'real life', that the industrial work done in the North is the only 'real' work, that the North is inhabited by 'real' people, the South merely by rentiers and their parasites. The Northerner has 'grit', he is grim, 'dour', plucky, warm-hearted and democratic; the Southerner is snobbish, effeminate and lazy—that at any rate is the theory (Orwell 1959: 110–11).

There is a special link between the value of music and authenticity. In music, more than in other areas of culture, authenticity is linked to poverty. Music created by artists living in impoverished areas and being working class comes across as more 'authentic' than that produced by those who are affluent or acquiesce to commercial pressures (Wiseman-Trowse 2008: 48). The myth of a musician-genius who lived and died poor can be traced back to the times of Mozart, but is still easier to activate in times and places where poverty is a predicament of a large part of the population, and the English North, in common with the American South, fits this bill well.

Inevitably, some authors are quick to point out that it ultimately does not matter whether a specific artist from the North of England is objectively working class and authentic due to that, because being northern automatically bestows on him or her such an honour. Irene Morra observes:

> John Lennon is rarely subjected to the accusations of inauthentic posturing that have plagued his other middle-class peers. Jarvis Cocker may have grown up in a former manor house in Sheffield, but when he moved to London, his Northern accent apparently enabled him the 'liberation' of 'discovering that he was working class, after all' (Morra 2014: 98).

The previously quoted song 'It's Grim Up North' can also be regarded as an ironic commentary on the idea that the North is sentenced to be a 'grimland', no matter how its history develops, especially given that it finishes with the sentence 'The North Will Rise Again'.

On one hand, music in the North of England is appreciated for its 'placeness'; on the other hand it is renowned for its openness to foreign influences. Its cosmopolitan character in part results from its history and in part from its desire to resist the pressure to conform to the values and fashions coming from the South, as previously mentioned. In relation to Manchester, Dave Haslam maintains:

> Manchester is a hybrid town, born all in a rush one hundred and fifty years ago, when those looking for work in the fast-growing factories, workshops, warehouses and foundries included large

numbers of Catholic Irish, as well as Scots, and German and East European Jews. These migrations have been replicated since, with incomers from the Caribbean in the 1950s and from the Asian subcontinent in the 1970s (Haslam 1999: xi).

One facet of this northern cosmopolitanism concerns foreigners bringing to the North something that they learnt at home and that the locals appropriated and reworked, as examined in the chapter by Tom Attah in this volume about blues in the North of England in the 1950s and 1960s. Another concerns northern artists seeking recognition abroad, bypassing London. The history of Factory, whose bands were often more appreciated on continental Europe than in the United Kingdom (Nice 2011: 91–114), demonstrates this point well.

The strength of music in the North concerns not only its production, but also appreciation and engagement by the local populations. Russell begins his chapter on 'Singing the North' with a quotation from Edward Elgar who in 1903 observed that:

> It is rather a shock to find Brahms' part-songs appreciated among the daily fare of a district apparently unknown to the sleepy London press; people who talk of the spread of music in England and the increasing love of it rarely seem to know where the growth of the art is rarely strong and properly fostered. Someday the press will awake to the fact, already known abroad and to some few of us, that the living centre of music in Great Britain is not London, but somewhere further north (Russell 2004: 208).

My own experience confirms this opinion. When in the late 1990s I hunted for a place to live in Glossop, a small market town in Derbyshire, every house I visited had a musical instrument, sometimes several of them, often taking up most of the space in the living room. However, these successes of northern performers, music producers and media personalities should not blind us to the fact that these were usually partial successes, when cultural capital generated by a specific initiative did not match its monetary capital. The troubled career of Tony Wilson best illustrates this problem. Although Wilson is widely seen as a godfather of Manchester's regeneration through music, his main enterprises, the Factory and The Haçienda, were commercial failures and even spectacular examples of economic incompetence (Nice 2011: 465–89). Moreover, the successes of northerners involved in music work took place against a background of the dominance of London, reflected in the fact that many northern artists relocated there in the course of their careers, regarding it as an opportunity to get better access to national and global markets, and gain fame and wealth. The trajectory of the Animals, The Beatles and Oasis perfectly illustrates this trend. Moreover, when the northern music businesses faced bankruptcy, their owners typically turned to their London competitors for help. Again, the history of Factory Records well illustrates this rule (Nice 2011: 473).

The ambition of this collection is to examine music *in* the North of England and *of* the North, namely as a reflection of other aspects of northern culture, economy and politics. Rather than focusing on its greatest stars and hallmarks, it seeks to reveal its less known facets. This results from the authors' recognition that there is a tendency to reduce music of the North to a limited number of artists, movements and places, such as The Beatles, Joy Division, Tony Wilson and The Haçienda. Such reduction, reflected in a high number of publications devoted to them, not only distorts the history of this music, but also, as Paul Long and Jez Collins observe in their chapter, presents a particular burden for contemporary creativity in the North. Nostalgia for heroic moments and iconic artists undermines the achievements of the allegedly lesser historical figures and the confidence of those who are about to start their career. Moreover, rather than treating the North as a homogenous whole, the idea behind this collection is to unpack the North by considering musics produced and consumed in specific places during specific periods. Unsurprisingly, among them Manchester receives the most attention, but other towns, such as Liverpool, Sheffield, Hull, Leeds, York or even Chorley are also discussed. In most chapters these northern locations are considered in relation to the South of England. The question posed explicitly or implicitly is whether northern popular music withstands the southern pressure. The authors also consider the internal dynamics of the North, for example the competition and collaboration between particular cities, such as Manchester and Liverpool, and Sheffield and Leeds. They also try to locate northern music and music business in terms of wider, European or global trends. By taking such an approach, *Sounds Northern* fills a significant gap in the research. Although music in the North is covered in numerous publications, both academic and journalistic, the prevailing approach is to examine music in a particular city, such as Manchester (Haslam 1999; Middles 2002, 2009; Nice 2011), Liverpool (Cohen 1991; Leonard and Strachan 2010) or Sheffield (Lilleker 2005), focusing on its uniqueness, rather than looking at it more holistically. Another purpose is to consider northern music from the perspective of policies affecting music production and consumption, careers of local stars, music festivals and reflection of local architecture. Each chapter is based on original research, usually combining ethnological study of music with studies of urbanism, tourism and political economy.

The first part of the book, 'Northern Music, Regional Politics and Entrepreneurial Culture', looks at the relationship between national and regional policies and the effect of the activities of music entrepreneurs on the state of the music industry and the successes of specific musicians. It begins with a chapter by Richard Witts, entitled 'Manpool, the Musical: Harmony and Counterpoint on the Lancashire Plain'. By using the term 'Manpool' Witts points to the similarity and cooperation of the two northern cities, Manchester and Liverpool, which are typically seen as rivals, including in terms of popular music. He draws attention to their histories, of which a significant part was building connections between them. Then he considers the careers of musical figures associated with one city, but who also played a vital, but forgotten, part in the life of the other: the boss of Factory Records Tony Wilson, Roger Eagle, associated with the Liverpool post-punk club Eric's, and the Griffiths brothers of the band Real People. Witts argues that while central governments tended to render the cities as adversaries, competing with each other for scarce resources, at the grassroots level cooperation was seen as the best way for their development and survival. Witts' chapter also advocates for combining ethnographic research with using a bird's-eye view in the study of popular music. This is because ethnography by itself, with its preoccupation with, for example, one scene, fails to acknowledge connections between different music phenomena or locate them correctly in a wider context. This collection, by contrast, argues that such context is needed to understand music in the North.

The second chapter by Paul Long and Jez Collins, 'Another Uniquely Mancunian Offering? Un-Convention and the Intermediation of Music Culture and Place', follows in the footsteps of Witts' investigation, by considering a local event, Un-convention, in a wider, national and international context. Established in 2007 in Manchester, it was conceived by its founder, Jeff Thompson, as an informal sideline to 'In the City', an annual industry event founded by Tony Wilson and described as 'the biggest music gathering of its kind in Britain'. By contrast, Un-convention was meant to be small and Manchester-centred. Its main purpose was to overcome the problem of fragmentation of the local music industry, compounded by the London-centric nature of the music business. Un-convention has been informed by the idea of collaboration and mutual self-help. Regular activities at Un-convention events included discussion panels and performances and it has extended its practices to events in other British cities and networks across the globe. It has organized events in places such as Uganda, Columbia and Venezuela, locations at the periphery of the world's music business. This fact points to a similar logic that informed much of Wilson's activities: rather than looking South, it tried to transcend the binary structure of the British music industry by becoming more international. Drawing on interviews, organizational analysis and reflexive participation Long and Collins explore how the practices of Un-convention are anchored in northern English identity, especially its self-deprecating and homely DIY ethos and penchant for informal and 'open space' practice, as captured by the very term 'Un-convention'. The value of Long and Collins' investigation also lies in examining the role of 'intermediaries' in creating vibrant music scenes and industries.

'They Say a Town is Just a Town, Full Stop, But What Do They Know? Architecture, Urbanism and Pop in Sheffield' by Owen Hatherley responds to Witts' call to combine micro- with macro-research. Hatherley links Sheffield's musical 'golden age', which lasted between the late 1970s and the early 90s, with the intensity of the postwar transformation of its architecture and urban design. He maintains that this Sheffield competes only with London, Glasgow and Birmingham for the intensity of its transformation in the immediate postwar decades. Under an effective Labour one-party state, the city embarked on a massive programme of rebuilding. Sheffield's housing schemes were produced by the city architect's department, and placed quite deliberately on the city's hillside peaks, giving the impression of a 'socialist citadel', independent and hostile to the capital—the 'socialist Republic of South Yorkshire', as it was only half-jokingly described. Hatherley argues that this architectural renaissance is reflected in the size, content and quality of pop-rock music produced in Sheffield. Various Sheffield bands deliberately evoked, celebrated and critiqued the city's architecture. Among them, the most famous is Pulp, and Hatherley focuses on their productions as a reflection of living and loving Sheffield. Hatherley, like Long and Collins, emphasizes the fact that in the North 'things are done differently' than in the South, largely because they are done in a communal spirit and with the conviction that profit should not be treated as the highest value of labour.

The second part of the collection is devoted to distinct, yet relatively little known soundscapes, scenes and artists, developed in the North of England and their relations to a wider world. The first chapter by Tom Attah, 'I Thought I Heard That up North Whistle Blow: African American Blues Performance in the North of England', examines the development of blues music in the North from the mid-1950s till the end of the 1960s. Attah notes that following tours by American musicians such as Josh White and Big Bill Broonzy, seminal artists such as Muddy Waters, Sonny Terry, Brownie McGhee and the Reverend Gary Davis brought their performances to Manchester, Sheffield, Leeds, Bradford and Newcastle at a time of racial and cultural upheaval. Attah emphasizes the demographic and cultural links between the rural and industrial poor of the United States who made contact with the disenfranchised youth of industrial northern Britain during this transformational period in British culture. Through original interviews with north of England performers still working in the field as well as reference to contemporary primary sources, he indicates how the blues was developed from a music of the African-American rural poor to a style that emphasized personal authenticity, providing a source of belonging and creativity across racial barriers in circumstances geographically removed from the United States.

The next scene explored in this part is in Hull. In his chapter 'The Contrasting Soundscapes of Hull and London in David Bowie's *Ziggy Stardust and the Spiders from Mars*', Peter Atkinson argues that the success of Ziggy Stardust rests on the perception of authenticity of the supporting musicians in the project, who came from Hull, a modest port town in North-East England. Examining this case study of a collaboration between artists from the South and the North (where the southerner has a dominant position) allows Atkinson to compare the soundscapes of Hull and London. He maintains that Bowie and his support cast were subject to different cultural settings, and thus influenced by different soundscapes. Atkinson provides an assessment of how the involvement of these Hull musicians in the Bowie project has impacted upon the city's historical music culture, and on heritage issues and cultural production in that town. He argues that the Hull musicians gave Bowie an authentic, urban rock sound which simultaneously addressed a young audience who felt excluded from the more middle-class music of the sixties counter-culture, and yet challenged their perceptions of gender and sexuality, because of his performance. He concludes by noting that the milieu may be changed by events in June 2016 following the EU Referendum as this issue impacts on the North/South divide and possible plans for investment in the region.

Ian Trowell in 'Hard Floors, Harsh Sounds and the Northern Anti-Festival: Futurama 1979–1983' discusses the post-punk festival in Leeds, which took place at the disintegrating Leeds Queens Hall. As a musical statement Futurama gathered the post-punk micro-scenes that were congealing in many cities in the North and beyond. These scenes built upon a vaguely coherent common strand of moving beyond punk, by adding a sense of industrial angst and futuristic ambiguity. It was a festival without an equal at the time, as large festivals emerging from the hippie and rock scenes had settled with events like Glastonbury and Reading and catered for audiences within those scenes. In turn, Futurama eschewed a vision of hope and celebration, settling for anxiety and claustrophobia, the brittle and spittle of deviant punk in grim cities. Futurama would take place over a weekend in September, with punters allowed simply to sleep on the dirty, concrete floor between each day. Trowell provides the first academic documentation of the five Futurama festivals (and a small number of spin-off events) through a multiple set of interpretations. In particular, he documents the post-punk vernacular as a regional phenomenon and considers Leeds as a lacuna of identity compared to Sheffield, Manchester and Liverpool. He draws attention to the violent, intimidating and terrorising nature of the fabric of life around Leeds at the time: a city crippled by the serial killer Peter Sutcliffe, a violent football culture and a community divided by racial antagonism, fear and hatred.

While in the majority of studies of the North, the South is treated as the norm, hence the yard stick with which the North should be measured, Simon Featherstone suggests that it should be the other way round, namely the North should be regarded as a norm, on account of its epitomising trends which had spread nationally and globally (Featherstone 2009: 89). Such a line of thinking informs the approach taken by Brian Baker in the last chapter in this part, entitled 'Scrap Value: Sleaford Mods, *Invisible Britain* and the Edge of the North'. The contemporary punk/hip-hop band Sleaford Mods, which is its subject, is not from the (proper) North, but at best (or worst) from its edge, namely the Midlands. However, Baker argues that the way the band self-represents itself and is represented in the film *Invisible Britain* (2015), which documents its tour of the UK, brings to mind the dominant narrative of the North as the neglected, broken-down and boarded-up parts of the country that British politicians have tried to forget for many decades, yet unsuccessfully, as the results of the Brexit referendum demonstrated. Rather than distance themselves from such an environment, Sleaford Mods, perhaps in search of authenticity, come across as spokespersons of the 'edgelands' and, by the same token, 'honorary northerners'. Baker's chapter thus, more than any other in this collection, points to the fact that the English North is an imagined community. In particular, Sleaford Mods take issue with white, working-class masculinity, a category that mainstream politicians from the right and the left and the British liberal, (ethnic, religious, sexual etc.) minorities-obsessed media try to forget, yet which stubbornly returns, complicating political plans and dominant narratives of British society and culture.

The third and last part of the collection is devoted specifically to the exploration of northern hip hop and grime. The point of departure of Adam de Paor-Evans' chapter, 'From Broken Glass to Ruf Diamonds: Manchester Hip Hop', is an observation that hip hop is marginalized in discussions about Manchester's 'golden age' of music during the 1980s and 1990s. Yet this phenomenon deserves closer examination because in this period Mancunian hip hop rapidly developed, establishing itself as an organic counter-narrative to two cultural positions—firstly the very local yet nationally explosive position of The Haçienda and Madchester and secondly the role of hip hop in London which was growing an international presence with professionalism. De Paor-Evans investigates the key developments in hip hop in Manchester, starting in 1984 with Broken Glass, a Mancunian breakdancing crew, and concluding with Ruf Beats and the Jeep Beat Collective in 1994. His exploration is informed by three questions: to what extent did the evolution of Mancunian hip hop complement or oppose the cultural dynamics of The Haçienda, Madchester and rave subculture? What was the relationship between hip hop in Manchester and London in terms of cultural representation, identity and value; and finally, is there a particular 'honesty' in Mancunian hip hop that differentiates it from the gravity of London hip hop and the spectacle of Madchester? By the same token de Paor-Evans critiques two interrelated (meta)narratives about the North of England and its music: that the North is a colonial periphery of the UK and its music imbued with authenticity. In common with other authors in the collection, de Paor-Evans also discusses the divisions within music in the North.

While de Paor-Evans looks at the hip hop scene, Les Gillon and myself focus on the career of one particular rapper from Manchester: MC Tunes. MC Tunes, born Nicholas William Dennis Hodgson, achieved commercial and artistic success while fronting a British electronic music group, 808 State. He played a significant role in the Madchester music scene during the 1980s and 1990s, yet failed to achieve global success or even sustain national fame, as demonstrated by the fact that his second record, to be released by ZTT Records in the early 1990s, was rejected by the label and only released in 2015 in a limited edition format. This chapter, drawing on interviews with MC Tunes, conducted by the authors, a documentary by Howard Walmsley and the existing research on music industry in Manchester during the period of Madchester and beyond, tries to account for the main factors in MC Tunes' meteoric fame and its decline, as conveyed in its title, 'The Missing Star of MC Tunes'. One is the weakness of the music industry in the North, also demonstrated by Tony Wilson's failure to sustain his project of creating a commercially successful popular music industry in Manchester. The second is the specificity of the genres with which MC Tunes was identified, namely rap. Finally we draw attention to personal factors in MC Tunes' decline, most importantly his rock and roll lifestyle.

The chapter about MC Tunes examines the reasons for the musician's failure (somewhat reflecting the fact that the North is connected with failure). By contrast, the chapter that follows focuses on the reasons for one artist's success. Its author, Kamila Rymajdo, transports us from the history of popular music in the North to its present day, analysing the career trajectory of Manchester rapper Bugzy Malone, the highest-charting grime artist to date. Rymajdo observes that, uncharacteristically for grime, Bugzy, not being a member of a crew, refuses to celebrate any sense of community. This poses a question about the ramifications of such isolation within a small urban scene such as Manchester's. Moreover, the rapper attributes Manchester's rise to prominence on the UK urban scene solely to himself, declaring that he 'put Manny on the map' (which provides the title of Rymajdo's chapter). He appears alone on the cover of his EP with his picture surrounded by a large border of negative space, suggesting that aside from him there is nothing of interest in the city. Rymajdo looks at Bugzy's success against the background of the history of Manchester and grime, as well as the ideology of neoliberalism which the musician wholeheartedly adopted.

Many of the chapters in this collection point to a paradox. Northernness constitutes a specific cultural capital for those working in the music business, but it signifies poverty or at least indifference towards money and what can be described as a 'sound business plan'. However, this means that if the North ever becomes affluent and business-oriented, it will lose its attraction.

## References

Cohen, Sara. 1991. *Rock Culture in Liverpool: Popular Music in the Making*. Oxford: Oxford University Press.
Featherstone, Simon. 2009. *Englishness: Twentieth-Century Popular Culture and the Forming of English Identity*. Edinburgh: Edinburgh University Press.
Haslam, Dave. 1999. *Manchester England: The Story of the Pop Cult City*. London: Fourth Estate.
Inglis, Ian. 2010. 'Historical Approaches to Merseybeat: Delivery, Affinity and Diversity'. In *The Beat Goes On: Liverpool, Popular Music and the Changing City*, ed. Marion Leonard and Robert Strachan, 11–27. Liverpool: Liverpool University Press.
Lennon, John, and Malcolm Foley. 2010. *Dark Tourism*. Andover, Hampshire: Cengage Learning.
Leonard, Marion, and Robert Strachan, eds. 2010. *The Beat Goes On: Liverpool, Popular Music and the Changing City*. Liverpool: Liverpool University Press.
Lilleker, Martin. 2005. *Beats Working for a Living: The Story of Popular Music in Sheffield 1973–1984*. Sheffield: Juma.
Middles, Mick. 2002. *From Joy Division to New Order: The True Story of Anthony H Wilson and Factory Records*. London: Virgin Books.
—2009. *Factory: The Story of the Record Label*. London: Virgin.
Morra, Irene. 2014. *Britishness, Popular Music, and National Identity: The Making of Modern Britain*. London: Routledge.
Nice, James. 2011. *Shadowplayers: The Rise and Fall of Factory Records*. London: Aurum.
Orwell, George. 1959. *The Road to Wigan Pier*. London: Secker & Warburg.
Rickman, Dina. 2015. 'Are 9 of the Poorest Regions in Northern Europe Really in the UK?' https://tinyurl.com/eJ0axHCqmx (accessed 16 November 2015).

Russell, Dave. 2004. *Looking North: Northern England and the National Imagination*. Manchester: Manchester University Press.
Shields, Rob. 1991. *Places on the Margin: Alternative Geographies of Modernity*. London: Routledge.
Smith, David. 1989. *North and South: Britain's Economic, Social and Political Divide*. London: Penguin.
Turner, Graham. 1967. *The North Country*. London: Eyre & Spottiswoode.
Wiseman-Trowse, Nathan. 2008. *Performing Class in British Popular Music*. Basingstoke: Palgrave Macmillan.

# Part 1
Northern Music, Regional Politics and Entrepreneurial Culture

# 1 Manpool, the Musical: Harmony and Counterpoint on the Lancashire Plain

## Richard Witts

Liverpool is officially a 'City of Music'. This UNESCO sobriquet was awarded in 2015 and it is alleged to bestow global status, though no funding comes with it.[1] There are nine such Cities of Music around the world as part of a UNESCO 'Creative Cities Network' of 116 members, each of which petitioned a committee in order to obtain this rather nebulous cachet (UNESCO 2016). Around the same time, and in contrast, Liverpool's neighbour Manchester was titled the 'Music Capital of Britain'. A survey jointly commissioned by Ticketmaster and the newspaper publisher Trinity Mirror produced this laurel (*Manchester Evening News* 2014). The two competing and troublesome titles contribute to a common view that the dual cities, thirty-five miles apart, are chronic economic and cultural adversaries, competing for grants, kudos and football cups.

In 2010 a BBC1 television programme titled *A Tale of Two Rival Cities* claimed that the feud was 'personified by sport and music' but that it had begun a century earlier 'with hard-headed financial calculations' (BBC 2010). In 2012 an online poll asked voters which music scene was better, 'The Haçienda or the Cavern? Morrissey or Macca?', resulting in a slim win of 50.96% for Manchester against Liverpool's 49.04% (*The Tab* 2012). For the record, both Liverpool's Cavern club and Manchester's Haçienda were long defunct, but their names had begun to represent typifying scenes of mythological dimensions. As for 'Macca' (Paul McCartney of The Beatles), the American magazine *City Journal* published '21 reasons why Liverpool outclasses Manchester', in which five of those claims featured The Beatles (*City Journal* 2015). The notion of

---

1. When in February 2016 a local MP asked the national government's Culture Secretary what support the government would give Liverpool for this accolade, the minister merely listed the Arts Council and Lottery grants the city had received that year.

Scouse chalk and 'Manc' cheese is now so legitimized in media discourse that it deserves scrutiny.

## The South North-West

The land that made up Lancashire, between the rivers Ribble to the north and Mersey to the south, was considered by the Domesday commissioners in 1086 to be a unified tract (Jewell 1994: 17). The two locales that would become Manchester and Liverpool formed the southern base of the Duchy of Lancaster's province from 1265, providing along the Mersey[2] a transport infrastructure for the region. Up to the seventeenth century the chief port of the area had been Chester, but the silting up of its river allowed Liverpool to take charge. By adding an innovatory wet dock system in the early eighteenth century, Liverpool merchants boosted an infrastructure for the economic development of the region, notably the export of Lancashire coal and Cheshire salt together with the import of raw cotton for the increasingly systematic production of cotton goods (Belchem 2006: 11). Replacing fabric workshops with mills and factories, the county's landscape 'changed … from green to black' (Alderson 1968: 11). The population of the county tripled from around 230,000 in 1700 to 700,000 by 1800.

In his visit to the region in 1727 the diarist Daniel Defoe hailed Liverpool as 'one of the wonders of Britain … a large, handsome, well built and encreasing or thriving town'. In turn he described pubescent Manchester as 'the greatest meer village … I cannot doubt but this encreasing town will, some time or other, obtain some better face of government, and be incorporated' (Defoe 1986). By 1795, chronicler John Aiken reported that Manchester had become 'the heart of this vast system' of mass production, 'the circulating branches of which spread all around it'. To Aiken, Manchester was a city of manufacture ('Cottonopolis') while Liverpool was its port, complementing it as a city of commerce (Aiken 1968: 3). As the cities expanded, thought was given to improving transport links between them. The history of improved access may be summarized as follows:

1. 1726: Turnpike road route operational between the conurbations.
2. 1772: The extension of the Bridgewater Canal to the Mersey, which heralds the 'canal boom'.
3. 1829: The Rainhill Locomotive Trials, leading in 1830 to the Liverpool–Manchester Railway, the world's first passenger train service.

---

2. The Mersey river runs from the edge of the Peak District near Stockport, forming a southern flank to Manchester, before entering the Irish Sea north-west of Liverpool.

4. 1897: Manchester Ship Canal opens.
5. 1914: Liverpool–Manchester Monorail (not realized).[3]
6. 1934: East Lancs Road, Britain's first inter-city arterial road (dual carriageway).
7. 1976: M62 motorway.

It is the Manchester Ship Canal at the end of the nineteenth century that raises the most controversy in any history of relations between the two cities. Some argue that the canal allowed goods ships to sail directly from the Mersey estuary to the Salford–Manchester docks and bypass the monopolistic Liverpool docking charges; it became the very source of the cities' commercial antagonism alluded to earlier in the BBC film. On the other hand, Manchester merchants were already avoiding Liverpool by using the east coast ports of Hull and Goole for some categories of freight; the ship canal circumvented the associated overland costs. By this time Liverpool had anyway reached its tonnage capability in handling 11,000 ships annually while it had massively developed its passenger traffic of emigrants to the Americas (Littlefield 2009: 15–16). The ambivalent economics of the ship canal was in any case off-set by the incremental improvements in road and rail access: the general direction of policy lay in co-operation and mutuality. How then is there a common assumption that the cultural story of the cities is one of autonomy and singularity, of friction and factionalism? To summarize my argument: rivalry principally exists between the conurbations at the administrative level and it was imposed relatively recently by central government dealing with the postwar de-industrialization and economic decline of the North-West region. A narrative of cultural distinction has been constructed to serve the current disposition of rival civic governance, competing directly in a climate of entrepreneurism for grants and guarantees. The remainder of this chapter attempts to explain this situation and its impact on two academic areas that may be unsuspectingly complicit in establishing the dominance of that narrative: popular music studies and ethnography.

**Liverpool *versus* Manchester**

To deal first with this hapless emphasis on division, it is well explained by C. B. Phillips and J. W. Swift in their long history of the region:

> Between 1920 and the late 1970s ... the decline of cotton, coal and, later, heavy engineering diluted the common vocabularies and shared experiences that had united the most populous parts of the

3. See http://discovery.nationalarchives.gov.uk/details/r/C2580564

region ... By the 1920s [Liverpool and Manchester] each had all the trappings of a regional capital ... The economic roles were, in many ways, complementary but their regional ambitions ... increasingly split the region between east and west (Phillips and Swift 1994: 302–303).

While postwar manufacturing was outstripped by the service industries—impacting on Manchester's vast manufacturing and engineering quarter Trafford Park—various attempts to save Liverpool dock life failed when the cargo vessels became too large for Victorian wharves (Phillips and Swift blame in part 'the dockers' resistance to change'), and both cities faced imperilling falls in population; Liverpool's 1938 tally of 880,000 was halved to 440,000 by 2001 (Munck 2003: 54). Local government appealed to central government to support a number of visionary schemes, a peak reached in 1969 when Manchester's Planning Officer proposed 'a giant dispersed city extending from the Pennines to the sea through Manchester and Liverpool', later labelled the 'Mersey Belt' (Phillips and Swift 1994: 339). Instead, the Labour government of the time, caught up in calls for total devolution in Scotland and Wales, had proposed a radical modernization of England's regional and constituency borders. The Redcliffe-Maud Commission's report of 1969 (Cmnd.4040) proposed a new system of unitary authorities to include a small number of grand metropolitan counties. But the recommendations were taken up for implementation by Edward Heath's Conservative government (1970–74), fiddled about with under the rubric of localism or subsidiarity and introduced in 1974 just as another Labour government took over[4] (Heath 1998: 447). Up to then the two cities had together formed the southern bed of Lancashire. Now they were split into Merseyside and Greater Manchester and placed in competition for funds in a period of acute economic decline and growing unemployment.

When the reformist Conservative Margaret Thatcher became Prime Minister (1979–90) she visited the North West for one whole day, stating confrontationally that people in Britain had to understand that improved public services could only be paid for out of higher levels of productivity (Thatcher 1979). This speech, in a region where unemployment of 16 to 24 year olds had hit fifty per cent, heralded the 'Thatcherite' neoliberalism of deregulation, the free market and the pull away from the communal to the individual (Belchem 2006: 428, 440). As for Liverpool, her Chancellor of the Exchequer (a finance minister) advised her that it was fit only for 'managed decline... We must not

---

4. '[The] new arrangement is a compromise which seeks to reconcile familiar geography which commands a certain amount of loyalty, with the scale of operations on which planning methods can work effectively' (*The Times*, leader, 1 April 1974).

expend all our limited resources in trying to make water run uphill' (Pye 2014: 179–80). Her cabinet saw the consequent 1981 riots in Toxteth and Moss Side as inner-city problematics. They set up centrally-controlled Task Forces and unelected Urban Development Corporations. In doing so they overrode the elected metropolitan councils and indeed abolished them in 1986 (Munck 2003: 60). Thatcher appointed cabinet member Michael Heseltine as 'Minister for Merseyside'. To his credit he thought up a dextrous reclamation project—an International Garden Festival in 1984—that foreshadowed cultural schemes which both cities would soon turn to, predicated on tourism, heritage and commercial investment (Heseltine 2000: 216–27; Pye 2014: 181–85).

Thatcher's successor John Major (1990–97) acknowledged that coherent provincial strategy had been lacking hitherto and announced a selective range of spending programmes. A *City Challenge* initiative was instated for which local authorities had to compete against each other to secure regeneration funding. Each contender had to engage a range of private and voluntary bodies in the programme's design (Munck 2003: 62). Manchester used this funding to demolish the modernist crescent flats of Hulme and return it to a traditional layout (Mackay 2006: 8).

Yet what the Major government achieved was little more than a 'hotchpotch of agencies', in Belchem's words (2006: 470). The cities were placed in contention for thematically unconnected portions of central government funds. Nevertheless, in both cases the informal development of advisory networks, local agencies and action groups involving the private sector (Liverpool First, Manchester Growth Company) galvanized a new entrepreneurial approach to renewing in gentrified fashion the city centres (Wainwright 2009: 67–68; Littlefield 2009: 36–41). These were based in part on 'success' stories of revitalization such as Lille and Barcelona in mainland Europe, together with the achievement of Glasgow as the 1990 European City of Culture (Quilley 2002: 77). In fact at this time Merseyside and Greater Manchester each started to receive structural funding from the European Union under the terms of its Regional Development Fund and Social Fund. However, the areas were treated, then (and now), as standing on different strategic platforms. This is somewhat ironic, as the regional policy's prime aim is 'cohesion'.

From 1993–94 Merseyside was designated Objective One status as a 'poor region' with a gross domestic product rating 75% or so of the European Union average; it received £1.25 billion of aid between 1994 and 1999. Manchester has attracted less funding as a 'More Developed' region attaining 90% or higher of gross domestic product against the European average. In the midst of this programme, Tony Blair's 'New Labour' government gained power (1997–2010) and brought new systems into play, changing the administrative shape and scope of both Liverpool and Manchester. These changes were carried through by the succeeding coalition government (2010–15). Manchester led the way as a 'statutory city region' with devolved economic powers in 2011 under the title Greater Manchester Combined Authority, serving a population of 3.3 million (AGMA 2009; GMCA 2016). The Liverpool City Region Combined Authority ('a local enterprise partnership') was set up in 2014 to serve a population of 2.7 million (LCRCA 2016), holding elections for a city regional ('metro') Mayor in May 2017, won predictably by Labour's Steve Rotherham (local.gov.uk 2017).

Back in 1997 New Labour had talked brightly of a 'New Regional Policy' and soon a North-West Regional Development Agency was established (Harrison 2006). It had been a tradition of parliamentary policy that where socialists see regions, Conservatives see villages. But the entrepreneurial turn in Manchester—pragmatic governance by local elites—sat well with New Labour and the business-friendly 'Third Way' of its policy architect Anthony Giddens (2010), and indeed may have contributed to such behaviour; one thinks, for example, of the jargon of 'boosterism' employed shamelessly by both. While Deputy Prime Minister John Prescott attempted to kindle regional devolution, he was 'hung out to dry' and the project collapsed when voters in the North-East region rejected its own devolution proposals by 78% to 22% (Wainwright 2009: 245–46). Voters in Liverpool, more supportive of Prescott's position than many, having in the 1980s moved beyond Old Labour to the 'hard Left' ways of the 1980s militant tendency, deserted the socialist camps and instead gave municipal power to the Liberal Democrats (1998–2008), before returning to Labour (2008–present). Thus, in summary, at every turn since 1974 the two neighbours have had no option but to compete with each other at the level of regeneration and 'growth'. Yet a comparative account of the political economies of Manchester's expedient New Labour and Liverpool's less stable regimes may well show in practice more similarities than differences, that is, competing to do identical things. While both regimes have played down homelessness and played up office space and tourists, they have both been using European Union funds, and now—as city regions—allocations devolved from the UK government which are channelled into specific, parallel objectives to benefit mostly an urban elite, before which each city dangles its cultural quarters, street food bistros and festivals.

**Manpool**

But there is a counter-movement. By observing the history of complementarity between the two cities, new analysis of the diarchy as a polynuclear metropolitan zone has focused also on the towns 'in between' such as St. Helens and Warrington. The potency of economic coordination has already been credited to projects in Germany, such as the Ruhr's 'region of cities': Düsseldorf, Cologne and Bonn have fostered between them a revitalizing polycentric balance along the Rhine. This in turn has been compared historically to Baden-Württemberg, the successful union of two 'rival' states in south-west Germany, first unified by a public referendum—of all things—in 1952. At a conference at Essen in 2015, the urban strategists Andreas Schulze-Baing, Sebastian Dembski and Olivier Sykes described Manchester and Liverpool as key nodes of the 'Mersey Belt' urban corridor. They examined how the potential of intermediate towns might gain from 'the emerging new forms of regional and sub-regional planning and governance' (Schulze-Baing *et al.* 2015).

This unifying principle has been dramatically translated into 'Manpool', where 'Liverpool and Manchester might bring together their populations and resources to create a "supercity" in the north', according to Lord (Jim) O'Neill of Gatley, who coined the term (O'Neill 2014). O'Neill is an outspoken macroeconomist well known for contriving acronyms such as 'BRIC' (Brazil, Russia, India, China) and chairing the coalition government's Cities Growth Commission (2013–14). He is most vocally associated with the notion of the 'Northern Powerhouse', whereby the chain of cities from Liverpool in the west to Hull in the east would apparently gain commercial traction by using devolved funds and foreign investment, in this way fuelling national growth. O'Neill's Manpool project has already taken visionary shape in the form of the massive 'Ocean Gateway' scheme of Peel Holdings. According to Tom Harper of *The Independent* newspaper, the Peel Group property parent is 'owned by the reclusive tax exile John Whittaker' and his aim is to:

> transform fifty miles of bleak industrial land between the Port of Liverpool and Salford Docks into a £50 billion redevelopment ... The scheme, which will take at least five decades to complete, will include a £5.5 billion overhaul of [Liverpool's] waterfront with 50 skyscrapers, four hotels, a marina and a cruise liner terminal (Harper 2013).

This commercial step, to return the two cities to their complementary roles, ironises the governmental practice of dividing them (*Economist* 2014). It is significant that, thanks to the ingress of neoliberal practice in local government policy, a speculative project on this scale can now be considered a way forward after forty years of contrived administrative rivalry. Yet there have been acts of co-operation, reciprocity and synergy between the two cities for all of that time. That these events have not been featured in accounts of the lives of the cities is surely down to the failure of these endeavours to conform to the governing narrative of difference and rivalry. Given the conventional claim from the BBC at the head of this chapter that this self-determination is 'personified by sport and music', and this being a book about music, I wish to turn to that subject, with apologies for the long but unavoidable preamble to reach this point.

## The Case of Popular Music History

The essentialist representation of the Manchester and Liverpool music scenes has crossed a wide range of media forms, from academic ethnography to tourist brochures. Whilst Manchester offers guided tours around the town to display post-punk shrines, Liverpool subsidises a permanent exhibition called *The Beatles Story* (Gill 2016). Commercial films have portrayed each city's music scene, such as the Liverpool characterised in *Powder* (2011) and *The City That Rocked the World* (2013), or *24 Hour Party People* (2002) and *Closer* (2007) depicting Manchester. One difference worth noting lies in the fact that Liverpool University has had since 1988 an Institute of Popular Music. There, Sara Cohen has researched splendid ethnographic accounts of the everyday music scene in the city (*Rock Culture in Liverpool*, 1991; *Decline, Renewal and the City in Popular Music Culture*, 2007). In contrast Manchester has had to depend on the precarious facility and bent of freelance journalists such as Dave Haslam and Mick Middles, while oral histories are limited there to the likes of Raquel Morán's *Mancunions and Music* (2011).

In the need to define and promote a distinctive, re-born cultural character for the millennium, Manchester's elite political networks started to construct a modern history for the city. They centred it on their entrepreneurial selves, opening the civic biography in 1996 with an Irish Republican Army bomb explosion in the city centre, a blast that permitted physical reformation of what it destroyed and the hinterland of that. This 'renaissance' story is predicated on urban renewal, lifestyle manifestations such as the gay village, the Atlas bar, the bohemian Northern Quarter redeveloped by the property entrepreneurs Urban Splash, and the promotion of the city by the Manchester Independents action group and others as a centre of popular culture, in order to advance student residency (Madenorth n.d.; Wainwright 2009: 67). This history replaced and exscribed the narrative of decline and collapse on the local music scene associated at the time with the bankrupt Factory Records (1978–92) and its troubled nightclub The Haçienda (1982–97) (Hook 2012: 239–40; Nice 2010: 437–40, 481–89; Reade 2010: 131). Both were the subject of drama and embarrassment, while Manchester's main band at the time, Oasis, made it clear that it had nothing at all to do with Factory (although it had tried; see Nice 2010: 457).

In retaliation, those journalists who had invested heavily in the Factory story were anxious to raise their heritage status in the Manchester revival. They constructed a 'noble failure' history centred around Factory, Joy Division (1977–80) and the lynchpin of the Factory brand, regional television presenter Anthony (Tony) Wilson (1950–2007). On Wilson's death three films were produced on the subject and no fewer than five books (Witts 2010: 19–20).[5] Since then a rapprochement has been made with Manchester's urban peers to incorporate the Factory story as a prehistory to the city's renaissance, and a new 'Northern Powerhouse' arts venue scheduled for 2019 will be called The Factory, placed as it is on the site of the television studio where Wilson worked. The project has been grandly promoted by the city fathers as 'the next critical piece of infrastructure to support the area's "creative eco-system"' (BBC 2015). To support this, local music journalism has been assimilated into the city's renaissance enterprise, promoting a narrow story of an eternally hip Manchester which now excludes on the one side the most successfully international of local acts, the nostalgic Simply Red, and on the other the highly radical yet inveterately scruffy band The Fall.

**The Case of Ethnography**

If we cannot rely on this menial brand of music journalism to provide transparency, then there is always the cooler-headed approach of ethnography. For some years ethnography has vividly advanced our understanding of music in everyday life and practice. As Sara Cohen has claimed, 'Music plays a unique and often hidden role in the production of place' (1991: 288). But there comes a point where ethnography can't see the wood for the trees. This occurs at that stage where the operative boundaries under study are set too tight, especially so in terms of genre and setting. Where the cohesive factor is music, there is a tendency to underestimate the extent of the patterns of interactions. The problem is that of the spatial relations between the administrative frame and the functional terrain of flows and interactions, one that this chapter is attempting to describe. Where a process of journalistic mythologizing is underway, such as that kind which presupposes that aesthetic difference is a defining condition of a city's identity, ethnographic study is not immune to this tendency, and indeed comes to be in danger of sanctioning it. Sociologist Michael Burawoy has persuasively advocated ways by which ethnography can grow outwards, 'releasing [fieldwork] from

---

5. In Grant Gee's documentary *Joy Division* (2007), Tony Wilson says, 'I don't see this as a story of a rock group. I see it as the story of a city... The revolution that Joy Division started has resulted in this modern city.' See Witts 2010: 22.

solitary confinement, from being bound to a single place and time', though his ambitions are global more than regional (Burawoy 2000: 4). Meanwhile George Marcus has elaborated on multi-sited ethnography which allows for an analysis of ideas that spread across space (Marcus 1998). Yet these practices are essentially comparative, and what I have experienced by living in both Manchester and Liverpool is that together they have retained across the decades a dynamic and mutual relationship, including in this the production, performance, reception and circulation of music of all kinds. For these neighbouring cities, time and space are often identical rather than contrastive.

*The Regional Circulation of American Popular Music*
As an example of how assumptions about distinctiveness may skew the historical narrative, let us consider the postwar traffic of American popular music in the region, a story that is often used to explain why Liverpool had The Beatles and Manchester had nothing to compare with them.[6] A claim often made is that the postwar circulation of American popular music was distinctive in Liverpool because it was a port where passenger liners crossed back and forth to New York. These liners were staffed by the 'Cunard Yanks' who brought back with them records as family gifts, with some for sale. Bill Harry, who founded the paper *Mersey Beat* in 1961, calls this 'something of a myth' (Harry 2009: 12–13). Given the postwar reduction in dock life, he considers the specialist record stores to be more important as agencies for foreign songs. Another source was the radio (Luxembourg, American Forces Network). Yet a far more direct supply of recorded and live music was available to Liverpool and Manchester in equal measure from a nearby American military base, that of Burtonwood. Sited north of Warrington, a small 1930s airfield, which started out as a joint civic venture to serve the two cities, was taken over in 1938 by the RAF which built a fake church and football field to hide Spitfires and Hurricanes. Burtonwood was handed over in 1942 to the United States 8th Airforce as a base air depot (BAD1). It expanded to accommodate 18,000 soldiers and air crew, and was soon known as 'Lancashire's Detroit'. A 1,000 seat theatre was built (there were six venues in all) and American stars were flown in, such as Irving Berlin, Frank Sinatra, Nat 'King' Cole, and The Ink Spots. It held public dances and a range of sports events. By the 1950s Burtonwood had grown to the size of a small town (Ferguson 1986). It was handed back to the RAF in 1965 when the Americans were planning to move to France. But President De Gaulle, unwilling to sup-

---

6. Groups associated with 1960s Manchester include the Hollies, Herman's Hermits, Freddie and the Dreamers, the Bee Gees, and Barclay James Harvest.

port the US war in Vietnam, refused to accommodate the military and they remained at Burtonwood until 1994.

Burtonwood had segregated procedures during World War Two, but not so afterwards. From 1942 to 1945, 1948 to 1965, and 1967 to 1994, black and white American military personnel lived there and took weekend furloughs to Manchester and Liverpool. Some of them were singers and musicians who performed in the legal and the illegal clubs, known as Blues and shebeens, which could be found mainly in Manchester's Moss Side and Liverpool's Toxteth. Manchester promoter Tosh Ryan remembers that 'you got Americans bringing albums over, you got Americans who were playing in bands at weekends—that includes dance band music, moving from dance bands to jazz, small groups' (Bourne and Tebbutt 2014: 26). One particular technique in the late 1950s and early 1960s that was passed on from servicemen to local black artists was doowop. Liverpool's group, the Chants, honed their skills in this way. Burtonwood Americans recalled visiting the various black and Irish clubs and bars associated with the cities, but private houses too, and teaching new popular songs to the locals (Ferguson 2016; Brocken 2010: 50). The fact that they moved between the two cities even-handedly suggests much more 'hip' activity in both scenes than writers have so far led us to believe.

I will now offer three sets of examples, at different levels, in order to challenge those indolent, mediated presumptions about rivalry and difference which ethnographic isolation has tended to enhance. They concern (first) entrepreneurship, (second) musical influence, and (third) political solidarity.

*Mutuality: entrepreneurship*
There were many minor entrepreneurs during the North-West's post-punk period (1978–84), some running club nights, others 4-track studios, agencies, rehearsal rooms, and writing for fanzines or the nation's music press. Two of the most famous of these figures remain associated entirely with 'their own' city. Roger Eagle ran a club in Liverpool called *Eric's* (1976–80); Tony Wilson was a Manchester-affiliated television celebrity who co-created *The Factory* club nights at the Russell Club (1978–79), Factory Records and The Haçienda nightclub. Yet, in fact, their work and projects affected both cities in tandem. Wilson's first job in the region was a reporter for the *Liverpool Daily Post*. When he started as a presenter at Granada Television in 1973 he covered Liverpool issues; an engaging video clip from 1974 survives of Wilson recording disbelieving Scouse 'voxpop' reactions to Bill Shankly's retirement as manager of Liverpool football club[7] (Reade 2010: 33). From his university days Wilson had

---

7. https://www.youtube.com/watch?v=rHrp8A3dYOk, from 01:06.

taken an interest in the anarchist current of Situationism. He savoured the notion of playing an entrepreneur who would ironise capitalism by inverting or transgressing mercantile conduct (Nice 2010: 29). Interested in musical trends more than in music, he was stimulated to develop *The Factory* nights at the Russell Club in Manchester (1978–79) by Roger Eagle's creation of Eric's in Liverpool two years before (Hook 2012: 68, 107). Eagle booked and supplied bands and other acts for the weekly Manchester club night (Nice 2010: 35, 42). This arrangement allowed visiting groups to play the two cities in sequence.

Factory Records was a joint enterprise Wilson created with freelance actor Alan Erasmus and designer Peter Saville (Nice 2010: 44). It had emerged from a plan to create an independent joint Liverpool–Manchester label managed by Roger Eagle, Peter Fulwell of Inevitable Records, and Wilson. An argument over which bands should be represented on the joint label led to a rift. Among bands considered were two from Manchester (Durutti Column, Joy Division) and, from Liverpool, Pink Military (Nice 2010: 43). Wilson evangelized for the Merseyside band Orchestral Manoeuvres in the Dark, which the others didn't rate. Wilson therefore chose to go it alone, yet it can be seen on the second (ERIC.S) and third column down (FACTORY) on the grid on the draft label of his first offering, *A Factory Sample* (FAC2), that it was intended to be a joint enterprise between Eric's and Factory (see Figure 1). Wilson continued to support the musical traffic between the two cities, attempting to find television slots for artists from both. He was always careful to call himself a 'Son of Salford' in Manchester but a 'Lancashire Lad' in Liverpool. At the untimely close of his life Wilson contributed a rhapsodizing, reflective chapter on Liverpool and the Mersey to an anthology on that river (Wilson 2007: 94–102).

While Wilson's career began in Liverpool, that of Roger Eagle (1942–99) started in Manchester. Born in Oxford, from 1960 this 'gentle giant', as Wilson called him, travelled around the country in beatnik fashion on his 350 Enfield motorbike, paying an influential visit to *The Scene* rhythm and blues (R&B) club in London's Soho, a place that developed the role of the record-based DJ. Moving to Manchester in 1962 ('I just thought I'd see a different city'), Eagle played R&B records in coffee bars and by chance met a family of brothers who were setting up an all-night city centre R&B club called The Twisted Wheel which eventually acquired with Eagle's help a near-mythical status as a progenitor of Northern Soul. Eagle opened his own rented club, The Magic Village, 'a psychedelic dungeon', in 1968, at the age of twenty-six. During all of this time in Manchester he would promote and look after visiting acts such as Muddy Waters, Chuck Berry, and the new hippie bands (Sykes 2012: 19, 88, 107). Struggling to make money, he 'moved on' to Liverpool in 1970. Table 1 lists the venues in Manchester or Liverpool associated with Eagle.

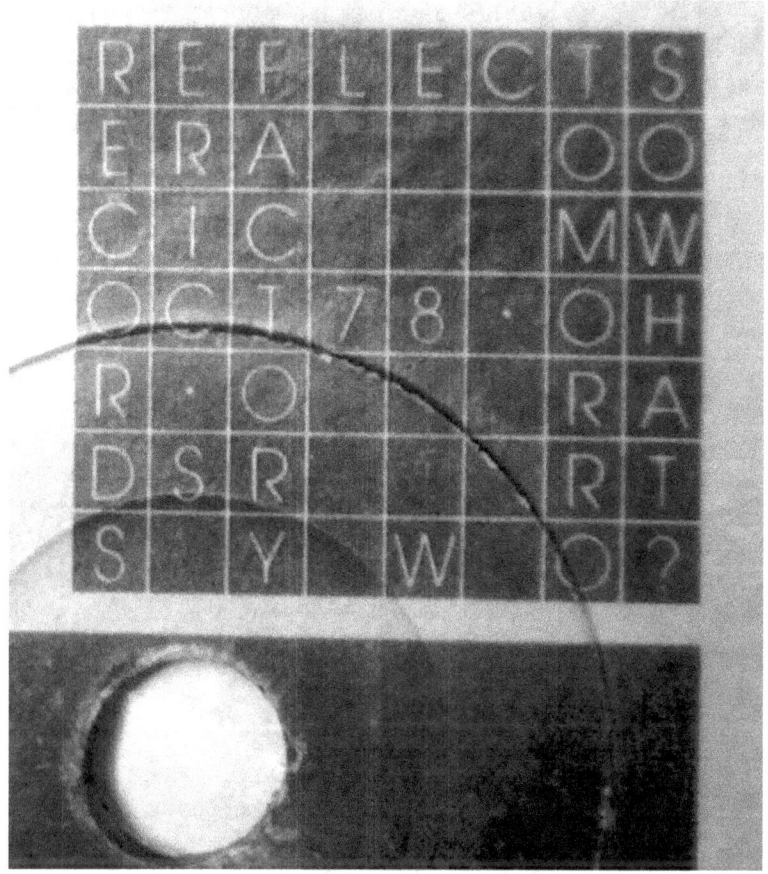

**Figure 1:** FAC2, *A Factory Sample*, detail of cover (1978)

**Table 1:** The career of entrepreneur Roger Eagle

| Year | City | Venue |
|---|---|---|
| 1963–66 | Manchester | Twisted Wheel |
| 1968–70 | Manchester | Magic Village |
| 1970–76 | Liverpool | Liverpool Stadium |
| 1976–80 | Liverpool | Eric's |
| 1980–82 | Manchester | Zodiac (Rafters) |
| 1980–84 | Liverpool | Crackin' Up |
| 1982 | Liverpool | Adam's |
| 1984–92 | Manchester | The International |
| 1986–90 | Manchester | The Ritz (RTR) |

In Liverpool Eagle ran a boxing stadium 'built out of corrugated iron' as a concert hall during what has been described as a 'fallow period' after 'the heavy rock boom and just before punk', although visiting bands included the likes of Captain Beefheart, Led Zeppelin and the New York Dolls (Biggs 2011: 102; Brocken 2010: 223–24; Sykes 2012: 123). He supported the few local groups then active, but by 1976 his desire to 'create a club for people who don't normally go to clubs' chimed with the punk and 'new wave' scene, and so with his business partners Peter Fulwell and Ken Testi he set up a crammed venue in the city centre at a site opposite the old Cavern Club, by then demolished. Eric's—a parody on names such as Annabelle's or Genevieve's, but apparently also a reference to the jazz pioneer Eric Dolphy—became a venue of high value to touring post-punk bands, who Eagle would then book for Manchester's Factory nights at the Russell Club (Nice 2010: 35). The formidable flowering of new bands at this time, such as Echo and the Bunnymen, Wah! Heat and The Teardrop Explodes, is traced back by Biggs to:

> the musical atmosphere of Eric's and its inspirational co-owner Roger Eagle. The club's eclecticism was an education, its DJs combining dub reggae, vintage rockabilly, New York punk and almost anything else in ways that would profoundly shape local musicians' tastes (Biggs 2011: 103).

Following a heavy police raid on Eric's in 1980 accompanied by a VAT tax bill which between them closed the club down, Eagle moved swiftly back to Manchester. In the 1980s he programmed Manchester's International Club at a time when Wilson had opened The Haçienda. The latter became notorious for its emptiness, while Eagle had the International patrons 'jumping and dancing' with quality live acts such as Lee 'Scratch' Perry, the Bhundu Boys, and Curtis Mayfield (Sykes 2012: 242–60, 344–53). In his biography of Eagle, Bill Sykes points out that the 'gentle giant' lived hand to mouth and never made any money. Yet the list at the end of the book of bands he promoted and cultivated is astonishing. And, as Table 1 shows, Eagle divided his energies fairly evenly between the two cities. Like Wilson, he enhanced the music life of both, and he nurtured music-making.

### *Mutuality: musical influence*

Here are two examples out of many where correspondence between the two cities has led to a significant musical turn. Firstly, the Frantic Elevators was a Manchester punk and post-punk band, formed in 1976 and fronted by the sweet-voiced Mick Hucknall, who was then seventeen years old. After failing to gain much attention, with one languishing single on a local label followed by another on Eric's Records, Eagle offered to manage the band. However, the project dissipated and resolved itself in an unexpected direction. Hucknall moved to Liverpool where Eagle used his extensive record collection of R&B and soul to foster the youngster's vocal style and knowledge of repertoire. In Hucknall's words, 'The jukebox in *Eric's* just summed Roger up … That eclectic thing had a huge effect on my attitude towards the music I make, because I don't make one type of music. They classify [Simply Red] as soul music but we have reggae tunes and jazz tunes' (Sykes 2012: 166). In effect Eagle closed down the Elevators and erected in its place Simply Red, so far the most internationally successful popular musical act from the Manchester area.

My second example is that of the Real People. This Liverpool band was formed in 1987 by the Griffiths brothers, Tony and Chris. They were in turn influenced by the Manchester band Inspiral Carpets, who they toured with. The Real People had a distinctive look, wore parkas and sunglasses on stage, used back lighting, and made a sound clearly derived from that of The Beatles. One of the Inspiral Carpets' roadies was the Manchester guitarist Noel Gallagher. The Gallagher brothers, Noel and Liam, stayed for a time with the Griffiths brothers in Liverpool. According to Tony Griffiths, 'They were quite naïve about recording, so we'd show them how to play the songs, how to think about the structure of the songs and the dynamics. We were just helping them because that's what bands do in Liverpool' (Moody 1996). The result was an eight-track music demonstration tape through which Oasis signed its first record deal. The Manchester band consensually took the sound, the light and the physical look of Liverpool's the Real People, including Liam's iconic posture in front of the microphone, and even songs. For example, the anthem 'Rockin' Chair' is in fact a Real People song, although it is doubtful if the stadium audiences who have sung it back to the Gallaghers were aware of this. While Oasis split up in 2009, the Griffiths brothers can still be found playing in Liverpool bars (McKechnie 2015).

## *Mutuality: political solidarity*

There are three examples of confederacy offered here. The first was a one-day festival that took place on August bank holiday 1979. It was titled 'Zoo Meets Factory Halfway'—a reference to the two regional record labels (Zoo being a Liverpool indie). It was Wilson's idea, telling Zoo's Bill Drummond, 'We do a festival, you bring your bands and I bring mine … Don't worry, Bill, people will come' (Drummond 2001). The affair took place off the East Lancs Road in Plank Lane, Leigh, which was approaching midway between the two cities but not easy to reach. The line-up included Liverpool's Echo & The Bunnymen and Manchester's Joy Division (see Figure 2).

> **ZOO MEETS FACTORY HALF-WAY**
>
> BANK HOLIDAY MONDAY
> AUGUST 27th
>
> LEIGH OPEN AIR POP FESTIVAL
>
> ADMISSION £2
> FIRST BAND 1.00 p.m.
>
> Zoo records and Factory records bring you the flesh
>
> Zoo records and Factory records bring you
> the flesh that brought you the vinyl . .
>
> THE DISTRACTIONS
> ECHO AND THE BUNNYMEN
> X-O-DUS
> ORCHESTRAL MANOEUVRES
> ELTI-FITS
> CRAWLING CHAOS
> LORI AND THE CHAMELEONS
> A CERTAIN RATIO
> THE TEARDROP EXPLODES
> JOY DIVISION
>
> Use your wits or use the bus;
> No. 26 from Manchester Victoria
> No. 39 from Liverpool
> Festival site—Plank Lane, Leigh, Lancs.

**Figure 2:** 'Zoo meets Factory half-way'. Leigh Open Air Pop Festival, 27 August 1979

Any profit was to be given to Rock Against Racism. However, the event made a disastrous loss (Middles 2009: 184–88). According to Nice:

> the bands found themselves playing to an empty field beside a disused colliery, where audience numbers never rose above 200. With punters outnumbered by police, the event raised no money for the good causes proposed, leaving the organisers virtually bankrupt (Nice 2010: 76).

The Leigh Open Air Pop Festival, its alternative title, may not be a successful symbol of solidarity, yet it remains an illustration of bands from the two cities sharing time and space. The second example took place at Liverpool's Royal Court Theatre on 8 February 1986 and was titled 'From Manchester With Love'. Tony Wilson was friends with Liverpool's militant council leader Derek Hatton. The concert, given by Manchester acts New Order, the Smiths, the Fall and John Cooper Clarke, was a fundraiser for the Family Support Group of the forty-eight Labour councillors who had been surcharged by Thatcher's government for not setting a balanced budget. This concert did raise money, and even the t-shirts made a profit (McKechnie 2015).

The final example is one that has only recently found resolution, in raising funds for the Hillsborough Justice Campaign. It was at the Hillsborough football stadium in 1989 that ninety-six Liverpool supporters were killed in a crush as a result of incompetent police control. The police subsequently fed the press a collection of untruths which *The Sun* duly printed on its front page four days later. Two weeks after that Tony Wilson (who, we should remember, was a former reporter) organized a successful benefit at Manchester's Haçienda, which the local band Happy Mondays headed. The twenty-fifth anniversary of the tragedy in 2014, together with the phone hacking scandals surrounding *The Sun*'s publisher News Corporation, revived the campaign against mendacious journalism. The Liverpool 'scally' (lad) band, The Farm, set up a small tour, on which they were joined by members of Manchester's band the Stone Roses, as an act of solidarity between the two cities whose four football clubs are often presented by the press to be the epitome of social and religious intolerance.

**Conclusion**

These seven examples of co-operation, reciprocation and solidarity between the two cities remain hidden when assumptions about separate 'scenes' are not tested by examining the common patterns of behaviour between sites of activity. This is nothing new, by the way. In 1963 the singer Billy J. Kramer teamed up very successfully with The Dakotas, though on a strictly business level. He was from Bootle; they were from Manchester. The Dakotas were the house band of the Plaza Ballroom in Oxford Street, where the manager had asked them to dress each week as American Indians, hence their name.

Actors and events that are vital to the stories of both cities get consigned to one. Ethnographic network analysis may be the way forward. But ultimately, when it comes to music, regional frameworks may offer richer stories about music-making than local ones.

## About the Author

Richard Witts is Reader in Music and Sound at Edge Hill University. He is the author of the biography of the German chanteuse Nico (1993, revised edition 2017), a study of the music of the Velvet Underground (2008), and a history of the Arts Council (1999). He has contributed many articles for journals, including recently *The Musical Times* (Summer 2015) and vol. 7/3 of *Popular Music History* (2012). His contributions to BBC radio include the documentaries *1968 in America* and *The Technocrats* where he discussed pop music with Stockhausen.

## References

AGMA (Association of Greater Manchester Authorities). 2009. *The Manchester Statutory City Region*. alma.gov.uk 2009-12-28 (accessed 14 April 2016).

Aiken, John. 1968 [1795]. *A Description of the Country from 30 to 400 Miles around Manchester*. Newton Abbot: David & Charles.

Alderson, Frederick. 1968. *View North*. Newton Abbot: David & Charles.

BBC. 2010. 'Rivals: Liverpool v Manchester'. https://tinyurl.com/bbc-8677547 (accessed 31 March 2016).

—2015. *The Factory £110m Arts Venue Approved*. http://www.bbc.co.uk/news/uk-england-manchester-33621486 (accessed 1 April 2016).

Belchem, John. 2006. *Liverpool 800: Culture, Character and istory*. Liverpool: Liverpool University Press.

Biggs, Bryan. 2011. 'Liverpool's Radical Music'. In *Liverpool: City of Radicals*, ed. J. Belchem and B. Biggs, 98–124. Liverpool: Liverpool University Press.

Bourne, Dennis, and Melanie Tebbutt. 2014. 'Shebeens and Black Music Culture in Moss Side, Manchester, in the 1950s and 1960s'. *Manchester Regional History Review* 25: 1–34.

Brocken, Michael. 2010. *Other Voices: Hidden Histories of Liverpool's Popular Music Scenes, 1930s–1970s*. Farnham: Ashgate.

Burawoy, Michael. 2000. 'Reaching for the Global'. In *Global Ethnography: Forces, Connections and Imaginations in a Postmodern World*, ed. J. A. Blum, M. Burawoy, S. George, T. Gowan and Z. Gille, 4–15. London: University of California Press.

*City Journal*. 2015. http://www.citiesjournal.com/top-13-reasons-liverpool-is-better-than-manchester (accessed 3 April 2016).

Cohen, Sara. 1991. *Rock Culture in Liverpool: Popular Music in the Making*. Oxford: Oxford University Press.

—2007. *Decline, Renewal and the City in Popular Music Culture*. Farnham: Ashgate.

Defoe, Daniel. 1986. *A Tour thro' the Whole Island of Great Britain, Divided into Circuits or Journies, Letter 10, 1727*. London: Penguin.

Drummond, Bill. 2001. *[(45)]*. London: Abacus.

*Economist, The*. 2014. 'Never Walk Alone: The Industrial North, Editorial'. *The Economist*, 9 April.

Ferguson, Aldon P. 1986. *Eighth Air Force Base Air Depot, Burtonwood*. Reading: Airfield Publications.

—2016. Communication with the author.
Giddens, Anthony. 2010: 'The Rise and Fall of New Labour'. *New Statesman*, 17 May. http://www.newstatesman.com/uk-politics/2010/05/labour-policy-policies-blair (accessed 14 April 2016).
Gill, Craig. 2016. http://www.manchestermusictours.com/about-us
GMCA (Greater Manchester Combined Authority). 2016. https://www.greatermanchester-ca.gov.uk/info/20064/about_gmca (accessed 15 April 2016).
Harper, T. 2013. 'The Biggest Company You've Never Heard of: Lifting the Lid on Peel Group—the Property Firm Owned by Reclusive Tax Exile John Whittaker'. *The Independent*, 18 October. https://tinyurl.com/ya2do87v (accessed 15 April 2016).
Harrison, John. 2006. 'The Political-economy of Blair's New Regional Policy'. *Geoforum* 37/6: 932–43.
Harry, Bill. 2009. *Bigger than Liverpool: The Story of the City's Musical Odyssey*. Liverpool: Trinity Mirror.
Heath, Edward. 1998. *The Course of My Life: My Autobiography*. London: Hodder & Stoughton.
Heseltine, Michael. 2000. *Life in the Jungle: My Autobiography*. London: Hodder & Stoughton.
Hook, Peter. 2012. *Unknown Pleasures: Inside Joy Division*. London: Simon & Schuster.
Jewell, Helen M. 1994. *The North-South Divide: The Origins of Northern Consciousness in England*. Manchester: Manchester University Press.
LCRCA (Liverpool City Region Combined Authority). 2016. https://www.liverpoollep.org/economic-strategy/combined-authorities (accessed 15 April 2016).
Littlefield, David. 2009: *Liverpool One: Remaking a City Centre*. Chichester: John Wiley & Sons.
local.gov.uk. 2017. https://tinyurl.com/merseyside-39804725 (accessed 1 June 2017).
Mackay, Lesley. 2006. *Re-appraising Hulme in 2004—a VivaCity2020 Report*. Manchester: Vivacity.
Madenorth. n.d. *Tom Bloxham Chairman and Co-Founder Urban Splash*. http://www.madenorth.co.uk/tom-bloxham-chairman-and-co-founder-urban-splash (accessed 15 May 2016).
*Manchester Evening News*. 2014. 'It's Official: Manchester is the Music Capital of Britain'. http://www.manchestereveningnews.co.uk/whats-on/its-official-manchester-music-capital-7813550 (accessed 31 March 2016).
Marcus, George E. 1998. *Ethnography through Thick and Thin*. Princeton, NJ: Princeton University Press.
McKechnie, Joseph. 2015. Interview with musician Joe McKechnie, Liverpool.
Middles, Mick. 2009. *Factory: The Story of a Record Label*. London: Virgin Books.
Moody, Paul. 1996. 'The Oasis Story'. *Vox* magazine (May). http://ireland.iol.ie/~kglennon/paper/mayvox2.htm
Morán, R. 2011. *Mancunions and Music: Tales of the Internet, the Underground and the Manchester Music Scene*. Ilford: LittleAsturias.
Munck, R. 2003: *Reinventing the City? Liverpool in Comparative Perspective*. Liverpool: Liverpool University Press.
Nice, James. 2010. *Shadowplayers: The Rise and Fall of Factory Records*. London: Aurum.
O'Neill, Jim. 2014. 'Could Merging Liverpool and Manchester Boost UK Growth?' *Daily*

*Telegraph*, 13 November. https://tinyurl.com/10654182-growth (accessed 15 April 2016).

Phillips, C. B., and J. W. Swift. 1994. *Lancashire and Cheshire from A.D. 1540*. London: Longmans.

Pye, Ken. 2014. *Liverpool: The Rise and Fall and Renaissance of a World-class City*. Stroud: Amberley Publishing.

Quilley, Steve. 2002. 'Entrepreneurial Turns: Municipal Socialism and After'. In *City of Revolution: Restructuring Manchester*, ed. J. Peck and K. Ward, 70–93. Manchester: Manchester University Press.

Reade, Lindsay. 2010. *Mr Manchester and the Factory Girl: The Story of Tony and Lindsay Wilson*. London: Plexus.

Schulze-Baing, Andreas, Sebastian Dembski and Olivier Sykes. 2015. *Urban Renaissance—What is the Prospect of Places in the Periphery? Manchester-Liverpool and the Spatial In-between*. In host publication, *Polycentric City Regions in Transformation—The Ruhr Agglomeration in International Perspective*, Essen, 11-13 July.

Sykes, Bill. 2012. *Sit Down! Listen To This!—The Roger Eagle Story*. Manchester: Empire Publications.

*The Tab*. 2012. 'Manchester v Liverpool: The Music Scene. You Decide'. http://thetab.com/uk/liverpool/2012/11/15/manchester-v-liverpool-the-music-scene-you-decide-1858 (accessed 3 April 2016).

Thatcher, Margaret. 1979. 'Remarks Visiting the North West (defending economic policy)'. *Financial Times*, 1 September 1979 by Rhys David, Northern Correspondent. Margaret Thatcher Foundation archive. http://www.margaretthatcher.org/document/104136 (accessed 14 April 2016).

UNESCO. 2016. http://en.unesco.org/creative-cities/home (accessed 31 March 2016).

Wainwright, Martin. 2009. *True North—in Praise of England's Better Half*. London: Guardian Books.

Wilson, Anthony. 2007. 'Westward Ho!' In *Mersey: The River that Changed the World*, ed. I. Wray and C. McPherson, 94–102. Liverpool: Bluecoat Press.

Witts, Richard. 2010. 'Building up a Band: Music for a Second City'. In *Mark E. Smith and The Fall: Art, Music and Politics*, ed. M. Goddard and B. Halligan, 19–31. Farnham: Ashgate.

# 2 Another Uniquely Mancunian Offering? Un-Convention and the Intermediation of Music Culture and Place

Paul Long and Jez Collins

To start a little way from the geographic North: in February 2017, 32 bands from across the UK came together to perform in the town of Hastings, contributing to the promise of an 'exceptional day of live music' (http://unconventionhub.org/uncon/89). Supplementing performance was a series of discussion panels about music, its organization and cultural value, and featuring figures such as musician and journalist John Robb, Lara Baker of the Association of Independent Music (AIM) and James Ketchell of Music Heritage UK. Panel themes were signalled in titles such as 'Music Tourism' and 'Building a Career in Music'. The event was badged as 'Off-Axis', a translation of the Portuguese phrase *Fora do Eixo*, referencing a Brazilian 'social movement of cultures' (quoted in Garland 2012: 510). The imaginative ambition represented by this conjunction of geographical and cultural reference points was brought together under the umbrella of Un-Convention, an organization based in Manchester.

Conceived as a one-off, Un-Convention was established with an event in Salford in October 2008: Hastings was the 89th event under the same banner and continuing its originating ethos. As claimed at Un-Convention's website, its activities annually involve thousands of music artists, contributing speakers and concert attendees. A wealth of activity takes place online, reaching a range of global interlocutors, many first engaged at events that have taken place in other UK cities and towns as well as a variety of international locations, including Mumbai (#Uncon7, 2009); Buenos Aires (#UnCon19, 2011); Haifa and Ramallah (#UnCon87 and 88 respectively, 2017).

Remarkable enough for its ambition and endurance, Un-Convention merits attention in the context of this collection for the manner in which it emerged from and can be understood to evince a particular set of qualities and practices associated with its roots and abiding anchor in the North of England. Exploring its foundation and character in this chapter, we assess what it means to understand this particular cultural enterprise as 'another uniquely Mancunian offering' (Hurst 2013). In so doing, we explore how Un-Convention is located at the confluence of a number of traditions and practices concerning identity and a politics of representation. Drawing upon statements from and interviews with founders and contributors, our approach is to conceptualize Un-Convention in terms of processes of cultural intermediation. Its makers are described here as representatives of Manchester's music sector who have contributed to the city's perception, identity and recent remaking. In practice they disseminate an ethos in their practice that is imbued with a sense of the city as a place of symbolic production. While so much about Manchester's popular music in particular is often narrated around a familiar set of actors and tropes, Un-Convention is resolutely 'off-axis', engaging with the city's heritage while seeking to forge innovations and alliances across music cultures, exploring cultural identities through practice in dialogue with metropolitan and indeed global peers. In examining Un-Convention, we can understand the dynamism of representations of the North that, as many have indicated, are far from homogenous but plural and often seen to be subject to negotiation from within as much as from without localities.

## The Specificity of Place and Sound

Un-Convention's co-founder, Jeff Thompson, has recently argued that this enterprise 'could have happened anywhere' (interview). In fact, he disavows any chauvinism about its local origins, reflecting on Manchester's influence that it is 'not inherently in the DNA of it'. Nonetheless, he recognizes conversely that the specificity of place *was* vital to its formation. Lacking a policy prompt or financial investment, Un-Convention was enabled 'because there was quite a big network even though there's not a huge infrastructure, no big money or big labels, but there was a lot of people doing the same thing'. Thompson's reflexivity is thus a helpful starting point for demystifying the relationship of ideas about Manchester, popular music culture and Un-Convention as a creative enterprise. His disavowal of any simple essentialist character invites the question: to what degree is any cultural symbol and geographically particular practice simply *of* a place rather that imbricated with any ethos and qualities specific to it?

Here, the mythos of place is important for making sense of how representations have real force in relation to experience and expression, played out in the cultural field in particular, which in turn serve as mutual reinforcement for social and economic imaginaries. Helpful here is Allen and Hollingworth's (2013) deployment of a concept of habitus to explore interrelations of space, place and identity, suggesting how the specificity of location impacts upon on one's dispositions, ambition and potential. As developed by Milestone (2016) in her exploration of gender, northernness and Manchester's creative industries, a place-specific concept of habitus helps understanding of how individuals might represent and embody particular localities. There are ways of being that are informed by shared traditions and orientations which are mobilized and performed as a means of defining oneself as within and without communities: as a Londoner, Liverpudlian or Mancunian for instance. In thinking of Manchester in particular, there is a range of associations that are repeatedly called upon to do work in referencing its character. These associations are suggestive here for illustrating conventional ways in which the city is afforded agency via an accretion of the actions and expression of members of its population. For example, MacKillop summarizes the link of business practice and image in the city, writing that 'Manchester was always about "making it happen" … displaying a "can do" attitude that goes beyond the usual civic pride that can be witnessed in other cities' (2012: 247). One can appreciate in turn how this identity has informed the habitus of place of Mancunians. As MacKillop writes, from the transformations of the late twentieth and early twenty-first centuries, 'Manchester accrued a proud reputation as a city-region of "firsts". This has permeated local attitudes and discourses on the part of the elite, defining a boosterist urban regime' (2012: 247).

The advent of this contemporary civic boosterism is summarized by Peck and Ward. They suggest how the tropes of Manchester's transformation echo broad challenges that have faced industrialized economies, encompassing an 'obsession with city-centre regeneration, the (re)emergence of elite decision-making networks and privatized governance, the can-do entrepreneurialism of local agencies, the search for "joined-up" responses to social exclusion' (2002: 3). A key element to this specific transformation is Manchester's celebrated cultural revolution and its employment in its narrative of reinvention and re-presentation. On this theme, Quilley distinguishes between the 'hard city' of flagship redevelopment and regeneration in the built environment and a 'more telling area of continuity' in relation to the 'soft city' (2000: 612). This distinction refers to how a sense of civic identity has been expanded in order to incorporate a shared pride in Manchester's vibrant popular culture for the part it plays in the image and agency of an 'entrepreneurial city'.

The creative industries have certainly been integral to establishing a view of Manchester as exceptional and in achieving competitive distinctiveness in the cultural sphere. Milestone (2016) for instance summarizes the current importance of the city as a 'creative hot-spot' and its atypical status by way of comparison with other northern cities. She cites local labour research that identifies Manchester as the city with the largest number of employees in the creative industries outside of London. There are success stories in digital media and broadcasting, designer fashion and photography for instance, as well as architecture and computer gaming, and which afford Manchester with economic vitality as well as symbolic value.

Gesturing to the politics of identity and representation important to the specific habitus of *this* place, Peck and Ward describe how the mobilization of creativity as asset in Manchester is one that draws on 'very deep and long-established roots', an appropriation, recuperation even, of 'what began as a series of counter-cultural movements' (2002: 4). Central to this development was the popular music culture of the city, the high point of which corresponded with the period of its reinvention. As Straw summarizes, in the 1980s and 1990s, Manchester 'was one of the most important western cities in the field of popular music, the birthplace of highly influential cross-fertilizations of post-punk rock and forms of dance music' (2004: 414).

The valuation of Manchester's music culture was nuanced too by a faith in its exceptionality, that it could only have happened *there*, so drawing upon familiar ways of thinking about sound and place. Holt and Wergin have written about the relationship of music and urban environments, of how sounds are regularly taken in popular narratives to be an expression of the particularities of a milieu (2013). As they point out, this imaginary is informed by 'origin myths of creativity' and ideas about people: 'phantom crowds in the streets' (2013: 2). As Halfacree and Kitchin suggest, this relationship of music culture and place is not born of abstract ideas: 'geography, through imagery, infrastructure and localised experiences, has been used by bands as a resource to develop their art' (1996: 51). Such relationships have abiding valence for consumers, in music journalism and the marketing strategies of the industries themselves. To these we might add the agents of cities like Manchester for whom music has a particular force. Again, echoing something of the force of the habitus of place, Bottà (2009) has written of the way in which city residents, tourists and leaders understand the way in which popular music has a role to play in defining the identity of place and its economy. He describes how its presence is manifest in city plans, project bids, promotional material, and realized in regeneration, renewal and preservation projects.

We would suggest therefore that this presence of music informs a version of what Quilley describes as a 'script' emerging from redevelopment and which 'entails a common language and conceptual vocabulary ... shared and adhered to by actors involved in all aspects of urban regeneration; a script which crosses institutional and political lines' (2000: 609). Such a script—which might in fact predate regeneration given the history of the counter-culture described by Peck and Ward—that tells of Manchester's narrative as a music city, might be enabling but potentially limiting too, depending upon its parameters. For instance, we would argue that the identification of Manchester with popular music has, to some degree, been over-determined and in turn over-determines the image of the city and its culture, focused as it often is on a narrow set of moments, iconic artists and individuals. There is, for instance, a prodigious range of popular narratives produced by music journalists and photographers such as Paul Morley and Kevin Cummins, intermediaries like Tony Wilson and musicians such as Peter Hook of Joy Division and New Order (Haslam 1999; Robb 2009). Alongside these works, more formal academic studies are extensive and, in total rather than as a result of any individual deficiency, relatively myopic in focusing on punk (Crossley 2009), Joy Division and New Order (Fraser and Fuoto 2012; Strong and Greig 2014; Nevarez 2013), 'Madchester' (Halfacree and Kitchin 1996) or these references together (Bottà 2009).

As we discuss below, the recurrence of these reference points presents a particular burden for contemporary creativity and cultural intermediaries in the city. However, we can appreciate how any 'script' for the city's music culture works in tandem with a boosterist ethos and its role in a habitus of place and modes of doing business. For instance, MacKillop's summary of Manchester's rejuvenation enlists a familiar and broad characterization of its agents, suggesting that policy innovations addressing the challenges of de-industrialization that faced the city were designed and executed 'in typical Manchester style, by talking loud and thinking big' (2012: 247). This trope is echoed in a description of the music field by journalist Stephen Dalton who describes the particularity of the city's scene in similar manner, of how, 'a kind of swaggering northern pride is also a crucial part of the chemistry. Many local musicians, even born again Mancs from outside the city, share this chippy arrogance' (2009).

In Quilley's account (2000: 606), the ambition identified by MacKillop involved re-pitching the focus of projects from a local to global vista, realized in place-making, marketing and strategy bids for the Olympics and Commonwealth, as well as entering competitive urban redevelopment schemes such as City Challenge and City Pride. One example of an ambitious and successful project in the field of music was focused not just on celebrating and promoting local bands but in attracting the attention of the wider music industry to Manchester as *the* place to do business on a global scale. Thus, 'In the City' was an annual industry event founded 1992 by Tony Wilson, head of Factory Records, and his partner Yvette Livesey and appositely described by the *Daily Telegraph* as 'the biggest music gathering of its kind in Britain, which each autumn drew decision-makers and opinion-formers from the London-centric music industry' (Anon 2007). In this specific reference point lies a conjunction of mainstream music industry, the dominance of the metropolis and an echo of the hyperbole of Manchester's boosterism, the exclusions, oversights and alienating message of which Un-Convention was designed to address.

**From Fat Northerner to Un-Convention**

Un-Convention emerged from Manchester's popular music culture and is imbued with its character and practices. Extending beyond those characteristics and references recognizable from the dominant representations of the city alluded to above, the establishment of Un-Convention thus exposes some of its tensions. For instance, in interview Thompson has said of the contemporary scene that 'people assume it's a lot more mature and ... professionalized than it really is', suggesting that in fact it 'hangs off half a dozen artists and the reputation of the Factory label'. His perception is of 'a big music city on a small scale. Everything's little but there's a lot of it'; and it was in this economy and on a micro scale that Thompson, along with business partners Ruth Daniel and Dan Thomas, first emerged as musicians and then from 2003–2010, as cultural entrepreneurs with releases on their record label Fat Northerner.

Currently in hiatus, the label identifies itself as in the tradition of British independents such as 4AD, Warp, Creation 'and of course Factory'. Daniel describes it as 'built from passion ... we weren't looking for the "next big thing" so it was music that we all really liked' (interview). While the label name is a tongue-in-cheek deployment of a familiar stereotype (the logo is accompanied by the face of a shouting, moustachioed and overweight man), Fat Northerner from its inception was committed to supporting local artists and the expression of a broadly regional identity in sound, roster and business practice. Responding to transformations in music production and distribution, the label was an early explorer of the challenge of digitization, offering downloadable music to international audiences. 'Digital Northerner', for instance, was an eclectic series of rock, soul and electronica promoted as featuring 'some of the most outstanding new artists and bands from the North of England'. Label signings included bands such as Bone Box, described as 'authentic and original', allusively evincing 'the sound of the "Deep North"' (bone-box.bandcamp.com).

In pursuit of its mission in support of music from Manchester and the Northwest, the label made some money but not enough to invest in achieving greater recognition for its artist roster with significant promotions or financial backing for extensive touring. This limitation, inherent to the micro-nature of the business, was illustrated to the label in a moment at the annual South by Southwest (SWSX) music industry convention in Austin, Texas. As Daniel recalls, at a workshop entitled 'Marketing on a Shoestring', the 'shoestring' referred to was £10-15,000, far in excess of the budget available to Fat Northerner (interview). Aware that such amounts were also beyond the reach of many others they dealt with, and with a focus closer to home, Daniel and Thompson approached the organizers of the 'In the City' event to request a session that spoke to the needs of those in the DIY and micro-business sector of music production. However, as Daniel recalls, this suggestion was not one viewed favourably by representatives of 'In the City', who advised Fat Northerner that concepts such as DIY were no longer relevant. In fact, she and Thompson interpreted this rebuttal as a comment on the value of their sector and a statement on what matters to the narration of the new Manchester and its economic ambition and preferred script. Daniel relates how the discontent of this moment was compounded by a perception that 'In the City' was generously supported by funds from the Cultural Redevelopment budget of the City Council. Furthermore, tickets for the event were priced at up to £600—a figure in excess of Fat Northerner's marketing budget at the time!

Crystallizing the sense of exclusion resulting from this refusal, Un-Convention was conceived in entrepreneurial spirit as a means of addressing a gap in the cultural field. It was also reflective of the scope and ambition of the sector; it represented 'a very small-scale idea … We thought it would just be an afternoon in the pub having a chat' (Thompson quoted in Anon 2008). This then offered an opportunity for those who felt ignored by 'In the City' and, in fact, the BBC's online coverage of Un-Convention's first event was titled 'In The Other City'—as much a reference to the established event as the setting in the city of Salford. However, Un-Convention's establishment was also a signal beyond the locality. As Daniel suggests, it offered 'two fingers up to the industry' and in so doing was an expression of a broader discontent about the place in the world of Manchester's music micro-businesses. This discontent had a long gestation in Daniel and Thompson's sense of the fragmentation of the local industry, compounded by the London-centric nature of the music business. As Thompson has said, there was a 'feeling of being excluded … by distance and by money and by our opportunity. And that was an impetus'. While he envied the dynamism and vibrant qualities of the capital's scene, he suggested at the time that locally, 'it feels like we constantly have to reinvent the wheel up here, so we wanted to try and get people together, not just from Manchester, but … those working at the same level as ourselves to share ideas and experience' (quoted in Anon 2008).

From its launch, Un-Convention was firmly anchored in the same tongue-in-cheek sense of Mancunian northern-English identity established by Thompson and Daniel's label. As noted at its original blog site, its original strapline promised events including 'Music and Pies', later 'With Cake' (http://unconvention.wordpress.com). Running in parallel to 'In The City' of 2008, the inaugural Un-Convention took place in the community setting of Sacred Trinity Church in Salford. It was organized in a style homologous to the approach of DIY music labels like Fat Northerner and the constituency it sought to attract. It showcased bands, 'some amazing local talent', as Thompson described it to the BBC, as well as industry representatives who would lead workshops and discussion: label owners, self-releasing bands, promoters, venue owners, designers, photographers, PR people, journalists. He described it pointedly as an inclusive event, which would welcome anyone who wished to attend: 'We really believe that the people who attend are as important—if not more so—than the people we have on the panels. Although we have panels to give it some structure, it isn't a case of people sitting there to listen—we want people to contribute' (quoted in Anon 2008). As Daniel commented in interview, the aim was to 'be more useful than going to a drinks reception ... with Britney Spears' manager!'

Thus, the prefix of *Un*-Convention can be interpreted as a pointed riposte to the slickness of 'In the City' as well as a signal of affiliation with the informalities of 'unconferencing', 'hack-days', 'BarCamps', and 'open space' practices. Billsberry *et al.* (2013) characterize such events as those in which participants organically and democratically determine the nature of what happens. As they suggest, this format is one that is effective when bringing together people who are well informed and passionate about a subject: 'When participant contributors are either experts or newly yet deeply engaged in the literature, they can get to the crux of the matter readily to talk about cutting-edge ideas' (2013: 178). While one wonders whether such a format is *so* distinctive, the signal of irregular approaches in unconferencing events prompts an undoing of the familiar and offers space for revisionist thinking and an exploration of ideas that are constrained by formalized contexts. Whatever it sought to achieve, for Daniel it was about 'doing things differently' and Un-Convention's position with regards to 'In The City' was predicated on the fact that *that* event was representative of a moribund traditional industry, un-responsive to the challenge of digital. Thus, Thompson's rationale for Un-Convention was a faith in the idea that 'smaller, DIY labels are the ones breaking new bands to the most savvy audience ever' and an empowering sense that while the industry was suffering, 'the power genuinely is shifting back towards the artist and there are a lot of positives to be had from that' (quoted in Anon 2008).

Evincing an optimistic view of a landscape revivified by digital and micro-labels and innovative practice, discussion informing Un-Convention's establishment also located the event as a further riposte to the booster image of Manchester as a creative hub built on a particular music lineage. A diatribe posted by Daniel at the Fat Northerner website in advance of the Salford event argued with reference to the founder of 'In The City' that 'STOPPING TALKING ABOUT TONY WILSON IS WHAT TONY WOULD HAVE WANTED' (http://fatnortherner.wordpress.com). She complained how a focus on the past 'gives no room for the new generation', arguing that at music industry events (i.e. In the City), 'it seems easier to wheel out the old Haçienda crew ... than speak to the people who are now actually doing it'. What was needed, she wrote, were accounts from those addressing issues such as the advent of digital, the contemporary live circuit, finance issues, piracy, and ending with a demand to the representatives of the past to 'Step aside and let the new creatives show you what they can do'.

**Un-Convention as Cultural Intermediation**

Such expressions are not uncommon in the context of a wider discourse about Manchester, its music scene and how this represents the city and its culture. They are expressions of frustration rather than absolute rejections of Manchester's icons or enduring aspects of practice, an awareness of exclusion and inequalities. The character of the organization, its organizers, proselytizers and its local scale can thus be understood in the context of debates about the politics and value of culture across a wider stage, in relation to processes of cultural intermediation.

As Taylor suggests, since the origination of the concept of the cultural intermediary in the work of Pierre Bourdieu, the roles and actors encompassed under this title have both expanded in range and conceptualization 'into a more general process of intermediation between the production and consumption of symbolic forms in all their diversity' (2013: 366). For Wright, this figure is 'a specific type of worker engaged, at different times, in the pursuit of both economic and symbolic profit' (2005: 106). In this light, the intermediary has proven to be an ambivalent figure. Apposite to the context of the tropes of the narrative of Manchester's reinvention, the intermediary has become a focal point of interest for comprehending changes in the cultural sector and the emergence of the discourse of creative industries.

O'Connor (2015) summarizes a variety of perspectives in describing intermediaries, as those who make a reality of the idea of a creative economy, shaping, regulating, organizing and governing it. They work amidst its power struggles and tensions, negotiating and reconciling its contradictions—

culture conceived in terms of economic value and return on investment for instance—bringing together agents from across fields to produce and transform knowledge, priorities and objectives. Furthermore, the intermediary is implicated in a wider set of issues allied to the culture sphere and its role in social reproduction. In Wright's analysis, for instance, the intermediary is integral to reproducing the privileged place for the creative genius and 'potentially exclusionary aspects of cultural value', eliding production's imbrication in 'systemic, organizational and, crucially, class relations' (2005: 109).

This negative assessment of the work of intermediaries across a range of commentaries, according to Perry *et al.*, results in 'a rather singular narrative of self-interested cultural workers, under-pinned by an interest in the relative autonomy or interpenetration of cultural–economic fields' (2015: 725). As they go on to argue, there is a concomitant limitation in the way in which the intermediary is positioned in relation to 'a formalised, professional sphere of culture' (2015: 726) with its economic priority, eliding other sites and modes of cultural practice that might be at the margins of practice, everyday or vernacular in character. They thus call for accounts of intermediaries that attend to the work and ethos of those who 'operate in diverse professionalised and everyday cultural ecologies' (2015: 726). Such attention would look for wider motivations than are allowed for in more negative assessments, whether political, social or moral, 'particularly those that seek not only to advance their own interests but also to develop connections with excluded, marginalised or disadvantaged communities' (2015: 726). Further to this nuanced consideration of the role of intermediaries, Taylor suggests that while these figures might be involved in the reproduction of inequalities, they are also responsible for bringing into being new modes of association. Theorists of neoliberalism identifying the failures of that project point to new formations, and the emergence of alternatives to it manifest in 'a practical politics of collectivity' and the emergence of 'alternative regimes of economic calculation', for instance, 'in the social dynamics of the creative economy itself' (Taylor 2013: 363).

We relate Un-Convention to these nuanced readings of the work of intermediaries, here representative of a constellation of interests. Its operatives and acolytes mobilize positive traditions drawn from the organization's roots in Manchester's culture and practices, from within the margins of the music industry and nurtured by its expanding global networks. Un-Convention's originators were prompted by the exclusions noted above—from a boosterist vision of Manchester as well as a metropolitan music industry. In many ways, Un-Convention's reaction to these exclusions involved a particular articulation of a 'habitus of place', evincing an interesting conjunction of northernness and an independent ethos apparently rejected by 'In the City'. For instance,

Buzzcocks, a Manchester band, formulated the DIY tradition that many associate with the moment of punk and that was bequeathed to the independent sector. Reynolds has written that the band's Spiral Scratch was more important than recordings by the Sex Pistols in the development of punk: 'the EP wasn't the first independently released record, not by a long stretch, but it was the first to make a real polemical point about independence. In the process, Spiral Scratch inspired thousands of people to play the do-it-yourself/release-it-yourself game' (2009: 92). As he continues: 'Spiral Scratch was simultaneously a regionalist blow against the capital (Manchester versus London) and a conceptual exercise in demystification' (2009: 92), the release containing information on the production process, how to 'do it yourself'.

Here, Fonarow's typology of independent music as aesthetic and production practice is helpful for thinking about Un-Convention as intermediation. The 'mainstream' of music as corporate business is characterized by centralized authority and organizational conglomerates, a global reach and distant, impersonal nature that is 'phony, generic', generalized and 'fat' (2006: 66). 'Indie' conversely is intimate, personal and modest, on a small scale and about specificity; it is authentic, lean and *local*. All of these qualities are apparent in the discursive practices of Un-Convention, conferred both by its roots and location in Manchester, and its associations and actions at home and abroad.

In spite of his ambivalence about whether 'the ethos is particularly Mancunian', Thompson has reflected in interview on the associations of the North as a region with 'that kind of idea of socialism or Do-It-Together community', captured precisely in Un-Convention's approach, 'that everyone will be better off by coming together on ideas'. These are qualities that were recognized by those at the inaugural event. In one commentary at Un-Convention's original blog site, Nick Fitzsimons of Penny Distribution shared with readers 'the most thrilling discovery' from his participation in Salford that concerned the mutual recognition between bands, labels and artists in a similar situation. The result was 'an immense sense of camaraderie, founded on the simple realization that everyone was pushing in the same direction' (https://unconvention.wordpress.com). Likewise, promoter Howard Monk addressed potential supporters that 'This is an attempt at doing something at a level which is not so far beyond your reach'. He notes how so much about the music industry seemed 'so far away from your real experience', or about who one might know, but 'This is talking about what you can do, now ... this is very real' (ibid.). This sense of integrity, of authenticity and accessibility has been a continued quality of Un-Convention. For instance, a typical session at #UNCON 17 proposed 'Thinking outside the box', stretching the boundaries of what constitutes the parameters of music industry and its conventions. Addressing 'strategies that normally do not get addressed at events such as this' (ibid.), it aimed to consider musicians outside of pop and rock and those operating outside the established cycle of recording, promotion, airplay and tour. A repeated attempt at events to produce albums at speed offered a means of demystifying the process of music industry mediation. Such activity manifests a collective ethos, demonstrating how 'many hands make light work', momentarily sidelining the dominance of the individual artist or band and indeed exploring the nature and scope of creativity itself.

Some of Thompson's reticence about the foundational qualities of Un-Convention and its character may be promoted by its debt to a wider group of contributors and the rather improvised manner in which the organization developed. Certainly, for Daniel, the informal status of Un-Convention has sometimes meant that it 'feels like a jumble sale', a quality also signalling how it has been sustained through voluntarism and anxious searches for funding to enable its not-for-profit status. Unplanned, its continuity has nonetheless produced reflexivity and focus, and thus as Daniel has said, 'we have a process, a methodology'. While this method often appears *sui generis* to every iteration, involving an adaptation of purpose, panels, performance and participation to the needs of each locale in which Un-Convention has occurred, the ethos was cemented early on by the creation of a manifesto. This emerged from dialogue between founders, the creation of an extended Un-Convention board and participants, and underpins its continuation in the form of 'a forum for ideas, for creativity, for shared experiences and knowledge and for seeing and hearing great artists' (http://unconventionhub.org). The manifesto exhibits the discourses of independence, opining how the 'mainstream' lacks relevance and 'the most interesting stuff happens on the margins'. Un-Convention is not about the 'traditional' music industry in that it is 'not about the business of music'. It prefers a sense of celebration of music *qua* music, the organizations existing 'to provide a forum for those of us who work at the grassroots. For artists and musicians who want to understand how to get their music heard and how to practice their craft … For people who want to work with music, be they promoters, publicists or creatives' (ibid.). Of course, such ideas are paradoxical, holding at bay the exigencies of the industrialized, commercial processes that enable the production, distribution and consumption of music. This approach is summarized by Wright by way of the work of Russell Keat in which intermediaries sidestep the overarching demands of marketization in which cultural goods are conceived to 'have a *transformative* rather than simply a *demand* value, i.e. they allow for the exploration of aspects of human experience and human well-being' (Wright 2005: 107). As detailed above, such ideas are not unfamiliar to the discourse of popular music, particularly evinced in the independent sector where cultural value and authenticity are presented as primary concerns. This idea is encapsulated in a comment attributed to Tony Wilson in his obituary: '"You either make money", he once shrugged with typical portentousness, "or you make history"' (quoted in Anon 2007).

### Going Global—Internationalizing Un-Convention and the 'Habitus of Place'

Moving towards a conclusion, it would be disingenuous to avoid the fact that many more people have been involved in making Un-Convention than the handful involved in its founding. On this basis we should be careful, like Thompson, of any over-assertion or slippage about its essentially Mancunian character. Clearly, its operations are the nuanced sum of a great many parts. However, the anchor of this origin and association with the city of Manchester and its music culture, of its negotiation of identity, traditions and contemporary exclusions, is one that comes into focus in its ventures beyond the UK.

This internationalization occurred in tandem with the realization that Un-Convention would continue beyond Salford with requests to organize similar events following in quick succession at home—from Belfast (#UnCon 2, 2009)—and abroad: Mumbai (#UnCon 7, 2009) and Groningen (#UnCon 8, 2010). Of particular note here is the attention that the British Council afforded Un-Convention in aiding its international engagements. In interview Daniel has recounted that this relationship developed as a result of her nomination for a young entrepreneur award and the resulting attention and invitations she received. Subsequently, while making some small-scale funding available, the British Council was able to lend cachet to development in places such as Jinja, Uganda (#UnCon33, 2012) and Kathmandu (#UnCon44, 2013), enlisting Un-Convention in its missions and liaison with its agents.

As related in Daniel's account, while the British Council's involvement presented its own challenge, and space does not allow for discussion in the present context, support for Un-Convention was clearly imbricated in its project to export the country's creative industries (Garnham 2005: 25). We infer that, in turn, Un-Convention's drive for digital innovation and association with Manchester lent cachet to the British Council's project. Nonetheless, this relationship poses questions about the ultimate value of Un-Convention for the agenda of an economic export drive, especially in light of its not-for-profit status and missionary aspect. This is captured in an online summary by the British Council describing Un-Convention's investment in music as a tool for social change, manifest in 'hip hop projects in the barrios of Colombia to innovative music projects in the streets of India' (http://creativeconomy.britishcouncil.org/people/ruth-daniel). Such altruistically focused applications of music culture seem far away from the interests involved in the drive for the generation of returns on intellectual property and economic advantage.

In these global expeditions, it might have been expected that the identity of Un-Convention, in emerging from the North, might have become subsumed to a broader category of Britishness, or at least Englishness. However, such is the identification of Manchester with particular ideas of alternative music and independent enterprise that even in the international realm, this has purchase. Ever reflective on this matter, Thompson suggests that the footballing success of the city and its international renown also underwrite the city brand but it has been nonetheless an important aspect of how Un-Convention has been understood. As Thompson has said, 'When we stage events in Europe, people are envious of Manchester ... It's funny because you don't always see that when you live here' (quoted in Hurst 2013).

Certainly, the associations of Manchester's music culture traditions and more recent script have been important to exporting Un-Convention. For instance, in reviewing an event in Columbia (#UnCon10, 2010) Gualdrón (2010) expressed an appreciation of the regeneration agenda. He wrote that forums, workshops, concerts and fieldwork by its representatives, 'enabled the city of Manchester to talk with the city of Medellín', learning of the 'cultural flowering that led to the English city to rebuild its economy through the arts and creative industries'. Its lessons would be empowering, countering 'the less fortunate practices of the musical establishment' such as insularity, self-interestedness, threats and payola. He concluded that Un-Convention would enable consciousness of social power relations, and of society and 'the capacity we have to take the reins and give art the space it deserves in society' (Gualdrón 2010).

Un-Convention's ethos was likewise welcomed in Jinja, engaging with Doadoa, 'the East African Performing Arts Market' that brings together creative talent and intermediaries (http://doadoa.org/about-doadoa). This has been lauded as an innovation in East Africa: 'Its core is the fight for independence in music. It will help musicians to sustain themselves without necessarily fighting for the narrow and limited place at the top' (Namakula 2012). While a more detailed examination might have more to say about the nature of these engagements by Un-Convention, they have proven to be far from an A&R excursion by those attending from Europe or an attempt (on their behalf) to export a creative industries boosterism to Uganda, or any other destination. Certainly, the ethos of Thompson, Daniel and others has always been pursued in the spirit of exchange rather than exploitation or search for gain or advantage.

Thus, Un-Convention's statement on these expeditions is that 'it has been our endeavour to find new and innovative ways for artists to connect, and build sustainable careers in the modern music industry'. This has reached its potentially most fruitful development in a connection with the Brazilian network *Fora do Eixo*, which is described as a mutual aid system outside of formalized 'mainstream' practices of the dominant music and media industries. It is described as a network which 'allows artists to play sold out shows across the whole country, even in cities they have never visited before. It is free to use and now involves 30,000 artists from across 200 cities, generating $44 million for the independent music sector'. While this zeal might be tempered by an awareness of critiques of *Fora do Eixo* (Garland 2012), in 2012 it entered into partnership with Un-Convention in order to develop a similar network in the UK. In this way, the intermediaries of Un-Convention have discovered, around the globe, like-minded individuals and organizations inspired by the ethos it represents and indeed the 'habitus of place' it embodies in terms of a DIY independence, invested in collectivism and mutuality.

## Conclusions

Milestone has written of encouraging researchers concerned with the creative industries to consider the culture of place as important to the operation of businesses, of how they are inflected by character and local dynamics (2016: 57–58). In this chapter's contribution to thinking about representations of the North therefore, the focus has been not on the familiar aesthetics and interpretations of music and the practices of musicians. Rather, it has concerned the nature of cultural intermediaries as actors in the practical representational economy of Manchester. Thus, it has been suggested that Un-Convention's events take an 'all-encompassing view of creativity', one that 'seems to be unique to Manchester; the city that excels in industry, music and science thanks to the creativity of its thinkers' (Hurst 2013). Such statements, while rhetorical flourishes, are also expressions of a collective faith in the value of place and its representation as manifest in both symbolic outputs and practices of the creative sector.

As we have argued, those behind Un-Convention and its character can be understood to manifest a location-specific habitus, operating as a beacon for independent, collective values—in the city, across the UK and abroad. In so doing, and now in partnership with *Fora do Eixo*, Un-Convention returns to its home base enhanced by a nuanced cosmopolitanism ostensibly at odds with the kinds of boosterist, neoliberal urban entrepreneurialism for which Manchester has become known. In so doing, it offers challenging ways for thinking about how individuals and organizations carry their local identity and impact on the culture and values around them. While it might be 'off-axis', Un-Convention, in engaging so many and in aiming 'to have the conversations other events don't', challenges us to think further about the manifestation and making of identity and representation, their utility and value.

**Acknowledgements**

Research for this paper was informed by work conducted on the AHRC-funded projects 'Cultural Intermediation: Connecting Communities in the Creative Urban Economy' (Ref: AH/J005320/1) and Knowledge Transfer Fellowship, 'New Strategies for Radio and Music Organisations' (Ref: AH/E006825/1).

**About the Authors**

Jez Collins is a Research Fellow in Birmingham Centre for Media & Cultural Research, School of Media at Birmingham City University. His published work focuses on the development of popular music as public history-making and the role of activist archivists who capture, preserve, celebrate and reveal the hidden narratives and alternate histories of popular music. Collins is Co-Director of Manchester-based Un-Convention, a global grassroots music network which has organized and participated in 90 events across the world calling on local music activists to create and sustain local music industries. Collins is also a media practitioner; he was Executive Co-Producer for the award-winning documentary Made in Birmingham: Reggae Punk Bhangra and the radio documentary *Bring It On Home: The Led Zeppelin Story*, and he has created and curated numerous music-related exhibitions, installations, tours and talks. He is a Trustee of the National Jazz Archive and sits on the national advisory board of the Community Archives & Heritage Committee.

Paul Long is Professor of Media and Cultural History at Birmingham City University. His research encompasses issues of cultural justice and informs his published work on the politics of representation and the past as they pertain to public history, popular music and the archive. He recently co-curated a major exhibition on Birmingham's music history. His current research builds on these themes in two areas: (i) the political economy and affect of contemporary archival cultures; (ii) the history of student unions and their role in British popular music cultures.

**Primary Sources**

Collins conducted interviews with Ruth Daniel and Jeff Thompson at several Un-Convention events. He is a board member and has been a participant at many Un-Convention events. Here we draw in particular on interviews with Daniel, 29 April 2013 and Thompson, 26 February 2017.

**References**

Allen, Kim, and Sumi Hollingworth. 2013. '"Sticky Subjects" or "Cosmopolitan Creatives"? Social Class, Place and Urban Young People's Aspirations for Work in the Knowledge Economy'. *Urban Studies* 50/3: 499–517.

Anon. 2007. 'Obituary: Tony Wilson'. *Daily Telegraph*, 13 August. www.telegraph.co.uk/news/obituaries/1560130/Tony-Wilson.html (accessed 1 January 2017).

—2008. 'In the Other City'. www.bbc.co.uk/manchester/content/articles/2008/10/02/051008_un_convention_feature.shtml (accessed 1 January 2017).

Billsberry, Jon, Amy L. Kenworthy, George A. Hrivnak and Kenneth G. Brown. 2013. 'Daring to Be Different: Unconferences, New Conferences, and Reimagined Conferences'. *Journal of Management Education* 37/2: 175–79.

Bottà, Giacomo. 2009. 'The City that was Creative and Did Not Know: Manchester and Popular Music, 1976–97'. *European Journal of Cultural Studies* 12/3: 349–65.

Crossley, Nick. 2009. 'The Man Whose Web Expanded: Network Dynamics in Manchester's Post/Punk Music Scene 1976–1980'. *Poetics* 37/1: 24–49.

Dalton, Stephen. 2009. 'This Charming Manchester (Manchester Music, Then and Now)'. *The National* (October). https://www.rocksbackpages.com/Library/Article/this-charming-manchester-manchester-music-then-and-now (accessed 3 July 2017).

Fonarow, Wendy. 2006. *Empire of Dirt: The Aesthetics and Rituals of British Indie Music*. Middletown, CT: Wesleyan University Press.

Fraser, Benjamin, and Abby Fuoto. 2012. 'Manchester, 1976: Documenting the Urban Nature of Joy Division's Musical Production'. *Punk & Post Punk* 1/2: 139–54.

Garland, Shannon. 2012. '"The Space, the Gear, and Two Big Cans of Beer": Off the Axis and the Debate over Circulation, Remuneration, and Aesthetics in the Brazilian Alternative Market'. *Journal of Popular Music Studies* 24/4: 509–531.

Garnham, Nicholas. 2005. 'From Cultural to Creative Industries: An Analysis of the Implications of the "Creative Industries" Approach to Arts and Media Policy Making in the United Kingdom'. *International Journal of Cultural Policy* 11/1: 15–29.

Gualdrón, Andrés. 2010. *¿Cómo Estuvo UnConvention Medellín?* 6 October. http://www.revistaarcadia.com/musica/articulo/como-estuvo-unconvention-medellin/22443 (accessed 1 January 2017).

Halfacree, Keith, and Robert M. Kitchin. 1996. '"Madchester Rave On": Placing the Fragments of Popular Music'. *Area* 28/1: 47–55.

Haslam, Dave. 1999. *Manchester, England: The Story of a Pop Cult City*. London: Fourth Estate.

Holt, Fabian, and Carsten Wergin. 2013. *Musical Performance and the Changing City: Post-Industrial Contexts in Europe and the United States*. London: Routledge.

Hurst, Phoebe. 2013. *The Un-Convention Manchester Weekender*, 4 October. https://tinyurl.com/weekender-0410 (accessed 1 January 2017).

MacKillop, Fionn. 2012. 'Climatic City: Two Centuries of Urban Planning and Climate Science in Manchester (UK) and its Region'. *Cities* 29/4: 244–51.

Milestone, Katie. 2016. '"Northernness", Gender and Manchester's Creative Industries'. *Journal for Cultural Research* 20/1: 45–59.

Namakula, Elizabeth. 2012. 'DOADOA: Taking African Music to the Global Scene'. *Start: Journal of Arts and Culture* (30 May). http://startjournal.org/2012/05/doadoa-taking-african-music-to-the-global-scene/ (accessed 1 January 2017).

Nevarez, Leonard. 2013. 'How Joy Division Came to Sound Like Manchester: Myth and Ways of Listening in the Neoliberal City'. *Journal of Popular Music Studies* 25/1: 56–76.

O'Connor, Justin. 2015. 'Intermediaries and Imaginaries in the Cultural and Creative Industries'. *Regional Studies* 49/3: 374–87.

Peck, Jamie, and Kevin Ward, eds. 2002. *City of Revolution: Restructuring Manchester*. Manchester: Manchester University Press.

Perry, Beth, Karen Smith and Saskia Warren. 2015. 'Revealing and Re-Valuing Cultural Intermediaries in the "Real" Creative City: Insights from a Diary-keeping Exercise'. *European Journal of Cultural Studies* 18/6: 724–40.

Quilley, Stephen. 2000. 'Manchester First: From Municipal Socialism to the Entrepreneurial City'. *International Journal of Urban and Regional Research* 24/3: 601–615.

Reynolds, Simon. 2009. *Rip It Up and Start Again: Postpunk 1978–1984*. London: Faber & Faber.

Robb, John. 2009. *The North Will Rise Again: Manchester Music City 1976–1996*. London: Aurum Press.

Straw, Will. 2004. 'Cultural Scenes'. *Loisir et société/Society and Leisure* 27/2: 411–22.

Strong, Catherine, and Alastair W. Greig. 2014. '"But We Remember When We Were Young": Joy Division and New Orders of Nostalgia'. *Volume!* 11/2: 192–205.

Taylor, Calvin. 2013. 'Between Culture, Policy and Industry: Modalities of Intermediation in the Creative Economy'. *Regional Studies* 49/3: 362–73.

Wright, David. 2005. 'Mediating Production and Consumption: Cultural Capital and "Cultural Workers"'. *British Journal of Sociology* 56/1: 105–121.

# 3 'They Say a Town is Just a Town, Full Stop, But What Do They Know?' Architecture, Urbanism and Pop in Sheffield

Owen Hatherley

In his 1994 novel of the Thatcherite Eighties, *What a Carve Up!*, Jonathan Coe describes his protagonist's first visit to Sheffield.

> The line was planted so thickly with trees that Sheffield itself took me completely by surprise, my first sight of it being a row of terraced houses silhouetted against a sky of Mediterranean blue, and perched on the top of a ridge, impossibly high, on a clifftop, almost. All at once a spectacular townscape lay before me: the steelworks and factory chimneys beside the railway were shrunk to insignificance beside the sheerness of the hillsides on which the city had been boldly raised, with phalanxes of tower blocks climbing steeply to their summit. Nothing had prepared me for such sudden, austere beauty (Coe 2007: 272).

This landscape is presented as a resistant one, which stands both politically and physically against the bland yet vicious sprawl of south-east England and the West Midlands. The narrator is amazed 'to find myself in a city so palpably and bracingly different from London'; arriving in the period of the self-described 'Socialist Republic of South Yorkshire', he 'was immediately filled with envy at the thought of a community which could so closely unite itself around a common cause' (Coe 2007: 272–73). This is not an atypical response of a left-leaning southerner with, shall we say, an open-minded approach to architectural aesthetics on first acquaintance with Sheffield. It comes across as an epically modern city, with its high-rises and concrete, but is integrated in a way rare among industrial cities with its landscape; the result, even regardless of its (then) embattled politics, is a city as citadel.

In terms of popular music, particularly in terms of musics that have emerged out of post-punk and electronic music, Sheffield is a city that punches some way above its weight. Compared, for instance, with the larger West Riding industrial city of Leeds, Sheffield has contributed vastly more to popular music—from the late 1970s on, a list that would include the Human League, Cabaret Voltaire, Comsat Angels, Heaven 17, ABC, Forgemasters, Sweet Exorcist (and the label Warp), Pulp, somewhat later the Arctic Monkeys and the Long Blondes. There are several groups of major importance from Leeds, but many of these were based primarily around Leeds University, such as Gang of Four, the Mekons and Delta 5. Tellingly, some of the more interesting groups from Leeds have sometimes been assumed to be from Sheffield, such as early techno acts Unique 3 or LFO. This is, on the face of it, a conundrum: why should Sheffield be the city that most rivals the large metropolises like Greater Manchester, London or Glasgow in the creation of modernist pop music? The argument of this chapter is that it may be the landscape described so well by Jonathan Coe that explains this preponderance. Sheffield competes only with London, Glasgow and Birmingham for the intensity of its transformation in the immediate post-war decades. Under an effective Labour one-party state, the city embarked on a massive programme of rebuilding, which had extremely melodramatic architectural results. Rather than being designed by volume builders or engineers, Sheffield's housing schemes were produced by the city architect's department, and placed quite deliberately on the city's hillside peaks, as if to announce the city and its priorities from a distance. Music and architecture are the only two places where Sheffield has had notable influence on the wider culture in Britain, something odd for a city that occasionally boasts of its insularity ('England's biggest village', as one cliché has it). The effect of architecture on music is hard to quantify directly—certainly, there is no evidence of it affecting the city's popular culture or popular music to any significant degree before the late 1970s. At that point, however, various Sheffield bands deliberately evoked, described, sometimes celebrated and sometimes critiqued the city's architecture and planning. Before we go on to music about architecture, though, we need to know exactly what architecture we are talking about.

**Empire State Humans**
The major building in any discussion of this kind is Park Hill (see Figure 1), an immense deck-access council housing complex on a hill above the city's railway station, at the time of writing in autumn 2016 still undergoing a

**Figure 1:** Park Hill, Sheffield (photograph by Owen Hatherley)

long-running process of redesign and privatization. For those that actually commissioned it—such as then councillor and later deputy Labour leader Roy Hattersley—Sheffield's most famous modernist (or any) building, Park Hill, was actually an attempt to emulate a Leeds building, the vast, Vienna-inspired interwar housing complex of Quarry Hill, which was demolished in the 1970s. For its architects, however, it was an early response to what were considered, even in the 1950s, to be modern architecture's failures. Empty spaces, isolation, a lack of street life, a middle-class 'this is good for you' ethos—all were critiqued by its planners and architects. Unfortunately for its advocates, the style of the buildings—reliant on 'béton brut', unpainted concrete—was christened 'the New Brutalism'. The New Brutalism's chief propagandist and associate, the writer and architectural historian Reyner Banham, pondered in a 1966 book whether the idiom was an 'Ethic or Aesthetic', so firmly marked was it by social concerns.

Banham argued that the Brutalists were the architectural equivalent of the 'angry young men' of the '50s, like the playwright Arnold Wesker or the novelist Alan Sillitoe. He pointed out that some of these architects were of 'red brick extraction', products of post-war class mobility, often Northerners, like its main theorists and occasional practitioners, the fiercely self-promoting Stockton-on-Tees and Sheffield-born intellectual couple Alison and Peter Smithson. Their Golden Lane scheme for a deck-access block of council housing defined Brutalism, and added a Pop Art touch, when the architects added images of Marilyn Monroe and Joe Di Maggio to the drawings for the unbuilt structure.

> In our zeal to erase the evils arising out of lack of proper water supply, sanitation and ventilation, we had torn down streets of houses which despite their sanitary shortcomings harboured a social structure of friendliness and mutual aid. We had thrown out the baby with the bathwater (Jack Lynn, co-designer of Park Hill, Sheffield, in 1962, quoted in Landau 1968: 30).

Reading the above quote, you have to remind yourself that Lynn is not talking about the building he designed at all, but the orthodox slum-clearance modernism he and his colleagues were setting themselves against. Park Hill was an early response to what were considered, even in the 1950s, to be modern architecture's failures. Park Hill was, alongside London's slightly larger but contrastingly affluent Barbican estate, the largest-scale application of Brutalism's ethic and aesthetic. It cleared a notoriously violent slum by Sheffield's Midland Station nicknamed 'little Chicago', but rather than rehousing the residents in isolated towers, the architects—Jack Lynn and Ivor Smith with Frederick Nicklin, selected by Sheffield's city architect Lewis Womersley—attempted to replicate in the air the tightly packed street life of the area. Students of the Smithsons, Lynn and Smith were enthusiasts for the close-knit working-class life supposedly being broken up by the new estates and new towns. As in the Smithsons' unbuilt Golden Lane scheme, claustrophobic walk-ups or corridors were rejected in favour of 12ft wide 'streets in the sky'. These 'streets' were almost all connected with the ground, on steeply sloping land. Street corners were included where the winding building twisted around, with the spaces around the blocks filled with shops, schools and playgrounds. Park Hill was closely monitored to see if it succeeded in its aims, and had its own tenants' magazine, the laconically named *Flat*.

Meanwhile the architectural aesthetic was shaped by a rejection of the clean geometries of mainstream modernism, in favour of roughness and irregularity. The marks of concrete shuttering were left, in the fashion of Le Corbusier's Unité d'Habitation, a monumental apartment block in Marseilles. Yet the use of multicoloured bricks, gradated from scarlet to yellow, abstract patterns aided by artist John Forrester, connected it with a specifically English, northern idiom. The blocks rose from four storeys at the highest point of the hill to thirteen at the lowest, giving a continuous roof line visible from much of the city: at the highest point they look out over the expanse of the city centre and the post-industrial Don Valley, and at the lowest they mingled unassumingly with Victorian terraces. Despite—or because of—Park Hill's aesthetic extremism, early responses to the blocks were very positive indeed. The 2009 BBC documentary *Romancing the Stone* features much footage of children and OAPs praising the place's modernity and community. Over old footage of the playgrounds, a South Yorkshire voice intones: 'there's no stopping this collective thinking. It's the future'. Encouraged by these responses, the architects designed a 'Park Hill Mark Two' built just behind the site—Hyde Park (see Figure 2), which rose to an eighteen-storey 'castle keep'. Later, a mark three, Kelvin Flats, was designed by other architects west of the city centre.

**Figure 2:** Hyde Park, Sheffield (photograph by Owen Hatherley)

In 1962, the book *Ten Years of Housing in Sheffield*, documenting Lewis Womersley's tenure as city architect, was published in English, French and Russian, rather extraordinarily. It is a curiously sad book, an object from what now seems a completely alien culture, but which makes clear just how tentative the planners and architects actually were—no grandiose declarations of success here. Park Hill was presented there as an experiment, albeit one about which the writers were cautiously optimistic. Noting that there was a huge risk in such a development of 'creating a vast inhuman building block', Womersley was at pains to point out how much they had attempted to lessen this effect, from the public park created between the estate and the street, to the way the courtyards opened out further as the storeys rose—though he noted that 'it must be left…to the occupants to judge to what extent the architects have been successful' (Womersley *et al.* 1962: 47). Meanwhile, along with the expected shops and schools, Park Hill and its sister scheme Hyde Park were unpretentious enough to include no less than four pubs.

Streets in the sky were only one facet of Sheffield's housing programme. The less futuristic but equally remarkable suburban counterpart to Park Hill's urbanity was Gleadless Valley, a collection of houses and flats making breathtaking use of the hilly landscape, resembling a strange socialist South Yorkshire version of 1950s Southern California. Park Hill makes sense best when seen as part of a larger project in town planning, aligned with other estates, also placed on prominent hilltop sites, such as the more straightforward tower block and maisonette modernism of Woodside and Netherthorpe. As the head of the city's Labour council, Howard Lambert, noted in *Ten Years*, all of these projects had a topographical specificity that, incidentally, was also at the heart of Brutalist preoccupations:

> most of our projects feature as important additions to the total environment—the more so because the topographical characteristics of the city allow many of them, such as Park Hill, Woodside and Netherthorpe, to be topographically related to each other. The careful exploitation of this topography—the building up of hill-top architectural compositions—is gradually producing something of the fascination of Italian Hill-towns. It is stimulating, exciting! (J. L. Womersley *et al.* 1962: 3)[1]

By the end of the 1970s, over half of Sheffield's housing was council-owned, and they were still building Brutalist deck-access housing, albeit on a warmer, smaller scale that can still be seen in Gleadless. This is a reminder that coun-

---

1. Woodside was demolished in the 2000s, Netherthorpe reclad in the '90s postmodernist idiom. The 'hill-towns' line, a persistent architectural cliché, most recently used in Will Alsop's proposals for Barnsley, apparently elicited the following from one Woodside resident after decades of poor maintenance—'the only similarity between this f---ing estate and a f---ing Italian hillside village is the amount of f---ing water running through the middle of it'. See online comments to my 'Sheffield: City of Skeletons', *Building Design*, 15 May 2009, http://www.bdonline.co.uk/story.asp?storycode=3140474 (accessed 23 June 2009).

cil housing was never intended to be the emergency measure it is now, but something that was genuinely 'mixed' in terms of social class and income.

Early criticism was almost overwhelmingly positive. One of the most penetrating articles on it was by Ian Nairn, who visited in 1961 and again six years later. His account of these visits notes something that is still apparent on visiting the building. Its sublime scale is initially intimidating—'they might not frighten the inhabitants, but they certainly frighten me' (Nairn 1967: 76)—yet up close, the human scale and intense sense of place is far more apparent. The problem is that few ever venture that close. Nairn's account was featured in *Britain's Changing Towns*, a book that attempted to weigh up the results of 1960s Britain's version of regeneration. On the whole, Nairn was deeply unimpressed by what he saw as the flashy, meretricious and loveless results of redevelopment. Sheffield, however, received unremitting praise from this most unsentimental of critics. He noted that 'an enlightened housing exchange system' (ibid.) (and the huge amount of council housing) meant that the young could freely choose flats; the elderly or families chose the lush suburbia of Gleadless and the like, with swapping as much as three or four times considered normal; while Park Hill itself, first seen in a slightly ambiguous light, is by 1967 viewed as an incontrovertible success. 'The surfaces are weathering well, and the multicoloured brick is achieving its purpose, as it disappears under the grime, of providing a gradual lightening of tone from bottom to top' (Nairn 1967: 80). Meanwhile Reyner Banham, a critic who could be expected to praise Park Hill, wrote that it was the nearest attempt to genuinely create an Other Architecture, unconcerned with conventional notions of elevations, design and elegance, instead creating 'a building more concerned with life than architecture'. It was the definitive monument of Brutalism, its finest moment: 'the moral crusade of Brutalism for a better habitat through built environment probably reaches its culmination at Park Hill' (Banham 1966: 132). Even so, this embodiment of the apparently avant-garde Brutalists' bloody-mindedness was opened by the centrist Labour leader Hugh Gaitskell, and praised by Conservative Prime Minister Harold Macmillan.

Obviously, Park Hill was not utopia. It had too few lifts, and the concrete on the taller sections was cracking by the 1980s. More arguably, it may have been too successful at recreating the space of the old rookeries—like them, it was full of escape routes and shadowy spots. The notion that it could preserve a working-class community being obliterated everywhere else is unsurprisingly unconvincing. However, there is no evidence that it ever became a 'sink' until at least the mid-'90s. Some of the critiques of Park Hill are barely worth taking seriously—the most famous, Nicholas Taylor's diatribe in the *Architectural Review* of 1967, appears to have been based on entirely imaginary statistics, and surveys into the 1980s showed a high level of satisfaction with the flats (see Saint 1996: 37–38). The aforementioned documentary *Romancing the Stone* claimed that the 'dream turned sour in the early 1980s', but didn't explore why that might be so—the transformation of the steel industry into a low workforce, the mass unemployment created by automated processes which turned Sheffield swiftly from a prospective City of the Future into a remnant of the past, or the 'Right to Buy' council housing which would turn unpopular estates into refuges of last resort. In an optimistic period Park Hill looked confident; as that world collapsed, it looked intimidating. In the 1990s Hyde Park was partly demolished, and its remnants became part of a wider project influenced by the work of the conservative geographers Alice Coleman and Oscar Newman (theorists of 'defensible space'), as part of the redesign of the city that coincided with the World Student Games held in Sheffield in 1991.[2] The 1960s terraces that were part of Hyde Park and the 1930s flats that preceded Park Hill were both reclad with new elevations that made them resemble the low-rise, introverted, aesthetically traditionalist speculative suburban housing created in the 1980s by developers such as Wimpey or Barratt. Hyde Park's decks were filled in, creating exactly the kind of desolate, soulless, depopulated space that 'streets in the sky' were designed to combat, its taller segments were demolished, and the whole thing was clad in brick and plastic (Dan Cruikshank in Saint 1996: 51).[3] Kelvin flats were levelled completely.[4]

## High-Rise Living's Not So Bad

At exactly the point that conventional architectural opinion was turning against the streets in the sky, popular music told a different story. The Human League were keen to have it on record on the sleeve that their shimmering, proto-techno instrumental 'Dancevision', described by Simon Reynolds in terms which describe contemporary Sheffield rather well as an 'ambiguous alloy of euphoria and grief' ((Reynolds 2005: 162), was recorded in front of Kelvin Flats; rather aptly, the later reissue of the group's early recordings as The Future featured a photograph of Park Hill. On their first album *Reproduction* (1979), 'Empire State Human' staged a strange confrontation between

---

2. For a critique of the notion of 'defensible space', here described as a policy that creates, rather than obliterates fear, see Minton (2009).

3. Note also Cedric Price's disdain for the 'pathetic Colemanville' that provided Park Hill's new hinterland (Saint 1996: 63).

4. Kelvin was, even more inexplicably, restored soon before it was demolished in 1995, and is interestingly described in Peter Jones' *Streets in the Sky* (2008). A former tenant of all three deck-access blocks in the 1980s and 90s, Jones claims Kelvin, the least famous and least publicly lamented of the three, had the warmest sense of community, while the reclad, heavily surveilled Hyde Park was the least enjoyable place to live.

man and architecture, where human being and building become interchangeable, while 'Blind Youth' reprimanded punks for their anti-modernism, insisting with tongue only slightly in cheek that 'you've had it easy, you should be glad/high-rise living's not so bad'. In their later career as bona fide pop stars, the group made great use of Sheffield's architecture in the video for 'Love Action', with a wedding taking place in one of Basil Spence's minimalist, concrete and brick churches, and setting the main romance of the video/song's narrative on a deck-access block of flats.

The more chilling, overwhelming aspect of Sheffield's post-war architecture and car-centred planning was obliquely referenced in the artwork and some of the songs on Comsat Angels' 1980 *Waiting for a Miracle*, as a rather glamorously oppressive space, on the model of Joy Division's Manchester. On the front cover, cars speed along a dual-carriageway; on the back cover, you can see that they're speeding past Park Hill, whose streets in the sky are illuminated with yellow sodium light. Lyrically, *Waiting for a Miracle* presents a much more familiar post-punk city—lives trapped, relationships tense and paranoid, and loomed over by the threat of nuclear war. On the album's centrepiece, 'On the Beach', the band obliquely imagine the city, with its motorways and high-rises ('a steel tide on an asphalt beach') devastated, so that 'no piece of glass or chrome remains... we'll wash this place right down the drain'; the intensity of the description of Sheffield in the song is dismissed by an interlocutor—'she says a town is just a town, full stop, but what does she know?' Oddly this chimes well with one of two major films made by TV director Mick Jackson in Sheffield in the 1980s—*Threads*, where Park Hill is among the Sheffield landmarks destroyed by a nuclear attack. In the other, *A Very British Coup*, a newly elected left-wing Labour Prime Minister and ex-steelworker is doorstopped in the first scene, in his apartment in Hyde Park flats. The city pivots between being dystopia and socialist citadel.

It could be argued that, when Sheffield City Council was no longer prepared to create an image of the future and a new way of life, Sheffield's electronic producers did so instead. Sheffield City Council had long had an enlightened policy with regard to ex-industrial spaces being used as studios and for raves, so it is unsurprising that the city became one of the major centres of house and techno at the turn of the 1990s. What is striking about this, however, is that the embrace of modernity by techno producers coincided with severe doubts about the modern landscape, and its progressive dismantlement. At the same time that Hyde Park's modern, cubist terraces were being given pitched roofs, Warp Records, and their early producers such as Richard H. Kirk or Rob Gordon, were creating an art form that was a continuation of the streets in the sky's vertiginous sense of new space and their brutalist, low-end rumble. It is also a sound that draws on the more 'high' modernist aspect of

Sheffield modernism, such as the American, metropolitan slickness of Sheffield university's Arts Tower and Library, designed by Gollins Melvin Ward in a style completely in hock to Mies van der Rohe in the early 1960s, the first wholly modernist university campus in the UK. This series of precisely engineered, machine-tooled, glass-and-steel pavilions and towers, recently renovated to their post-war splendour, is closer to the aesthetic of early Warp, rather than the Human League's (or Pulp's) more Heath Robinson pop modernism. Rob Gordon's group Forgemasters took their name from a particularly large Sheffield steelworks; their clean, clear, optimistic sound derived directly from Kraftwerk's *Computer World* and the more utopian moments of Detroit techno—Model 500's 'No UFOs', Rhythim is Rhythim's 'Strings of Life'. In one of their harshest metal-on-metal constructions, 'Stress', they sample Cybotron's 'Techno City', as if to lay claim to Sheffield as Detroit's British correspondent. A similar sense of metallic grandeur can be found in Sweet Exorcist, a collaboration between DJ Parrot and Cabaret Voltaire's Richard H Kirk. Notably, the videos for many of these were made by local musician Jarvis Cocker, and present a modernity that increasingly bypasses the present in favour of purer images from the recent past—Space Invaders, 1970s children's television. The music is still 'futurist', but a 'retro' prefix is starting to creep in.

The group that most thoroughly fixated with the built landscape of Sheffield was Cocker's group Pulp, whose name, as we will see, was traduced in the marketing of Park Hill to media professionals. Long after the demise of post-punk, starting with the tour-de-Sheffield in their 1990 single 'My Legendary Girlfriend', Pulp would return again and again to the ambiguous post-war landscape of their hometown, seeing it alternately as utopia and dystopia. In their 1992 'Sheffield: Sex City', Jarvis Cocker intones a series of Sheffield place names, with luridly sensual relish—from 'Intake' onwards, each one of them emphasized for any possible double-meanings. Frechville, Hackenthorpe, Shalesmoor, *Wombwell*. The next voice you hear is Candida Doyle, deadpan and Yorkshire, reading—of all things—from one of the sexual fantasies in a Nancy Friday book. Here, the city itself is the focus for all libidinal energies. 'We were living in a big block of flats... within minutes the whole building was fucking. I mean, have you ever heard other people fucking, and really enjoying it? Not like in the movies, but when it's real...'. Then, the 'sun rose from behind the gasometers at 6.30am', and we're on a tour of the carnal possibilities in a post-industrial city.

The most important sounds in it (aside from Cocker's own increasingly astonishing groans, howls, gasps and ecstatic squeals) are Doyle's, too—the banks of synths, interspersed with some more recent artificial instruments. It is these smears of indistinct, tinny keyboard atmospheres, the arpeggiated stutters, the repetitious house vamps and Russell Senior's queasily treated violin, which simulate the vertiginous feeling of nervousness, anticipation and mania which underpin the ridiculous, magnificent lyric, an obsessive, clammily sexual ambience. Underneath, a metronomic kick drum pounds, and deep, relentless low-end throbs, which the group got Warp Records' in-house engineer to lower to sub-bass levels. As it pulses, the whole city is 'getting stiff in the building heat', and Jarvis walks through its entire extent trying to find his lover. So overwhelmed is he by the sheer sexuality of Sheffield that he finds himself 'rubbing up against lamp-posts, trying to get rid of it'. The places made sexual are exemplars of non-utopian everyday life, as we traverse the semis, the gardens, and hear 'groans from a T-reg Chevette—you bet...you bet...', and in a particularly memorable moment stop to penetrate 'a crack in the pavement'. This transfigured space is cut with moments of frustrating mundanity: 'crumbling concrete bus shelters' and tedious nights indoors watching television. The pursuit is interrupted, because 'the fares went up at seven'; our protagonist loses his lover while 'sentenced to three years in the housing benefit waiting room'. The frustration and fascination build and build and build to the point of explosion, leaving the city's topographical extremes as location for the final consummation, with the city abstracted below them. 'We finally made it, on a hilltop at 4am. A million twinkling yellow street lights. The whole city is your jewellery box. Reach out, and take what you want...'. The city has not survived its orgy, and our lovers survey the wreckage left over. 'Everyone on Park Hill came in unison at 4.13 AM, and the whole block fell down. A tobacconist caught fire, and everyone in the street died of lung cancer.'

A 'Guide to Sheffield' that Pulp compiled for *NME* in 1993 partly concentrates on its role as centre of the 'Socialist Republic of South Yorkshire', when the red flag famously flew above the town hall. This comes out in a particularly quotidian way through these songs, where the all-but-free public transport is recalled as a way of seeing the city as a totality, only to be destroyed by deregulation and privatization:

> I remember when the buses were only 10p to go anywhere. That's why buses are mentioned quite a lot in our songs. Anyway, it all stopped in the mid-80s. There are about six different bus companies now, like Eager Beaver, Yorkshire Terrier... it's ridiculous—if the driver sees the stop they're supposed to be going to hasn't got any people at it, they change the number and go to one that has. People came from Japan to see our bus service—it was the envy of the Western World (Morris 1993).

As much as Pulp's Sheffield songs were the voyeur's view into an interior, they were an all-surveying view from the top deck of a bus.

More particularly, their gazetteer is about the city's failure to become the modernist metropolis that it once promised to be. Sometimes this happens in the most mundane examples, such as the Castle Square 'Hole in the Road', an underpass-cum-shopping-centre, whose early 1990s demolition was lamented by Pulp in the music press as an attempt 'to make everything like Meadowhall', the postmodernist out-of-town mall constructed on the site of a former steelworks; or you could find it in the montage-based modernist edifices designed under Womersley, constructed as assemblages of walkways, multiple levels and almost kitsch details. There is the Castle Market (see Figure 3), since demolished, where Cocker worked on the fish stall in his youth, the subject of a short local TV item where he held it up as an example of what makes Sheffield unique and specific. Then there are the housing estates, the monumental, interconnected collective housing blocks placed on the city's hilltops. Park Hill, we know about; but there are also its successors, Hyde Park and Kelvin, the latter of which gets a markedly less ecstatic Pulp song devoted to it. The suburban version at Gleadless Valley was the place where Russell Senior was raised.

**Figure 3:** Castle Market, Sheffield (photograph by Owen Hatherley)

Read another guide, any Shell Guide or Pevsner from the 1960s or 1970s, and it is this that they will tell you to look for—aside from a single Georgian square and a couple of Victorian civic buildings, they all point the traveller to that visionary series of housing estates and markets, or to a new town hall designed as a concrete honeycomb and soon nicknamed 'the egg box'. This vision was propagandized in the 1971 City Council promotional film *Sheffield: City on the Move*, a confident, convincing, if undeniably clunky vision of civic futurism that was sampled as a 'what were we thinking!' joke at the start of the 'dance, prole, dance' genre's most noted product, the 1997 comedy film *The Full Monty*. Many schemes were shelved for lack of money—at one point, the council were making plans to run street decks and walkways across the entire Sheaf Valley. By the 1990s, buildings that had a lifespan of barely 20 years, whose futurism was suddenly dated—the aforementioned town hall, the 'wedding cake' registry office next to it, the concrete housing estates of Broomhall, Hyde Park and Kelvin—began to be demolished, leaving huge scars across the city which haven't fully healed two decades later.

Another early 1990s *NME* interview makes it especially clear just how much of an effect this construction and destruction had on the future members of Pulp: "Sheffield's full of half-arsed visions of cities of the future that turn into a pile of rubbish', Russell Senior reflects, standing on the biggest traffic roundabout in Europe. 'We grew up reading the local paper and seeing "Sheffield, city of the future", with a map of how it's going to be and pictures of everyone walking around in spacesuits, smiling. But we're the only ones who took it seriously...'. 'When I was younger I definitely thought I'd live in space', says Jarvis Cocker ruefully. 'But when you realise you're not going to, it colours your life; you can't think, "It's alright if I'm signing on because I'll be on Mars soon", you have to try and get it down here' (Mulvey 1992). What runs through all of this is the lament of true believers in modernism, holding the present to account for its failure to create a viable future, and the pinched vision of the possible that then instils in those born after the future; as Cocker would yelp in 1998, obliquely apropos New Labour's workfare schemes, 'we were brought up on the space race—*now they expect you to clean toilets*'. *Intro* opens with a song that confronts this directly, 'Space', where an ambient drift of indeterminate hums and flutters imagines the previously longed-for journey above the earth's surface, where all the trash of bedsit life is left behind—'this is what you've been waiting for', he whispers, 'no dust collecting in corners or cups of tea that go cold before you drink them...it doesn't matter if the lifts don't work or the car won't start. We're going to escape'—and then Cocker suddenly rejects the reverie, stiffening into a determination to 'get my kicks down below'. It is this that lies behind all the obvious retro sounds and signifiers—the Farfisas, Stylophones and Moogs, the jumble sale clothes, the tower blocks, space hoppers and luridly bright artificial fabrics that pervade Pulp's music videos—a sense of being cheated out of the future, responding by fetishising the last time that a viable future appeared to exist. Yet Pulp's songs did delve into 1970s nostalgia, not least as a way of talking about the stripped-pine compromises and bland conformities of the 1990s.

'Deep Fried in Kelvin' (1993) is like a ten-minute reversal of 'Sheffield: Sex City'. Like the latter, it centres on one of the three huge collective housing blocks designed by Jack Lynn and Ivor Smith for Sheffield City Council. Kelvin Flats, which were, as we have seen, approvingly mentioned in the Human League's sleeve notes for the sublime 'Dancevision', were demolished in the 1990s and replaced by low-rise, low-density Barratt Homes, the sort you could imagine housing the soap-on-a-rope sagas of 'His & Hers'. In marked contrast with 'Sheffield: Sex City', there is little interest in the utopian possibilities of brutalist megastructures in 'Deep Fried', which instead depicts a people congenitally unable to live in anything other than houses with gardens, centring on a man destroying his flat by filling it with soil, trying to turn it into a garden, walking 'on promenade with concrete walkways, where pigeons go to die'. It is a vision of a consumerist, barely literate proletariat destroyed by Thatcherism, where children are 'conceived in the toilets of Meadowhall'. It has equal disdain both for the 'fizzy orange and chips' youth of this 'ghetto' and for those who might improve it (memorably, 'we don't need your sad attempts at social conscience based on taxi rides home at night from exhibition openings. We just want your car radio and bass reflex speakers. Now'), and eventually the contempt seems to be aimed at the narrator himself and his social concern.

Similarly bleak as a portrayal of a modernist environment is 'Mile End', palatably translated into genial space-skiffle. Here it is the old East End of London, repository for Blur's proleface sentimentality, which is, when surveyed from the top of a tower block as the 'pearly king of the isle of Dogs', 'just like heaven, if it didn't look like hell', and where maintaining your difference, rather than blending in, is the only way to keep sane. 'Nobody wants to be your friend, cos you're not from round here, oh no—as if that wasn't something to be proud about!' They are all songs that appear, to the untrained eye, more or less autobiographical, tales of dole life when you could still get a council flat without having to lose an arm or a leg or have a family in double figures. Sometimes these London estates become neither utopian nor dystopian, but have a more everyday romanticism; Jarvis Cocker and Martin Wallace's elegantly self-deconstructing 1992 video to 'Babies', for instance, takes place in Southwark Council Architects' Department's Sceaux Gardens Estate, Camberwell, where Jarvis and Steve Mackey were living at the time, and like Park Hill, somewhere with much architectural reputation when it was built.

Its low and high-rise curtain-walled blocks, with their elegant, cubic green panels and their Francophone names, were spread across green space taken over from former back gardens and overgrown bombsites. Ian Nairn wrote of Sceaux Gardens in 1966 that because of this, 'the magical transformation has happened, an estate transformed into a place' (Nairn 1966: 198). The block named 'Voltaire' gets a particularly wry shot in the video, as do the patches of green and swaying flowers in front of the towers, creating a place perfect for the song's rum, giddy nostalgia. One of the blocks caught fire in 2009, killing several people. The recent investigation blamed the council for installing as-cheap-as-possible UPVC panels on the whole block, which melted in the heat, spreading the fire. These council flat dystopias are, for all their justified bitterness, the correlate of the failed utopia that is longingly re-imagined in 'Sheffield: Sex City', indicators of what has happened to the working class and the places it lived in after (then only fifteen years of) Thatcherism.

## An Extra Special Place

**Figure 4:** The National Centre for Popular Music (photograph by Owen Hatherley)

It is almost certain that Park Hill would have suffered the same fate as Kelvin and Hyde Park had it not been listed in 1998. Practically inescapable in Sheffield, it is an overwhelming reminder of what it once wanted to be—the capital of the Socialist Republic of South Yorkshire—rather than what it wants to be now, a local service and cultural industries centre. Yet, like all British cities, it spent the following decade undergoing the dubious ministrations of 'free market' urbanism. This too was done with reference to pop music. The first attempt at centring 'regeneration' around the musical heritage of the city was actually Branson Coates' 1999 National Centre for Popular Music (see Figure 4), intended as a permanent exhibition, akin to Frank Gehry's Experience Music Project in Seattle. Designed in 'iconic' form as three titanium-clad drums, it originally contained exhibits on pop music history such as costumes, instruments and suchlike. It was hugely unpopular, and closed within two years, to be used by Sheffield Hallam University as a student's union. A much more successful example of neoliberal, 'iconic' urbanism using the city's pop history is actually the privatization and redevelopment of Park Hill by the Manchester-based developers Urban Splash.

Park Hill was transferred—for free, not sold—to Urban Splash in 2008. The Manchester-based property developer is best known for turning derelict mills, office blocks and factories into city-centre 'lofts', and according to its own account grew out of a pop poster stall run by founder Tom Bloxham, a former Labour Party Young Socialist. It has long been an interesting amalgam of two New Labour fixations—the 'creative industries' and property speculation, as opposed to Old Labour's heavy industries and social housing. Urban Splash has always stressed a link between its work and the Manchester of post-punk and acid house, and its brochure for Park Hill was elegantly rendered by Warp Records' and Pulp's sleeve designers, the Designers Republic. Full of quotations from Sheffield bands like the Human League and ABC, the whole document was written in infantile music-press clichés that contrast tellingly with the popular but non-patronising language of a document such as *Ten Years of Housing in Sheffield*. 'Don't you want me Baby?' it asks, and proceeding through numerous factual errors, it promises to restore 'the love' to Park Hill. 'Make it a place', it says. 'Make it a special place. Make it an EXTRA special place'. Although at least they're honest enough to admit 'we're in this to make a profit' (Johnson 2006: 75). At the time of writing in 2016, despite a Stirling Prize nomination, the redevelopment of the building can surely be seen as a spectacular failure. Thousands of people have been 'decanted' from social housing, in a city with a council waiting list of tens of thousands, and only one part of the building has been renovated and sold—to great fanfare, and with major public funding from English Heritage and the Homes and Communities Agency. However, while the redevelopment has been taking place, Park Hill's derelict hull has become a frequent set for music videos, films and television series of the 1980s, something surely connected to the proximity of Warp

Records' film production arm, Warp Films, at the converted 1930s buildings of The Showroom, just the other side of Sheffield station.

However, while Park Hill was partially renovated, another building of the era was destroyed. Castle Market, designed by Andrew Darbyshire under Lewis Womersley in the early 1960s, was by the 2010s a multi-level cavern full of surprises, a timewarp of smells and sights, one part the 'high' '60s of chic modernist design, one part a 'low' '60s of pop typography, and another part a thrown-together design spanning rave culture and the more basic, brash aesthetics of the 1980s. Like a lot of buildings from its time, it was perhaps a little too weird and ambitious for its very mundane purpose, with its complex layout a potential irritant. The first of its many peculiarities is the way it was built into its sloping site, with entrances from three different levels. Another was the way that it morphed into several different things at once, incorporating an older fish market and pulling a Brutalist office block into its composition. Another was its existence as the fragment of a vertical city, with the walkways connecting its upper levels to other upper levels elsewhere in the city (many of which were closed long before the market itself was).

Probably most intriguing of all, though, was spotted by Ian Nairn at the time of opening in the early '60s—that the designer was 'wise enough to know when to stop designing'. Castle Market's architects designed a highly ambitious, three-dimensional piece of architecture, which could only have existed on this particular site in this particular city at that particular time, one that contorted itself to do fifty things at once, while never drawing attention to that feat with the kind of fancy engineering fashionable both in the '50s and today. It was of particular interest as a showcase of a grass roots modernism, a pop modernism. The signs, or in the case of the cafés, the interior fittings that stallholders brought to the building, were as modern as the building itself. Right up to the end, there was a sweet shop using the same font as *The Prisoner*, original signs at Castle News, the intriguingly named Grocock's, and N Smith & Sons, who sold an array of things from toys to baskets to travel goods, with more on the outside galleries, like Lew Burgin's Ladies' Salon or the New County Hair Stylist, seemingly untouched since 1965. Funnily enough, the only anti-modernist design gestures were imposed by the Council, in the form of the florid metal signs installed on the walkways in the 1980s. Around the time it was demolished, Castle Market appeared to be ubiquitous as a design object in the city's bookshops, galleries and boutiques; the sense of imminent loss created a pre-emptive nostalgia. It is here that the main connection between pop music and architecture in the contemporary city can be found, and certainly not in any engagement with the 'luxury flats' and student housing developments of contemporary Sheffield architecture.

Pop culture of the last decade in Sheffield has still maintained an unusual preoccupation with the city's built landscape, even when the music has become increasingly retro. Richard Hawley's longing, knowingly nostalgic ballads have been sheathed in sleeves photographed in the (then) surviving, yet down-at-heel mundane modernist spaces of the city, like Coles Corner or Castle Market, which featured on the cover of his *Late Night Final*. Seemingly alongside this is an increasing interest in the city's post-war design as the material for nostalgic design objects—Jonathan Wilkinson's 'We Live Here' series of prints present clear, blueprint-like outlines of Sheffield's particularly rich seam of post-war Brutalism, such as Park Hill, Castle Market or the Tinsley Cooling Towers. One of the bands that most exemplified this was the Long Blondes, who attempted to take up where Pulp had left off in the mid-1990s in their stories of blocked lives, suburban romances and concrete fetishism. Their singer Kate Jackson also produces prints of modernist architecture, brightly melancholic images of flyovers, New Towns and West London's Trellick Tower; her new record at the time of writing, *British Road Movies*, is an explicit tribute to the post-war British landscape, both at the time of its destruction—Castle Market was demolished in 2014—and at a time when it is increasingly appreciated as an object of design history, with a wave of coffee-table books and exhibitions. The Sheffield experience is valuable for complicating the tendency to read modernism and pop, state planning and small-time enterprise, as intrinsically opposed. It also provides a way of reading the history of the modernist city in one British industrial city—from euphoria to dystopia, from nostalgia for the nineteenth century to nostalgia for a destroyed future, and finally, to pop music as a means of marketing property development through 'iconic architecture'.

## About the Author

Owen Hatherley received a PhD in 2011 from Birkbeck College, London, for a thesis on Constructivism and Americanism, which was published in 2016 as *The Chaplin Machine* (Pluto Press); he has had scholarly articles published in the *Journal of Architecture*, the *Journal of the Society of Architectural Historians* and the *International Journal of Urban and Regional Research*, among others. He writes regularly for *Architects Journal*, *Architectural Review*, *Dezeen*, *The Guardian*, the *London Review of Books* and *New Humanist*, and is the author of several books: *Militant Modernism* (Zero, 2009); *A Guide to the New Ruins of Great Britain* (Verso, 2010); *Uncommon—An Essay on Pulp* (Zero, 2011); *Across the Plaza* (Strelka, 2012); *A New Kind of Bleak—Journeys through Urban Britain* (Verso, 2012), which was set to music by the group Golau Glau; *Landscapes of Communism* (Penguin, 2015); *The Ministry of Nostalgia* (Verso, 2016) and the forthcoming *Trans-Europe Express* (Penguin, 2017). He also edited and introduced an updated edition of Ian Nairn's *Nairn's Towns* (Notting Hill Editions, 2013), and wrote texts for the exhibition *Brutalust: Celebrating Post-War Southampton*, at the K6 Gallery.

## References

Banham, R. 1966. *The New Brutalism: Ethic or Aesthetic?* London: Architectural Association.
Coe, J. 2007. *What a Carve Up!* Harmondsworth: Penguin [1994].
Johnson, N. 2006. *Park Hill: Made in Sheffield, England*. Manchester: Urban Splash.
Jones, P. 2008. *Streets in the Sky: Life in Sheffield's High-Rise*. Sheffield: self-published.
Landau, R. 1968. *New Directions in British Architecture*. New York: George Braziller.
Minton, A. 2009. *Ground Control: Fear and Happiness in the Twenty-first-century City*. Harmondsworth: Penguin.
Morris, G. 1993. 'Pulp's Guide to Sheffield'. *New Musical Express*, 3 April.
Mulvey, J. 1992. 'Ten Years in a Jumbo-Coloured Shirt'. *New Musical Express*, 10 June.
Nairn, I. 1966. *Nairn's London*. Harmondsworth: Penguin.
—1967. *Britain's Changing Towns*. London: BBC.
Reynolds, S. 2005. *Rip It Up and Start Again: Postpunk 1978–1984*. London: Faber.
Saint, A., ed. 1996. *Park Hill—What Next?* London: Architectural Association.
Womersley, L. *et al*. 1962. *Ten Years of Housing in Sheffield*. Sheffield: Corporation of Sheffield.

# Part 2
Pop-Rock Soundscapes, Scenes and Artists

# 4  'I Thought I Heard That Up North Whistle Blow': African American Blues Performance in the North of England

Tom Attah

### Introduction

Many narratives concerning the transatlantic cultural exchange which carried blues music and blues culture from the United States to the United Kingdom focus on the southern cities of the UK, particularly London and the South East. This chapter argues that the music producers, consumers and cultural workers of the northern United Kingdom, especially Manchester, but also Leeds, Newcastle and Liverpool, were equally significant as part of the cultural convection currents that precipitated and sustained the blues boom of the 1960s. Further, this chapter argues that the construction of blackness undertaken by performers, cultural workers and consumers during the 1950s and 1960s in the North of England was a fundamental strand in the discourse of authenticity that surrounded African American music, such as it was presented in the United Kingdom.

Broadly, the presentation of early blues performers in the UK of singing guitarists Josh White and Big Bill Broonzy to secondary audiences in the United Kingdom during the early 1950s was at odds with the reality of blues music and blues culture as presented by Muddy Waters and Otis Spann at Leeds in 1958, and by the musicians who took part in the subsequent American Folk Blues Tours of the early 1960s. Additionally, the performances televised by Manchester-based Granada Television also problematized the understanding of blues music and blues culture, whilst contributing to its spread beyond the United States. Manchester's Twisted Wheel Club and Free Trade Hall also provided an opportunity for a predominantly white British audience to engage first-hand with the live performance of African American artists.

In science, convection occurs when particles with high heat energy in a liquid or gas move and take the place of particles with low heat energy. This continual movement of particles may be used to characterize the processes of cultural acculturation, appropriation and exchange which saw blues music and culture exported from the United States during the mid-twentieth century, adopted in the United Kingdom and mainland Europe as an exotic and authentic music of a subaltern race, and subsequently re-imported to the United States under the guise of the 'British Invasion' and consecutive 'blues boom' of the mid- to late-1960s.

## Social and Demographic Links between Northern United Kingdom and Southern United States

Following the Treaty of Paris which ended the American Revolutionary War (American War of Independence) in 1783, trade links between the United States and the United Kingdom quickly recovered and by 1785 were at the same levels as before the war. Specifically, the transatlantic trade in cotton between the US and the UK was of particular importance to the southern states of America and the northern counties of the United Kingdom. The hot climate of the southern United States meant that American cotton was the best quality in the world, and the presence of slave labour made the crop economically advantageous to farm and produce. The cotton trail which started in the fields of the South proceeded through the ports of Liverpool and, from a manufacturing perspective, ended in the North of England. Specifically, the raw cotton produced in the US was spun into cloth by the emerging British working class who operated the mills of Manchester and Lancashire. By the mid-nineteenth century, Manchester (and its environs) was known as 'Cottonopolis' in recognition of its position as an international textile trading centre (Lloyd-Jones and Lewis 1988).

Despite the strength of the textile-based economic links between the southern US and northern UK, tensions over the use of slave labour to produce cotton became evident during the American Civil War (1861–65). As part of the northern offensive, the Union Army under President Lincoln blockaded the trading ports of the South, preventing the export of raw cotton to the United Kingdom; the intention being to prevent the southern states generating income from the sale of its raw materials. The southern states led by Jefferson gambled that the United Kingdom would join the war on the side of the confederacy in order to protect its investment and trade in cotton; as slave-owning Governor of South Carolina James Henry Hammond indicated in his 1858 speech to the United States Senate: 'You dare not make war on cotton—no power on earth dares make war on it. Cotton is King' (Hammond 1858).

This gamble exposed not only the naivety and hubris of the confederate government, but also the extent to which the workers of northern England were in sympathy with the abolitionist cause. Cotton workers met in Manchester on 31 December 1862 and voted to support those fighting against slavery, despite the implications for their own livelihoods. The resulting period, known as the Lancashire Cotton Famine or Cotton Panic of 1861–65, led to the closure of many mills through the lack of raw materials for refining and manufacture, as well as the emigration and diversification of a significant portion of the Lancashire cotton-based workforce and industry.

This brief overview of the Lancashire Cotton Famine is intended to illustrate the financial, socio-political, historic and ideological links between the northern British working class and the African American slaves of the southern United States. These links, however, do not equate to a direct and analogous comparison. Despite a common bond in labour, the nineteenth-century British working class, whilst being at the sharp end of the emerging industrial class system, was not subject to the appalling vicissitudes of slavery (Grist 2007: 210). What is of interest here, however, is the clear moral decision to support the abolitionist cause, which might be viewed as the establishment of a sympathetic context for African Americans in the North of England. During this period, the anti-slavery novel *Uncle Tom's Cabin* (Stowe 1852) was a bestselling book in the region, and escapees from slavery such as Frederick Douglass and Henry 'Box' Brown gave public speeches in the 'Cottonopolis' to an overwhelmingly positive reception (Burchard 2003; Robbins 2009). In simple terms, from the nineteenth century onwards there are clear indications that the workforce of Manchester was broadly sympathetic to the plight and efforts to alleviate the negative socio-political position of African Americans in the United States.

The socio-economic division between the industrial North and the affluent South of England fell into sharper relief in the years after the Second World War as the country's manufacturing base declined in significance and output through the 1950s. As globalization favoured cheaper manufacturing centres, the industrial cities of northern Britain entered a period of decline, superseded nationally in wealth and visibility by the newly fashionable consumer culture of 'Swinging London' (McGinley 2014: 161–62). By the beginning of the 1960s, northern Britons were very aware of their marginal position in relation to the South. Speaking from Newcastle in the industrial North-East of England, Animals drummer John Steel commented that the area's diminishing industry and working-class despair provided 'an instinctive emotional identification with black American blues' (quoted in Schwartz 2007a: 74). This binary, regional juxtaposition of marginalization with pre-eminence is mirrored in the relationship between the postbellum South and the affluent

North in the United States. The southern US appeared marginalized in favour of a stronger economic power base in the North, just as the northern United Kingdom appeared left behind by the economically powerful and globally visible South. Whilst segregation made second-class citizens of African Americans, *The Manchester Guardian* was concerned that opportunities, education and healthcare for those living in the post-industrial North were significantly poorer than for those resident in the South (*Manchester Guardian* 1962, cited in McGinley 2014: 162).

The northern United Kingdom was broadly welcoming to black Americans during and after WWII. As white American soldiers attempted to import the United States' unequal racial power structures to the UK, there are accounts of native British men and women resisting such racist behaviour and siding with black American soldiers as individuals, communities, in the press, and in the legal system (Hervieux 2015: 184–85). At the same time, there are reports of racism enacted against immigrants from British colonies who chose to settle in the UK in the post-war period (Gilroy 2002). The distinction here appears to be between individuals of African descent who were visiting the UK as part of the allied forces in wartime, as opposed to colonial nationals settling in the country in the post-war period. Ethnicity data was not formally recorded in the UK until the 1991 census in which it appeared that only 8 per cent of the UK was non-white. Of this number, less than a quarter were black Caribbean, black African, or black (other). In other words, in the post-war period black people made up less than 2 per cent of the UK population (Lupton and Power 2004: 4).

In simple terms, between 1945 and 1965 there was a substantial growth in the immigrant population of the UK, focused on urban centres such as London, Manchester, Lancashire, South and West Yorkshire, and other northern industrial areas. This growth also meant a rise in racial tension in areas of urban decline and competition for housing. The influence of visiting African Americans during the war and the proliferation of sound recording and broadcast technology led to the increased consumption of blues music and blues culture amongst the youth demographic of the day, giving rise to an increased multi-cultural engagement and the beginnings of cultural exchange and appropriation (Potter 1999: 79). Despite these changing demographic and cultural forces, black people were in a significant minority in Great Britain in the post-war period, and the ethnic mix of the audiences for blues music in the UK was overwhelmingly white.

**Early Blues Performers in Post-war Britain**

Although African American musicians such as jazz player Louis Armstrong had visited the United Kingdom during the 1930s, it was not until Josh White's visit in 1951 that the UK witnessed a blues-based performer in the flesh as a featured artist in a series of promoted concerts. White's 1951 tour took him across the UK to favourable reviews posted in the music paper *Melody Maker* and, importantly, his visits to the UK generated radio shows for the British Broadcasting Corporation (BBC), in which White performed sacred and secular material and explained the history of African Americans in America through folk music (Wald 2000: 213). These shows featured not only blues-based Negro folk material performed by White as a solo artist accompanying his warm baritone vocal with acoustic guitar, but also well-known traditional folk songs such as 'On Top of Old Smoky' performed in a way that highlighted elements of the blues style in both vocal performance and musical accompaniment. The significance of this is that audiences were able to hear White's Americanized interpretation of familiar material and thus widen their musical boundaries as part of a process of education and cultural exchange. White's performance of African American religious music in the BBC radio Easter special *Walk Together Chillun* (1951) and folk songs in the following series *The Glory Road* (1951) presented an instructive but non-confrontational introduction to African American music and the socio-political context of its development (Schwartz 2007b: 156). In this way, White was a potentially less problematic character than African American singer and actor Paul Robeson, whose forthright public representation of American civil rights issues saw him blacklisted and confined to the United States in this same period, despite a period of cultural success on stage and screen in the UK (Robeson 1988).

White's gentle yet distinctive style played a crucial role in acclimatizing postwar popular culture consumers in the UK to the mainstream presence of African Americans beyond jazz. Quite apart from the commercial success generated by his albums and tours, White's cultural influence extended to young guitar players in the UK, among them Eric Clapton who claimed that White's arrangement and recording of 'Scarlet Ribbons' was one of the first songs he learned to play on the guitar (Clapton and Sykes 2007: 22). In addition, the first blues instrumental instruction book to be published in the UK was *The Josh White Guitar Method* (White and Mairants 1956), in which Polish-born jazz and classical guitarist Ivor Mairants transcribed seven of White's songs, outlining a basic guide to White's style and 'offering a window into the world of blues guitar for young players on both sides of the Atlantic' (Wald 2000: 245–46). Quite aside from White's influence on Clapton, the book was a key influence on English guitar player John Renbourn (1944–2015), who was one of the most important guitarists to come out of the UK folk revival. Renbourn's interest in blues had been stirred by seeing White in concert, and the book 'provided the basis for the style of many of the players of his generation' (Wald 2000: 246).

White's popularity persuaded other blues artists, most notably Big Bill Broonzy, to make the journey from the US to the UK to perform. Broonzy presented himself in performance as a sun-hardened delta blues musician. Despite his history as a slick urban performer with a proven history as a songwriter in the US, the UK audiences and critics praised Broonzy for his authenticity. Returning to the UK in 1952, Broonzy took in Manchester and Liverpool, where critics remarked that 'at first hearing, his art seems unconscious, – but this is not strictly true – Bill has been singing his blues, work songs and spirituals so long that he has developed a form of presentation (call it showmanship if you will) that really sells his stuff' (Pythian 1952, quoted in Schwartz 2007a: 42). In other words, although some of his audience were well aware that Broonzy's work was a knowing construction, for many this stage-performance of black masculinity became the standard of authenticity by which other visiting blues performers were judged.

Broonzy returned to the UK in 1953, 1955 and 1957, each time to larger audiences and each time emphasizing his credentials as the 'last of the original delta bluesmen' (Riesman 2011). His last concert tour was arranged by Chris Barber, a British jazz trombone player instrumental in bringing African American artists to the UK and thus kick-starting the first British blues boom. At the end of the fifties, Barber hosted Sister Rosetta Tharpe—a groundbreaking artist not only in that she performed an up-beat, progressive and propulsive hybrid of blues and gospel whilst playing an electric guitar, but also for her presence as a female musician in a male-dominated space. Barber also arranged UK concerts for the influential harmonica and guitar vocal duo Sonny Terry and Brownie McGhee during this period. Additionally, Barber was the musician who provided the catalyst for the formation of Blues Incorporated—often named as the first British blues band—by giving its founder members guitarist Alexis Korner and harmonica player Cyril Davies stage time as part of his own jazz band's regular engagement at London's Marquee Club. Of further significance for this chapter, Barber also arranged for the first UK concert tour for the 'father of the electric blues', Muddy Waters.

### Leeds, Muddy Waters and the Electric Blues

McKinley "Muddy Waters" Morganfield is widely regarded as a transitional figure in the blues, and was first recorded in Stovall, Mississippi by folklorist Alan Lomax during his song-gathering field-trips of 1941 and 1942 (Lomax 1993). Recognizing his own potential as a recording artist, Waters travelled to Chicago in 1943. Realizing that urban sound-levels drowned the sound of his acoustic guitar in the small clubs where he opened for Big Bill Broonzy, Waters purchased an electric guitar and amplifier and began to adapt the acoustic delta blues into a harder-edged, dynamic and forward-looking ensemble sound which emphasized the bass and drums—hence the term '*rhythm and blues*'. By 1948 Waters had scored hits with 'I Can't Be Satisfied', 'Feels Like Going Home' and his signature tune, the relentless, pulsing 'Rolling Stone'. With these seminal recordings, Waters showcased both the potential of the extended electric blues band in the studio for the Chess label, and expressed a new facet within the persona of the bluesman: a modernized, hyper-sexual and insatiable character who announced his recorded performance with a barrel-chested vocal roar backed by a stinging, electrified slide guitar (Gioia 2008; Palmer 1981).

Waters made his UK debut at Leeds Town Hall on Thursday 16 October 1958 as part of the city's Triennial Music Festival—an incongruous setting which featured chamber music and jazz on the bill (Schwartz 2007a: 79). Accompanied by his pianist Otis Spann, Waters proceeded to perform the type of electric blues popular in his home city, backed by British jazz musicians led by trumpeter Kenny Baker (Gordon 2003: 158). The blues lovers who had made the journey north to see the performance were allegedly unprepared for the volume and ferocity of the electric guitar sound that Waters had cultivated:

> [Muddy] fiddled with the knobs [of his guitar]. The next time he struck a fierce chord, it was louder, and I realised that this was the established order of things. As he reached for the volume knobs again, I fled from the hall (Gordon 2003: 161).

This reaction of 'a well-known critic', is atypical however, and that the audience was shocked into paralysis and fear has been refuted by blues scholar and writer Paul Oliver:

> anyone who had heard Muddy Waters [up until that time] would have heard him playing acoustic [on record]. When he played electric, it was a surprise ... a lot of people still thought of blues as part of jazz, so it didn't quite match their expectations (quoted in Schwartz 2007a: 80).

Certainly, for those expecting a performance in line with Josh White and Bill Broonzy's conversational acoustic style, Waters' high-octane sets in Leeds and Newcastle-Upon-Tyne, culminating in shows in London, were a revelation. For listeners used to a more sedate, contained and controlled performance of blues music such as they had experienced on record and from previous acoustic touring artists, to be confronted with the raw power of Waters' performance first-hand offered a new perspective on blues music and blues culture. This was not blues tempered for an audience of Europeans; this was music performed in its raw state, as it was delivered to its primary audience in the urban clubs of Chicago. As Jack Florin of the *Manchester Evening News* complained:

> Although his singing is authentic and he uses his voice as an instrument for conveying melancholy and dissatisfaction, *I cannot class him as a true blues artist*. Apart from the beautiful 'Blues before Sunrise', most of his songs seemed to me to owe too much to the rhythm and blues style (Florin 1958, cited in Tooze 1997: 165; emphasis mine).

This paradoxical reaction highlights the tendency of some blues fans, sometimes referred to as the 'Blues Police' (O'Connell 2013), to regard blues music and blues culture as a set of synchronic stylistic slices, rather than as an evolving diachronic continuum of African American musical expression. In other words, although Waters clearly came from the Delta acoustic tradition, his work was to extend the boundaries of what constituted the blues for his current primary audience in the US—and that meant playing loud, up-beat music which focused on the thumping pulse of an amplified rhythm section in order that the music could function in its new urban setting. The tendency of a section of the blues audience to assume a gate-keeping ontological position whose purpose is to define what does and does not have the right to be called blues became a more heated debate with the publication of the scholarly texts *Blues Fell This Morning: The Meaning of the Blues* (Oliver 1960) in the UK, and *The Country Blues* (Charters 1959) in the US, and the subsequent purist and polemic early writings of the so-called 'Blues Mafia' in the US (McKune 1960). Here we see in action what sociologist Pierre Bourdieu calls *distinction* (2010); within a group that coheres around a common interest, in this case blues music, there are power relations reified by social and aesthetic judgements which are exclusionary. In simple terms, those who are really in-the-know recognize 'real' or 'authentic' blues when they see it. The further challenge here is that authenticity in popular culture performance, certainly since the proliferation of mass communications and sound recording from the end of the nineteenth century, is a problematic construct (Auslander 1998; King 2011; Ryan 2011; Wang 1999), as 'authenticity' is not inherent in a popular music performance, but is conferred upon it by the audience or consumer (Moore 2002: 214). Further to this, these UK commentators were not the intended primary audience of this live music performance, as indicated above; they were in fact part of a *secondary audience*. Secondary audiences are distinct from primary audiences by being culturally removed from a performance or artwork by reasons of geography, society or time; their interaction with the cultural practice is mediated and acontextual rather than lived (Gennari 2006); in this case the largely white British consumers of the blues in the early 1960s had no lived experience of blues music and blues culture, and were offering subjective judgements based on their consumption of a foreign culture achieved through technologically mediated means—phonograph records and radio shows. Put simply, in terms of judging blues performances, UK blues purists by and large had a very limited basis for comparison and in most cases seemed to be comparing live, contemporary performances of blues music with phonograph records that were in some cases up to thirty years old.

Waters' electric performance was sufficiently well-received to convince him to return to the UK as part of the American Folk Blues Tours of the 1960s which will be discussed briefly later in this chapter. The significance of these first shows played out across the North of England is to mark a transitionary phase in the UK understanding and engagement with blues music and blues culture. As Waters remarked, 'They thought I was Big Bill Broonzy. I wasn't' (Waters 1958, quoted in Gordon 2003: 158). What Waters did bring to the table those first nights at Leeds and through the rest of the tour, however, was a new set of rules about what could be counted as blues; his electric performances signed a warrant for younger white players such as Alexis Korner, Eric Clapton, Brian Jones, Keith Richards and Jimmy Page to turn up their amplifiers and take their first steps beyond mimicking the music of their heroes, toward developing these musical gestures into a new blues-based style through the use of high volume, distorted electric guitar(s) and a prominent rhythm section.

It is possible to view Josh White, Big Bill Broonzy and Muddy Waters as three points on a continuum which presented blues music performance as a living entity for an audience who had hitherto consumed the music purely as sound recordings. Between Josh White's first UK tour in 1951, Big Bill Broonzy's last appearance in 1957 and Muddy Waters' first performances in 1958, the blues was shown to be an increasingly wild, amplified and specific voice which resonated with certain groups of disenfranchised youth within post-war Britain. Of these three artists, Muddy Waters had perhaps the most immediately visible impact in the South and North of the UK. In other words, Waters had electrified the blues in his home country during the 1940s and mid-1950s, and in 1958 he electrified an audience of young musicians in the UK through his live performance. His influence in particular and that of the blues in general would continue to spread throughout the country and popular music culture with the specific intervention of the producers, cultural workers and consumers of Manchester.

## Manchester

Manchester's contribution to blues music and blues culture is perhaps under-represented within the transatlantic narrative on blues, although recent work by McGinley (2014) concerning the role of the city during the blues boom builds on that of Brocken (2010) and goes some way to redress this balance. As indicated in the introduction, Manchester's socio-political links to African Americans in the southern states were perhaps stronger than any other city in the UK, as demonstrated by its willingness to support the abolition movement and the northern states during the US civil war. In the post-war period immediately leading up to the UK blues boom, these links with African American culture can be illustrated by three specific examples. Firstly, Manchester's Free Trade Hall, which hosted the first American Folk and Blues Festival that brought black American blues performers to the city's major music venue in 1962. Secondly, Granada Television (based in Manchester) did much to disseminate blues music and blues culture regionally and nationally through a series of performance-based programmes, particularly in *The Blues and Gospel Train* show of 1964. Thirdly, the live performances and recorded music played at the Twisted Wheel club allowed a young, largely white audience exposure to African American music in the context of socializing and dancing—arguably, the music's first function for its primary audience in the US. Whilst each of the above examples made a valuable contribution to the incursion of African American music to the British Isles, the 1962 American Folk Blues Festival and *The Blues and Gospel Train* of 1964 are potentially problematic in terms of the way that the musicians concerned were presented on stage and on camera. In other words, the performances were delivered within an unfamiliar context for the artists concerned—to a majority white audience in a foreign country—and certainly in the case of *The Blues and Gospel Train*, the stage setting was designed to represent ideas of blackness and the American South that were simulacra, rather than specifically representative of reality.

*The American Folk Blues Festival*
The American Negro Folk Blues Festival Package Tours (later known as the American Folk Blues Festivals) were a series of concerts originally organized by German promoters Horst Lippmann and Fritz Rau. The tours ran annually from 1962 to 1970, then again in 1972, before a diminishing interest in the style and rising costs necessitated an eight-year hiatus. The tours resumed in 1980–83 and the final event took place in 1985. By the end of the 1950s, jazz was of huge interest in post-war Germany, and the blues was seen as its more exotic and dangerous precursor (Adelt 2008: 960). In addition, jazz in

Germany (and to a similar extent, Russia) held connotations of rebellion and resistance, having been proscribed by the Third Reich:

> so-called jazz compositions may contain at most 10% syncopation; the remainder must consist of a natural legato movement devoid of the hysterical rhythmic reverses characteristic of the music of the barbarian races and conducive to dark instincts alien to the German people (so-called riffs) (cited in Skvorecky 1977: 10).

Thus the public presentation of its musical forebear, the blues, might be regarded as a very clear message of defiance which pre-dated the UK and US counterculture movement of the mid- to late 1960s.

The aim of the American Folk Blues Festivals was to bring the original blues artists from the US to Europe in a package that would allow direct contact with the vernacular performances of African Americans and for this, Lippmann and Rau enlisted the help of bass player, composer and producer Willie Dixon as a recruiter and tour director (Dixon and Snowden 1989). The first tour was set for 1962 and concerts were scheduled in Germany, France, Denmark, Switzerland and Holland. Conspicuous by its absence this first year was Britain. UK blues fans reacted with disbelief to this omission and hastily scheduled a show at the Manchester Free Trade Hall on 21 October 1962.

So popular was the prospect of the Manchester show that British blues artists including Alexis Korner, John Mayall, Mick Jagger, Keith Richards and Brian Jones cancelled their shows in London in order to attend (McGinley 2014: 160). On the bill that night were Willie Dixon, John Lee Hooker, Helen Hulmes, Shakey Jake, Memphis Slim, Sonny Terry & Brownie McGhee, and T-Bone Walker. The significance of this 'Cavalcade of Blues' (Murray 2000: 267) was twofold. Firstly, the American Folk Blues Festival once again exposed young, largely white fans and nascent artists to performances that subsequently informed their activity and approach to blues music, thereby providing the raw materials that would fuel their own creativity and the blues boom and subsequent British Invasion of the US. Secondly, that the concert took place at all was an act of supreme good fortune given that Dixon and Rau were under the impression that 'there was not much enthusiasm [in Britain] when we came up with the idea ... only Paris right away liked it' (O'Neal 1993, cited in Schwartz 2007a: 146). The review of the Free Trade Hall show in *Jazz Monthly* was broadly complimentary, and noted 'the absence of deliberately "folky" episodes' and praised the performers for avoiding the use of 'Whiteisms', a clear acknowledgement of the constructed nature of Josh White's performance style which was now some ten years in the past (Lambert 1962).

This first American Folk Blues Tour show in Manchester was sufficiently successful for another concert to be staged in the same venue a year later, October 1963. This time the performers were Lonnie Johnson, Memphis Slim, Matt 'Guitar' Murphy, Victoria Spivey, Big Joe Williamson, Sonny Boy Williamson, Otis Spann—and Muddy Waters. The expanded line-up and European tour dates indicated that there was an appetite for these blues performances. Of interest for this tour, however, is Muddy Waters' decision to alter his performance based on his previous experience in the UK of 1958, as discussed above. This time, Waters brought an acoustic guitar and played softer, more folk-based music rather than electrified rhythm and blues. To his dismay, audiences offered only a lukewarm reaction:

> After the concert, [Muddy] sat shaking his head in disbelief. Just what did they want, these [British] white folks? He'd brought along the acoustic guitar they'd demanded. He'd given them the old down-home country blues this time – and now all they could ask him was, "Why'd you leave the Telecaster behind?"' (Val Wilmer 1963, cited in Gordon 2003: 184).

Part of the explanation for this confusion is that in the five years since Waters had last been in the UK, young British blues players had been expanding on what they had learned from him during his first visit. Bands such as the Rolling Stones—named after one of Muddy's songs—had formed; the blues boom was gathering steam, and the expectation was that Waters would bring his electric show rather than harking back to the performance milieu of Josh White and Big Bill Broonzy. In other words—times had moved on, and Muddy was no longer required to revert to a performance style that was, for many young fans, old hat. Despite this challenge, Muddy was keen to play *his* music—the electric blues—in the UK again and so agreed to return to the UK the following year to take part in another package tour—this time, with the possibility of appearing on British television.

*The Blues and Gospel Train (1964)*
Based in Manchester, Granada Television was a commercial organization founded in 1958 by brothers Cecil and Sidney Bernstein and was one of the first UK television companies to use production facilities purpose-built for television. By the early 1960s the company served an area stretching from Liverpool and Blackpool on the west coast of England to Kingston Upon Hull on the east coast, and including Manchester, Bradford, Leeds, Sheffield, Doncaster, the West and East Ridings of Yorkshire and the city of York. This considerable slice of northern Britain was often referred to as 'Granadaland' within

the reach of the company's broadcasts (Brocken 2010). Given BBC television's generally middle-brow, 'one-nation', style programming, Granada sought to emphasize the character of the North by making programmes with strong regional character. In contrast to the relatively conservative BBC, Granada produced investigative journalism series *World in Action* (1963–98), groundbreaking documentaries such as *The Up Series* (1964–), and the enduring soap opera, *Coronation Street* (1960–).

Under the stewardship of light entertainment producer Johnny Hamp, Granada produced a number of shows that focused on popular music in general and African American music in particular. In this, Granada were not the first television company to produce music-based programmes, but in line with the company's intuition for regional stories with characterful content the shows were lively and attracted a young audience in tune with the emerging popular culture of the day. As an example, Hamp fortuitously sent a camera crew to Liverpool in 1962 to capture the first show of local band The Beatles with their new drummer Ringo Starr, thus inadvertently creating a document that highlighted the vitality of the Liverpool beat scene of the time by filming its soon-to-be most famous sons in the first performance of their world-dominating line-up. Of interest to this chapter, Hamp also produced *Sarah Sings and Basie Swings* (1963) with Sarah Vaughan and Count Basie; *I Hear The Blues* (1963) which featured the artists who participated in that year's American Folk Blues Tour; and *The Blues and Gospel Train* (1964) (Brocken 2010: 201).

Given that both of these shows feature Muddy Waters, the key distinction between *I Hear The Blues* and *The Blues and Gospel Train* lies in the way that the shows are presented. *I Hear the Blues* is a studio recording, with the band playing on a stage erected in a blacked-out studio. An audience of young people is seated almost amongst the performing musicians, although a demarcation line between performers and audience is maintained. Memphis Slim opens the show improvising at the piano, and introduces the musicians who take the stage one by one, adding their instrumental voice(s) as they arrive; Billy Stepney on drums, Matt Murphy on the guitar and Willie Dixon on the double bass are called to the stage in turn (see Figure 1).

Once the band is in situ, the soloists are called and each performs a song. Lonnie Johnson, Victoria Spivey, Sonny Boy Williamson and finally Muddy Waters all take the stage as featured artists in their own right, before returning for a large ensemble presentation to close out the show. In a very real sense, the presentation is one of televised theatre.

This contrasts sharply with *The Blues and Gospel Train*, a 40-minute special which was filmed at the disused Wilbraham Road train station in May 1964 (see Figure 2). The show as presented on TV emphasizes the communal nature

**Figure 1:** (l to r) Memphis Slim (p), Sonny Boy Williamson (h), Willie Dixon (b), Manchester 1963

of the blues. The audience are mostly young blues fans and the footage shows them to be overwhelmingly white. The opening shots depict the audience travelling towards the fictional 'Chorltonville' station on the train, whilst the African American performers are conveyed by motor-coach. Muddy Waters is shown playing his guitar and singing on the fictional train station platform with his band out of shot (see Figure 3), and, as the train pulls into the station on its disused sidings, he is swamped by young people who crowd around him enthusiastically, some singing, others clapping, but all smiling and seemingly glad to be part of the spectacle.

The message here is utopian; although Waters is fulfilling his role as a blues performer, he is playing to a new and unsegregated generation of fans who are seemingly unaffected by the crippling social issues predicated on race in the US; here is a world where Waters is respected as a musician before he is reviled for the colour of his skin. Here is a world where African Americans are not untouchable and in fact inspire the young people around them; here is a world where—to paraphrase a recent marketing slogan—there is 'No Black. No White, just Blues' (Cirlot Agency 2006).

4 'I Thought I Heard That Up North Whistle Blow'  91

**Figure 2:** (l to r) Ransom Knowling, Muddy Waters, Lionel Hamp, Manchester, May 1964

**Figure 3:** Muddy Waters being filmed in Chorlton, Manchester, for *The Blues and Gospel Train*, May 1964

Additionally, the use of a train and the station is appropriate for this utopian vision. The significance and symbolism of the train in blues mythology is one of power, of progress, and of mobility; its presence in blues music and blues culture speaks of industry, autonomy and progress. In this way, *The Blues and Gospel Train*, in terms of stage sets alone, tells a tale of integration and cultural movement towards a better future where age and race are not divisive characteristics, but cause for celebration and inclusion. Despite the blurry hyper-reality used to convey these suggestions, the positive outlook appeared to resonate with some of the youthful audience:

> It was incredible because we loved these blues players in those days ... even the Rolling Stones were still playing blues then. People only heard about the concert through word of mouth but there was a huge crowd and it inspired people to go off and make their own music (James Chapman-Kelly, cited in Brocken 2010: 208).

In short, despite the artifice of the construction at play in the presentation of *The Blues and Gospel Train*, its subtle yet pervasive engagement with the problematic discourses of the blues depicted a potential alternative reality where music and humanity prospered. No less fictional than the presentation of Big Bill Broonzy, the difference here appeared to be that this particular social reality, grounded in music and acceptance rather than tolerance, was still under construction, rather than being a satirical, sly caricature of the present. In other words, it was possible for the audience to engage with the performance as builders of a better future, rather than observing a sarcastic, political mocking of the socio-political context.

## Conclusion

Between 1951 and 1964, the performance tours of African American blues performers in the North of England helped to initiate the cultural convection current which gave rise to both the blues boom of the 1960s in the UK and the British invasion of popular music acts to the US during the middle part of that decade. Whilst 'Swinging London' continued to draw attention as a cultural centre during the period under discussion, the role of northern cities such as Leeds and particularly Manchester should not be overlooked in this process of acculturation and influential exchange of blues music and blues culture. Certainly London played a major role in the development of the popular culture of this period through its density of performance venues, broadcast agencies and recording studios—but at a time of regional economic decline, the North of England made a significant contribution to the dissemination and development of blues music and blues culture in the UK and, by extension, to the wider world.

## About the Author

Dr Tom Attah is a practising musician, and BMus Popular Music Course Leader at Leeds Arts University. His PhD was awarded by the University of Salford, and his research interests include the effects of technology on popular music, particularly blues music and blues culture.

As a guitarist and singer, Tom performs solo, with an acoustic duo and as part of an electric band. Tom's performance practice includes his own original blues compositions and has led to performances at major international music festivals. Tom's multiple national radio appearances include performances and documentaries for the BBC and Sky Arts.

## References

Adelt, Ulrich. 2008. 'Germany Gets the Blues: Negotiations of "Race" and Nation at the American Folk Blues Festival'. *American Quarterly* 60/4: 951–74, 1153.

Auslander, Philip. 1998. 'Seeing is Believing: Live Performance and the Discourse of Authenticity in Rock Culture'. *Literature and Psychology* 44/4: 1–26.

Bourdieu, Pierre. 2010. *Distinction: A Social Critique of the Judgement of Taste*. London: Routledge.

Brocken, Mike. 2010. 'Granada TV, Johnny Hamp, and the Blues and Gospel Train: Masters of Reality'. In *Popular Music and Television in Britain*, ed. A. I. Inglis, 197–212. Abingdon: Routledge.

Burchard, Peter. 2003. *Frederick Douglass: For the Great Family of Man*. New York: Atheneum.

Charters, Samuel Barclay. 1959. *The Country Blues*. London: Michael Joseph.

Cirlot Agency. 2006. *Mississippi Believe It!* http://www.mississippibelieveit.com/portfolio-item/no-black-no-white-just-the-blues/ (accessed 12 August 2015).

Clapton, Eric, and Christopher Simon Sykes. 2007. *Eric Clapton: The Autobiography*. London: RNIB.

Dixon, Willie, and Don Snowden. 1989. *I am the Blues: The Willie Dixon Story*. London: Quartet.

Gennari, John. 2006. *Blowin' Hot and Cool: Jazz and its Critics*. Chicago: University of Chicago Press.

Gilroy, Paul. 2002. *There ain't No Black in the Union Jack: The Cultural Politics of Race and Nation*. London: Routledge.

Gioia, Ted. 2008. *Delta Blues: The Life and Times of the Mississippi Masters who Revolutionized American Music*. New York and London: W.W. Norton.

Gordon, Robert. 2003. *Can't be Satisfied: The Life and Times of Muddy Waters*. London: Pimlico.

Grist, Leighton. 2007. 'The Blues, Modernity and the British Blues Boom'. In *Cross the Water Blues: African American Music in Europe*, ed. N. A. Wynn, 202–17. Jackson, MI: University Press of Mississippi.

Hammond, James Henry. 1858. Congresional Speech, United States Senate. http://memory.loc.gov/ammem/awhhtml/awmss5/d08.html (accessed 18 December 2016).

Hervieux, Linda. 2015. *Forgotten: The Untold Story of D-Day's Black Heroes, at Home and at War*. New York: HarperCollins.

King, Stephen A. 2011. *I'm Feeling the Blues Right Now: Blues Tourism and the Mississippi Delta*. Jackson, MI: University Press of Mississippi

Lambert, G. E. 1962. 'Blues Festival in Manchester'. *Jazz Monthly* 8/10: 13.

Lloyd-Jones, Roger, and M. J. Lewis. 1988. *Manchester and the Age of the Factory: The Business Structure of Cottonopolis in the Industrial Revolution*. London: Croom Helm.

Lomax, Alan. 1993. *The Land Where the Blues Began*. London: Methuen.

Lupton, R., and A. Power. 2004. 'Minority Ethnic Groups in Britain'. In *Case-Brookings Census Briefs*, vol. 2. London: Centre for Analysis of Social Exclusion.

McGinley, Paige A. 2014. *Staging the Blues: From Tent Shows to Tourism*. London: Duke University Press.

McKune, James. 1960. 'The Great Country Blues Singers'. In *In Search of the Blues*, ed. M. Hamilton, 182–83. London: Cape.

Moore, Allan F. 2002. 'Authenticity as Authentication'. *Popular Music* 21/2: 209–223.

Murray, Charles Shaar. 2000. *Boogie Man: The Adventures of John Lee Hooker in the American Twentieth Century*. London: Penguin.

O'Connell, Christian. 2013. 'The Color of the Blues: Considering Revisionist Blues Scholarship'. *Southern Cultures* 19/1: 61–81.

O'Neal, Jim. 1993. 'I Once Was Lost but Now I'm Found: The Blues Revival of the 1960s'. In *Nothing but the Blues: The Music and the Musicians*, ed. L. Cohn, 347–88. New York: Abbeville Press.

Oliver, Paul. 1960. *Blues Fell This Morning: The Meaning of the Blues*. London: Cassell.

Palmer, R. 1981. *Deep Blues: A Musical and Cultural History from the Mississippi Delta to Chicago's South Side to the World*. New York: Penguin Books.

Potter, Russell A. 1999. 'Race'. In *Key Terms in Popular Music and Culture*, ed. T. Swiss and B. Horner, 71–84. Malden, MA and Oxford: Blackwell.

Riesman, Bob. 2011. *I Feel So Good: The Life and Times of Big Bill Broonzy*. Chicago and London: University of Chicago Press.

Robbins, Hollis. 2009. 'Fugitive Mail: The Deliverance of Henry "Box" Brown and Antebellum Postal Politics'. *American Studies* 50/1-2: 5–25.

Robeson, Paul. 1988. *Here I Stand*. London: Cassell.

Ryan, Jennifer. 2011. 'Beale Street Blues? Tourism, Musical Labor, and the Fetishization of Poverty in Blues'. *Ethnomusicology* 55/3: 473–503.

Schwartz, Roberta Freund. 2007a. *How Britain Got the Blues: The Transmission and Reception of American Blues Style in the United Kingdom*. Aldershot: Ashgate.

—2007b. 'Preaching the Gospel of the Blues: Blues Evangelists in Britain'. In *Cross the Water Blues: African American Music in Europe*, ed. N. A. Wynn, 145–66. Jackson, MI: University Press of Mississippi.

Skvorecky, Josef. 1977. *The Bass Saxophone*. Toronto: Anson-Cartwright.

Stowe, Harriet Beecher. 1852. *Uncle Tom's Cabin: A Tale of Life among the Lowly; or, Pictures of Slavery in the United States of America ... Embellished with Eight Spirited Drawings*, 2nd edn. London: Ingram, Cooke.

Tooze, Sandra B. 1997. *Muddy Waters: The Mojo Man*. Toronto: ECW Press.

Wald, Elijah. 2000. *Josh White: Society Blues*. Amherst: University of Massachusetts Press.

Wang, Ning. 1999. 'Rethinking Authenticity in Tourism Experience'. *Annals of Tourism Research* 26/2: 349–70.

White, Josh, and Ivor Mairants. 1956. *The Josh White Guitar Method*. London and New York: Boosey & Hawkes.

# 5 The Contrasting Soundscapes of Hull and London in David Bowie's *Ziggy Stardust and the Spiders from Mars*

Peter Atkinson

**Soundscape and Place**

Long and Collins use the term 'soundscape' to refer to 'the relationship of music, space and heritage' (Long and Collins 2012: 145). Their work follows theoretical approaches to the examination of soundscapes undertaken by the likes of Murray Schafer (1994 [1977]) and Thompson (2004). Thompson defines the soundscape as 'an auditory and aural landscape' which is 'simultaneously a physical environment and a way of perceiving that environment' (Thompson 2004: 1). Physical aspects of a soundscape consist not only of the sounds themselves, she notes, but also the material objects that create, and can sometimes destroy, these (Thompson 2004: 1). To this we can add that there may be an evolution of the soundscape which is derived from both the development of material objects, the creative use of these objects, the social uses of this creative production, and the subsequent cultural outcomes of all these things within culture. An example of this may be found in a town ballroom, used in the 1930s and 1940s for dancing to the tunes of live dance bands featuring brass and/or string instruments. The premises may have adapted in the late 1950s and 1960s and staged rock and roll, or pop, events which featured amplified electric guitar and vocals. The same buildings in the 1970s may have been converted into other uses, such as disco, where the music played was loudly amplified records. Thus, there is an evolution of the local soundscape. A cultural outcome in this case is that those people at the discotheque are not listening to live music, but to recorded product—music from another place, quite possibly another country. This has consequences in relation to the listener's sense of belonging to the place where s/he hears the music. As Thompson states,

> A soundscape's cultural aspects incorporate scenic, and aesthetic ways of listening, a listener's relationship to their environment, and the social circumstances that dictate who gets to hear what. A soundscape, like a landscape, ultimately has more to do with civilization than with nature, and as such, it is constantly under construction and always undergoing change (Thompson 2004: 1–2).

Developing Thompson's theory, Long and Collins (2012: 146) conclude that,

> Sound ... is to be accounted for not only as a matter of what we hear, but also as those practices that produce, use and make sense of it. This framework offers a suggestive means of making sense of the role of music in and about the city, of musical cultures and encounters with a polyphony of tunes (and other noises), of *how* they are heard and the meanings they have for creators, consumers and those who would avoid or ignore them, amplify, mute, commodify, preserve or indeed recall and map them as an aspect of experience.

Long and Collins' use of the concept of soundscapes is to map 'historical music cultures' (Long and Collins 2012: 145). Summarizing Whiteley's analysis of the relationship between music and place, they note that the interweaving of music and space has a role in the construction of national identity, the interrelationship of the local and global and 'the formation of the cultural industries that produce and circulate commodities and meanings'. In this way, the soundscape of popular music 'has a role to play in the branding and selling of place' (Long and Collins 2012: 146). *Ziggy Stardust* was shaped by an interaction between two *distinct* soundscapes: metropolitan London and provincial Hull. I analyse the relationship between the two soundscapes here in terms of the discourses that derive from the juxtaposition of the two. Long and Collins analyse the mapping of the Birmingham soundscape in the Birmingham Popular Music Archive. They consider the dissemination of information in and from that project and assess the cultural uses that derive from this. I provide some analysis of how the Hull soundscape impacts on heritage issues in that town and on cultural production there. Soundscape is always assessed retrospectively; a particular moment in sound is always already gone. And assessment of a soundscape is a discursive activity, whereby meaning is assigned to particular arrangements of sound for the purpose of conducting analysis, usually of socio-cultural circumstances and/or phenomena. I now compare the soundscapes of London and Hull and assess their influence on the practitioners who created *Ziggy Stardust*.

A lost clip of David Bowie performing his single 'Jean Genie' on *Top of the Pops* on 4 January 1973 was quite recently unearthed. The performance is not only notable because it remained inaccessible for more than forty years, but also because in it, the band is playing live (although the programme was recorded the day before). This is unusual for *Top of the Pops* and the clip provides a useful record of the band's musical style at the time. In it Bowie, dressed glam, plays the fictitious Ziggy Stardust, the character role he performed in 1972 and 1973 before killing it off in that year. He fronts the nominally fictitious backing band The Spiders from Mars who, in reality, are all from Hull. 'The Spiders' chug away delivering this Bo Diddley-inspired number, their rhythm and blues sound a derivation of electric Chicago blues to which Bowie also contributes blues harmonica.[1] At one point in the *Top of the Pops* clip, Bowie includes the harmonica melody line from The Beatles' first single, 'Love Me Do' and it is notable that The Beatles were engaged to play the Majestic Ballroom in Hull at the time of that record's release—October 1962—not because they were famous (the record had only been a minor hit), but because the venue needed a group to attract an audience for its bingo. The inclusion of a reference to the first Beatles record, a formative influence in English pop music, is self-conscious and knowing on Bowie's behalf as, indeed, is his entire performance. *Ziggy Stardust* was, precisely, a knowing post-modern manipulation of the conventions of the process of stardom. But Bowie's interpretation was one transferred wholesale to the rock genre which had developed a strong ideological dimension since the mid-1960s as it became the common currency of a so-called cultural revolution and a vehicle for the expression of the views of the counter-culture.

**David Bowie, the Suburban London Boy**

The success of *Ziggy* was the culmination of the artist's years spent absorbing the sounds and the culture that England's capital had to offer. David Jones was born in Brixton, south London, in 1947 and his career was shaped by his experience growing up in suburban Beckenham and Bromley. The youngster followed the well-trodden path of finding escape, fulfilment and new career prospects in the town centre. Doggett writes that, as a teenager, Bowie 'emerged in 1963 in the planet's most vibrant city' ready to witness—and be a part of—the 'brief flowering of freedom and creativity' of what has become mythologized as 'the sixties' (Doggett 2012: 17). Bowie hung around the fashionable areas and was introduced to the bohemia of Soho and to jazz clubs by his brother Terry, who later suffered from mental illness. He was in a band, The Kon-Rads, by the time

---

1. My thanks to Leslie Gillon for pointing out that the Hull musicians, although from a different geographical area, may have experienced some of the same media dissemination of music as Bowie in London. For example, radio, and pirate radio, were influential in promoting particular music forms, thus affecting local soundscapes.

he was fifteen and, after seeing the Rolling Stones on the Bo Diddley tour of 1963 and getting hooked on rhythm and blues, formed The King Bees, the name deriving from the Stones' cover of a 1957 Slim Harpo blues song, 'I'm a King Bee', a popular number covered live or on record by numerous other British groups. Bowie at the time had a lowly post at an advertising agency but prospects were good and the job taught him the art of self-promotion, which he used to sell himself and the group to a minor imprint of Decca Records, Vocalion. Proximity to the industry in the capital creates opportunity and inspires a confidence perhaps lacking in the provinces. Bowie was in a string of other London groups: The Mannish Boys (who supported The Kinks on tour), The Lower Third and The Buzz. He adopted the stage name 'David Bowie' in 1965 to avoid being confused with other artists that shared his real name. Bowie identified strongly with the Mods in the fashion-conscious cauldron of pop London, with its vibrant new music scene that produced one of the most distinctive soundscapes in the history of music. This was a city that spawned a host of bands and artists who became internationally renowned and have provided an enduring legacy: The Rolling Stones, Pink Floyd, The Who, The Kinks, The Small Faces, Elton John, Eric Clapton, Jimmy Page, Rod Stewart and Jeff Beck. In addition to this, the scene also produced a host of artists who attracted, and continue to attract, a cult following: The Yardbirds, Julie Driscoll, The Pretty Things, Arthur Brown, The Action. The soundscape and culture permeated Bowie's consciousness, inspiring him to write, and he produced the harrowing 'slice of Soho life' song 'The London Boys' in 1965 (Doggett 2012: 36).

Frith (2007: 139) claims Bowie is the 'quintessential suburban star'. The suburbanite, he suggests, may map her/his 'obsessions and alliances' onto the city streets of places such as Soho in an 'enactment of escape'. This in effect happened when Bowie's disciples, the so-called New Romantics, descended upon Soho at the beginning of the 1980s, setting up a series of club nights with a cult following in small venues such as Blitz, Billy's and The Wag. For Frith, this is effectively a 'suburbanization of the city' (Frith 2007: 140). Suburban culture is predominantly white, middle-class and 'white south-eastern English culture', he notes, and continues that the term describes:

> An urban phenomenon, the dominance of London, the concentrated site of both political and cultural power. The sub-urban sensibility ... is sub-London sensibility. From this media perspective other English cities (and even Scottish, Northern Irish and Welsh cities) are themselves effectively suburban.

Frith concludes with a specific reference to the perceived subordinate status of the north in relation to this London hegemony, observing that the point about

(Manchester Britpop band) Oasis, and The Beatles 'is not that they are ... from the north, but that they are seen and heard' by the south, to be 'northern' (Frith 2007: 138). It may thus be seen how, in light of this argument, a significant and culturally important work produced by an association between the suburban Bowie, and a group of musicians homogenized by their common roots in the northern town of Hull, is discursively double-coded. The meaning of *Ziggy Stardust* can only be interpreted with references to the two, distinct, places. The essence of the difference between the two soundscapes is economic—wealthy metropolitan London both imported and produced much music, and was culturally diverse; whereas the provision of music in the less wealthy, provincial Hull was more limited, and the town less diverse. London had the elaborated soundscape; Hull had a soundscape that was secondary to this, one subject to the former's influence.

Returning to the narrative of Bowie's evolution as a musician, the singer was introduced to London's wider social and cultural influences, as well as literary influences, by Kenneth Pitt, who became part of his management in 1966. Pitt was agent for acts such as Manfred Mann and Bob Dylan, but had also acted for London all-round entertainer, Anthony Newley—whom Bowie idolized. Alongside his work in musicals, on stage, film and television, Newley had released some novelty singles (such as a version of the music hall classic 'Pop Goes the Weasel') in which he adopted an 'exaggerated London barrow-boy' cockney accent (Doggett 2012: 12, 39). Bowie copied this affected vocal style for some of his songs. He produced the Deram LP *David Bowie* (1967) which failed to establish him as a name artist (the LP was released on the same day as The Beatles' *Sergeant Pepper's Lonely Hearts Club Band*). The LP has subsequently been associated with music hall, with its short story-like cameos and observations of the quirkiness of English, and London, life. The work was widely derided—especially for such items as the song 'The Laughing Gnome'—but Pegg observes that these cameos are consistent with the work of Pink Floyd's Syd Barrett and also The Beatles at the time. The Kinks must be added to this list and Pegg notes that these music hall-like Bowie songs were also an influence on quirky novelty act, the Bonzo Dog Doo-Dah Band (Pegg 2011: 295). *David Bowie* is an example of what Cloonan, and others, have labelled 'Pop Englishness', and is a part of that canon of work (Cloonan 1997; Bennett and Stratton 2010).

By 1968 Bowie's own interests were divergent, and he was encouraged by his proximity to London's arts and cultural production and to the country's major media providers. He wrote a radio play, a musical, planned a TV documentary, aimed to become a cabaret star, worked with mime artist Lindsay Kemp and, finally, got into folk in that year. He worked with several permutations of acoustic folk bands—Turquoise, Feathers—and in a duo with Yorkshireman John Hutchinson. He also participated fully in the counter-cultural milieu and was a co-founder of the Beckenham Arts Lab. However, he became disillusioned with the ideology of the counter-culture. His disenchantment coincided with an ebbing away of sixties utopianism, this being the result of several factors: the end of The Beatles; the Stones' debacle at Altamont—the antithesis of Woodstock 'love and peace'; the student riots; and the sharp downturn in the economy. Elsewhere, Syd Barrett, of whom Bowie was a fan, had been eased out of the hip Pink Floyd because of his erratic, drug-induced behaviour.

### *Hunky Dory*, with Hull Help

Bowie's next project was to record for his new label Mercury and, having been turned down by The Beatles producer George Martin, he was to work with American music producer Tony Visconti. A song 'Space Oddity' had been identified as a first single, which Visconti did not like and thus Gus Dudgeon produced the song which capitalized on the contemporary public interest in the moon landing of that year. When 'Space Oddity' became a surprise hit and Bowie quickly needed a backing band to record more material and promote it, Junior's Eyes were commissioned, who featured Hull musicians, guitarist Mick Wayne and drummer John Cambridge. Their album, *Battersea Power Station* (1969) was produced by Visconti (who also produced Bowie's friend Marc Bolan with his acoustic folk duo Tyrannosaurus Rex and the later electric rock version of the same band, T Rex). After confusingly releasing a second LP titled *David Bowie* (1969), so named to build the brand name, Bowie formed The Hype so that he could tour his new work. This featured Visconti on bass and Cambridge on drums who, after singing the praises of Hull guitarist Mick Ronson, travelled there to persuade the guitarist to join. Ronson had recently played guitar on an LP by a Hull folk musician, Michael Chapman, the album being produced by Dudgeon who had been impressed with Ronson's contribution. The Hull guitarist performed with Bowie on the John Peel *Sunday Show* on 5 February 1970 and from this point until 1973, the Hull guitarist played a prominent role in the production and performance of Bowie's music, as would other musicians from the northern town.

From the Peel appearance, Ronson is credited with having contributed his 'muscular' guitar 'power chords' to the song 'Width of a Circle', then in embryonic form, but which appeared on Bowie's new LP *The Man Who Sold the World* (Mercury Records 1970) (Weird and Gilly 2009: 45). Cambridge was sacked from the band after performing poorly and returned to Hull to be replaced by 'Woody' Woodmansey, also from Hull, who had played in Hull band The Rats with Ronson. For the recording sessions that eventually produced the songs for *The Man Who Sold the World* the musicians were largely left to create the music themselves as Bowie's input during the production of the musical element was minimal. He would come into the studio, present them with little more than some chord sequences, and then leave (Weird and Gilly 2009: 50). Woodmansey recalls that the band put the tracks down with guitar, bass and drums, having no idea what song would be put on top. He refers to the Hull soundscape, saying that he and Ronson had 'just come out of this hard rock area'—that was what 'we were influenced by'. Bowie, by contrast, 'had never touched' that musical area and Woodmansey indicates that Visconti had not either (Weird and Gilly 2009: 51). What resulted was a dark LP of heavy rock, totally distinguished from Bowie's former acoustic aesthetic, and the melody of the second *David Bowie* LP. The title of the song 'Black Country Rock' on *The Man Who Sold the World* references a regional variation in soundscape. The singer felt that the music sounded like that of The Move, who were from Birmingham, in the Midlands region of England, and 'spontaneously' gave the music that title, before he had written lyrics for it. The Midlands includes a district known as the Black Country because of its heavy industrial environment (Doggett 2012: 91). This is significant in the chronology of Bowie's development as an artist, and in relation to the impact of regional soundscapes upon popular music. 1970 was also the year of release of Black Sabbath's eponymous first LP, and a year in which there was a discernible shift in the rock genre. Cope (2013: 4) argues that heavy metal began with Black Sabbath in Birmingham in the 1960s. He suggests that, and gives examples of how, the austere, working-class industrial environment of noisy factories and limited opportunity for upward social mobility impacted upon the production of rock music there (Cope 2013: 26). There is a similarity here with the way in which the soundscape of Hull influenced Bowie's music, giving the former folk artist a 'heavy' sound, derived from an environment of lesser economic and cultural expectation than London.

Ronson and Woodmansey were invited back to London to work on Bowie's next album, *Hunky Dory*. Celebrated keyboard player Rick Wakeman was also asked to join the band but declined because of commitments. This may have been significant as Wakeman had a high profile as a musician and possibly would have influenced Bowie to take a different musical direction than the one he did with the Hull musicians. Ronson's own classical training in piano and violin meanwhile enabled him to do arrangements for some of the songs on this LP, including lauded productions such as 'Life on Mars'. 'Queen Bitch' meanwhile points forward to the rockier numbers on *Ziggy Stardust*, Ronson's power chords a raunchy diversion from the sweet melodies, piano and acoustic guitar prominent on the rest of the LP. Woodmansey concludes that:

> *Hunky Dory* is a bit too 'songwriter-like'. The eventual sound that we ended up with on Ziggy Stardust had more of a group sound. Although it was still David Bowie, it was more of a group thing. That's really what he needed. Mick [Ronson] was instrumental in much of that because he was able to take Bowie's chord sequences and put it into a rock thing (Weird and Gilly 2009: 65).

Woodmansey's comments confirm the nature of the contribution the Hull musicians made to the project. Their integration into the visual and ideological aspects of the spectacle proved more problematic however, as differences became apparent between the approach and stance of the suburban London boy, and the lads from the small northern town, as will be discussed later. Firstly, it is necessary to consider the properties of the Hull soundscape that influenced these musicians.

**The Hull Soundscape**

Hull in effect mirrors Liverpool on the west side of northern England. Like that port, the east coast town of Hull is built on an estuary, the Humber—which faces the North Sea and Europe, as opposed to the Mersey, which faces the Atlantic and Ireland and America. This caused Liverpool to be greatly affected by Celtic migration and shipping links with America, these factors influencing the development of the distinctive music scene and character that was so influential in 1963–64. Hull was not affected by such port links and yet suffered from a similar decline to Liverpool in the 1920s and 1930s. This, the Hull History Centre website notes, was 'exacerbated by overproduction in the fishing industry'. During World War II Hull was the heaviest bombed city outside London, thus necessitating considerable post-war reconstruction. The profile of the town's port trade meanwhile changed after the War, the smaller and older docks being closed while the Queen Elizabeth Dock opened in 1969 to handle container traffic. Hull continues to thrive, servicing large ships and providing a ready link with Europe (www.hullhistorycentre.org.uk).

The Hull soundscape in the 1960s and early 1970s did not have the elaborated character of London's, nor the cocky energy of Liverpool's beat scene. London was still the home of the UK entertainments industry, despite the challenge of The Beatles and the Merseybeat groups in 1963–64. The Beatles moved to London immediately when they first achieved fame. Hull was not yet linked directly by motorway to London and a train journey between them would take some five hours. Here, local provision of music co-existed with music provided by the London industry. Local music venues booked both local acts and touring acts. Thus, groups such as The Beatles and Rolling Stones and many others visited the area in the early-to-mid 1960s, and were in some cases supported by local groups. Ronson's first gig was with The Mariners, supporting the Stones at Bridlington in 1963. The Spa Hall in Bridlington, a few miles from Hull, held all-nighters in the early to mid-1960s. An event on 14 February 1964 is advertised as being between 20.00 and 06.30, with late bars until 03.00; early breakfasts from 03.30. Top of the bill of the eleven bands performing was (what is wrongly claimed to be) 'the Merseysound' of Tony Sheridan and the Sundowners (although there was a Hamburg connection between Sheridan and The Beatles). One of the support groups was Dean Webb and the Spidermen; the event, as with others at the time, thus featured a mixture of national touring acts and local bands. Tully's ballroom in Market Place, Hull meanwhile, had Rock Night every Saturday, with 'Hull's top groups' and in the same period jazz was popular in Hull clubs. Most of the local bands played cover versions of songs by nationally known British and American artists. The bill of the Skyline Ballroom featured a mixed-usage provision referred to earlier, with ballroom dancing on some evenings, but featuring rock and roll on Thursdays in 1963. The same venue held rock and roll and pop singing competitions around the same time as Beatlemania newly enthused the nation's aspiring musicians. Later, the same venue would host The Small Faces, The Kinks, Cream, Pink Floyd, and Jimi Hendrix who was, Palmer notes (2012), supported by a host of local bands.

Hull also had a well-established folk scene—as, indeed, did London. The publicity for the Hull Folk and Maritime Festival in 2016 stated that:

> Hull has a strong folk tradition; its status as a major port over the centuries meant that ideas and influences from different cultures and nationalities have been readily assimilated, adding to the diversity and richness of those traditions, while the city played an important part in the post-war folk revival, with the establishment of The Folk Union One Club above Ye Old Blue Bell pub in 1963 by The Watersons, who would go on to forge one of the most influential family dynasties in British folk music (www.hull2017.co.uk).

Meanwhile The Who's performance at Hull University in 1968 is the stuff of local legend; local attendee Mike Lawton tartly notes, however, that it was their performance at Leeds University that was committed to record in that year (The Who, *Live at Leeds*) and not the one at Hull. The local scene, and thus its soundscape, was plainly affected by the hegemony of the London-based entertainment industry and, in national terms, was secondary to it. The documentary DVD *Hot Coca-Cola with a Slice of Lemon* (2012) has been enthusiastically produced by Hull Museums and Heritage Volunteers with an accompanying leaflet by Alan Palmer. The title is a reference to a popular drink served in the Gondola club, which staged live rock and pop in the 1960s, but did not have a licence to sell alcohol. Ronson and the rest of the Spiders are the most prominent local musicians featured in the booklet but it also references other local acts from the period including Michael Chapman, The Hullabaloos (who enjoyed success in the USA as a part of the 'British invasion'), The Aces, The Small Four and the girl-group Mandy and the Girlfriends.

## 'Then We Were Ziggy's Band'

By the time Bowie and his band began recording songs that would eventually be included in *Ziggy Stardust*, they had been joined by another Hull musician, Trevor Bolder. Bolder had played in Ronson's short-lived project, his band Ronno, in Hull. Meanwhile Bowie's idea of creating a fictitious character came from the short-lived 1971 Arnold Corns project. This was his attempt to con the audience by creating a star, Corns—who in reality was his fashion designer friend Freddie Burretti—who did not actually sing on his own records, which would be performed by Bowie himself. The scheme undermined the 'hippie ideology' of authenticity that underpinned the relationship between rock musicians and their audience by the late 1960s, Auslander argues (2006: 132).

Bowie associated himself with what was termed 'underground music' in the London of the late 1960s. This was characterized by progressive development of technique, experimentation, movements towards cross-fertilization of genres, increased investment in the ideological meaning and significance of music, and an increasing political role for music. Popular music was the lifeblood of the so-called counter-culture, something Bowie was acutely aware of—indulging in its activities, but eventually rejecting its ideology. The latter was facilitated by exposing the inherent theatricality of the very performative nature of rock stardom with his *Ziggy Stardust* creation. This began to take shape in autumn 1971 with the recording of songs for the album. By early 1972, as recording continued, the look of the performance was also coming together as Bowie cropped his long hair to the famous spiked and dyed look and began performing in space-age attire. Woodmansey notes meanwhile that 'the pace of recording [the songs] was unprecedented' (Pegg 2011: 318). Bowie and the band would enter the studio and record songs one day, listen to them back, then record the final version the next. This suggests that Bowie and his band were a tight and integrated little unit by this time—actually an *authentic* rock band, the significance of which is discussed below.

The successful union of an authentic, homogenous band and the conceptual creation of fictitious persona derive from two soundscapes being juxtaposed in the dressy *Ziggy* project: those of Hull and London. Stereotypical north/south binaries are evident in the discourses that derive from the contribution of the Hull musicians as examined below, yet their provinciality was the taut canvas upon which the metropolitan Bowie painted his glitzy fiction. Writing of the

*Ziggy* era, Waldrep concludes that Bowie's presentation of self is futuristic, a utopian project that 'does not have an actual origin. It is a performance of gender and/or sexuality that is a simulacrum' (Waldrep 2015: 29–30).

Bowie had announced himself to be gay in January 1972 but Ronson had forcefully rejected the singer's request that he too should 'pretend' to be gay and to announce that they were in a bi-sexual affair, his wife Suzi Ronson has recalled (Weird and Gilly 2009: 67). However, the Hull Spider Ronson participated significantly in the performance of queer identity in the *Ziggy Stardust* stage show. In footage of the concerts he struts the mid stage area, at once evidently tied to his working band slightly behind him and to his right, their unity displayed in looks exchanged between the members as Ronson drives the music. He periodically joins Bowie at the microphone to share vocals (as illustrated in Bowie and Rock 2005). This produced iconic images which echoed those of The Beatles, and of the Rolling Stones' Jagger and Richards who similarly shared a microphone whilst looking straight at one another face-to-face. Such images were always dually coded as signs of homosocial comradeship, but also with homoerotic connotations. Famously, Bowie would perform mock fellatio on Ronson's guitar during his soaring solo on 'Moonage Daydream' (which was the original Arnold Corns single, but included in *Ziggy Stardust* in altered form).

Waldrep asserts that the central tenets of Ziggy Stardust are 'queerness, Orientalization and futurity' (Waldrep 2015: 30). The Spiders, whilst not conforming to the exotic image the main character of the show presented, nonetheless delivered raunchy rock and roll for an early seventies audience disaffected by the middle-class hippy ethos and the counter-culture of the 1960s. The costumed space-thing performed by Bowie bawls out the American slang phrase 'Ahhhhh, wham, bam, thank you ma'am' as the band belts out 'Suffragette City' to a climax. It is a misogynistic rock and roll past, meeting an androgynous future in a cathartic rock spectacle that highlights the very artificiality and pretence of its own delivery. The essence of the *Ziggy Stardust* project and its meaning is a double coding of 'alterity' (embodied in the metropolitan suburbanite Bowie's performance) and authenticity (embodied in that of the northern, provincial band) (Auslander 2006: 132). This enabled a high art statement to be suggested in what was really just another rock show. Such ambiguity pointed forward to the commoditized future of the enterprise culture of the 1980s and beyond, as is examined below.

## From Counter-Culture to Commodification

Taylor and Wall (1976: 115) note that underground artists who expressed the sentiments and ideology of the 1960s counter-culture, 'stressed an intellectual commitment to their music' and frequently eschewed 'direct influence from commercialism'. Part of Bowie's art in creating himself a star with *Ziggy* was for his management, MainMan, to treat him, 'the product', as a star 'even if nobody knew who he was yet' (Taylor and Wall 1976: 116). Although Bowie's figure of alterity raised ideological questions relating to gender, sexuality and the nature of performance, this was achieved mainly through processes that involve consumption: discipline of the body in trained dance and physical fitness; extravagant clothing and fashion; cosmetics and styling; and the visible trappings of stardom (an opulent celebrity lifestyle, publicized by press and media). The art of *Ziggy Stardust* was a prefiguration of the consumerist, fashion-obsessed, celebrity-centric, 'makeover' culture of today. Taylor and Wall (1976: 116) note that Bowie fused the commercial form of glam rock with the content of underground music (the music strongly associated with the counter-culture) but sharply conclude that:

> Bowie ... colluded in consumer capitalism's attempt to re-create a dependent adolescent class, involved as passive teenage consumers in the purchase of leisure prior to the assumption of 'adulthood', rather than being a youth culture of persons who question ... the value and meaning of adolescence and the transition to the adult world of work (Taylor and Wall 1976: 117).

The Hull musicians were complicit, although unwittingly, with the project, permitting a ready address to a working-class audience through their association with myths of the north, northern working-class resilience and openness, but also sexual conservatism. Yet the connotations of their working-class northern presence permitted an identification with the *Ziggy Stardust* project by an audience who may have been otherwise alienated by the work had the supporting musicians been recruited from the middle class and, like Bowie, been from southern England.

*Ziggy Stardust* pointed forward to the post-industrial society in which the industrial economy of manufacture was (forcibly) replaced by a service economy of lifestyle consumption. Martin Roth, Director of the Victoria and Albert Museum, writes that:

> One of his greatest impacts on our cultural life has been as a proponent of individualism—that we should be who we want to be, look how we want to look, and lead, not follow, without depending always on the views of others (Roth 2013: 17).

Yet Hewison notes that, in the movement to the free market, consumerist, enterprise society of the 1980s the freedom of the individual is 'purely economic', and

> The market becomes the only sphere of social action, and the economic becomes the only motive of morality. Ultimately, economic activity becomes the principal form of human expression. As the obsession with 'style' during the eighties shows …—you are what you buy (1997: 212).

In the eighties gender distinctions became less strictly defined in terms of dress and the performativity of traditional male and female roles. In this respect Bowie's performance of *Ziggy Stardust* is prescient. For Waldrep, Ziggy 'seems to present an alternative to gender encoding as it might exist in the future'. He continues:

> Bowie seems to imagine a universe in which sexuality is no longer a binary choice. To some extent, Bowie simply looks ahead to a more tolerant time, but it is not clear that he is queering straight identity so much as positing an identity that does not yet exist. His performance fractures gender and sexuality, but does not put them back together into a coherent whole (Waldrep 2015: 30).

He concludes that, with *Ziggy*,

> Bowie emphasizes the artificiality of all performances, including those of gender and sexuality. He realigns politics so that it is not just about electoral politics but identity politics as well. The personal becomes political in the seventies, and Bowie plays his part in making this fact known (Waldrep 2015: 31).

In the work, David Bowie anticipated modern-day liberal attitudes and metropolitan lifestyles that circulate around modes of conspicuous consumption. *Ziggy Stardust* also anticipates the centrality of spectacle to modern culture, not only in music, but in many public spectacles: in festivals, carnival, parades and other specially formulated public events. His influence in this respect is such that the Victoria and Albert Museum created the spectacle of a five-month exhibition exploring 'the broad range of Bowie's collaborations with artists and designers in the fields of fashion, sound, graphics, theatre, art and film' (www.vam.ac.uk). The exhibition later toured; there was a documentary film made around the exhibition, a lavish publication—*David Bowie Is* (from which the Roth quote above is extracted), and a range of merchandise made exclusively available. In the year of his death, forty-four years after *Ziggy Stardust*, spectacles have been created across the globe in his honour. At Glastonbury 2016 his trademark Ziggy and Aladdin Sane lightning-flash logo topped the Pyramid Stage and many artists covered songs of his in tributes.

Yet in the period of his career that is commonly held to be 'the most important historically', his *Ziggy* representation, crucially, was grounded in the authenticity of the music provided by the backing musicians who were, collectively, from a small northern town (Waldrep 2015: 28). This unexceptional town could therefore be discursively interpreted as being a signifier of the *genuine*, a balancing counterpart to the fictionality of the *Ziggy Stardust* project which justified its relevance. The transgressive 'rise' of *Ziggy Stardust and the Spiders from Mars* is conceptually supported by the notion that this authentic band of provincial musicians from Hull are doing just that: rising to stardom under the leadership of the more cultured Bowie. It is notable that The Rats recorded a song 'The Rise and Fall of Bernie Gripplestone' in 1967. The northern name of the protagonist here is consistent with the north's association with social realism in the first half of the decade and contrasts with the exotic nature of Bowie's derivation in the full name of the *Ziggy* album with its cosmic connotations.

## Coda: Hull's Heritage and UK Capital of Culture 2017

In later years a list of more recent music acts has been added in the continuing mapping of Hull's historical music culture, these being organically related to its soundscape. The likes of The Housemartins, Everything but the Girl, Red Guitars and Fila Brazillia are celebrated as having some origin in Hull, and Palmer (2012) notes that there was a vibrant music scene in the city, as the Hull Music Archive confirms. There is an historically proud, parochial enthusiasm within the scene which is reflected in the town's aspirational culture programme. Forty-five years on from *Ziggy Stardust*, Hull became UK Capital of Culture 2017, the second town to enjoy the status, the first being Derry-Londonderry in 2013. Fila Brizillia's Steve Cobby provided the soundtrack for the UK City of Culture 2017 bid film, 'This City Belongs to Everyone', which illustrates the importance of music to local culture and the democratic tone of the town's offer. Hull's cultural programme in 2016, the year leading up to the City of Culture spectacle, included—as well as the Hull Folk and Maritime Festival—the Hull Jazz Festival which promised to bring 'the best in jazz, funk, soul, reggae and improvised music to venues across the city' (www.hull2017.co.uk). There was also Humber Street Sesh, the annual street festival including music which promotes and celebrates the excellence and diversity of Hull's creative community. The festival played a significant role in raising the city's cultural ambitions and the City of Culture bid. Hull's Freedom festival also featured music.

The City of Culture scheme was inspired by the success of Liverpool being named European Capital of Culture in 2008, an European Union initiative. This brought significant social and economic benefits to Liverpool, as well as demonstrating how well a cultural spectacle could be delivered in a city that had previously been blighted by a pronounced economic downturn. The organizers of Hull 2017 put 'the transformational power of culture' at the centre of their offer (www.hull2017.co.uk). They promised that the arts and cultural programme would 'celebrate the unique character of the city, its people, history and geography', and that they would 'work with the artists of Hull and celebrate the culture of the city and its place in the wider cultural offer of the North, and make Hull a cultural destination for must-see events'. The website also talked of a Hull 'redefined within the Northern Powerhouse, but with a voice and confidence of a people on the up' (www.hull2017.co.uk). It has been demonstrated here that Mick Ronson and the other Hull musicians who contributed to Bowie's music from 1969 to 1973 played a vital role in developing the city's musical heritage, and also in redefining English music as two contrasting soundscapes merged in the creation of the seminal *Ziggy Stardust* production.

As a part of BBC Music Day on 15 June 2017 a blue plaque commemorating the Hull musicians in The Spiders from Mars was unveiled at Hull's Paragon station, from whence the band set out for their trips to London to work with Bowie. A plaque commemorating Bowie was also unveiled at the site of the Trident Studios in London.

## About the Author

Dr Peter Atkinson is Senior Lecturer in Film and Media at University of Central Lancashire, specializing in popular music and television. Peter has published on the role of broadcasting in the creation of The Beatles and Merseybeat myth of the early 1960s and on the topic of Abbey Road Studios, tourism and Beatles heritage. Most recently he has published a book chapter on the influence of the 1930s agit-prop theatre and radio documentary work of Ewan MacColl on the 1980s Manchester aesthetic of The Smiths and on the topic of ITV soap opera and representation of northern England.

## References

Auslander, Philip. 2006. *Performing Glam Rock: Gender and Theatricality in Popular Music*. Ann Arbor, MI: University of Michigan Press.

Bennett, Andy, and Jon Stratton. 2010. *Britpop and the English Music Tradition*. Burlington, VT: Ashgate.

Bowie, David, and Mick Rock. 2005. *Moonage Daydream: The Life and Times of Ziggy Stardust*. London: Cassell.

Cloonan, Martin. 1997. 'State of the Nation: "Englishness", Pop, and Politics in the mid-1990s'. *Popular Music and Society* 21/2: 47–70.

Cope, Andrew L. 2013. *Black Sabbath and the Rise of Heavy Metal Music*. Farnham: Ashgate.
Doggett, Peter. 2012. *The Man Who Sold the World: David Bowie and the 1970s*. London: Vintage Random House.
Frith, Simon. 2007. 'The Suburban Sensibility in British Rock and Pop'. In *Taking Popular Music Seriously: Selected Essays*, ed. Simon Frith, 137–47. Burlington, VT: Ashgate.
Hewison, Robert. 1997. *Culture and Consensus: England, Art and Politics since 1940*, rev. edn. London: Methuen.
Hull Music Archive. www.hullmusicarchive.co.uk (accessed 30 June 2016).
Hull UK City of Culture. 2017. www.hull2017.co.uk (accessed 24 June 2016).
Long, Paul, and Jez Collins. 2012. 'Mapping the Soundscapes of Popular Music Heritage'. In *Mapping Cultures: Place, Practice, Performance*, ed. Les Roberts, 144–59. London: Palgrave Macmillan.
Murray Schafer, R. 1994. *The Soundscape: Our Sonic Environment and the Tuning of the World*. Rochester, VT: Destiny Books.
Palmer, Alan. 2012. *Hot Coca-Cola with a Slice of Lemon*. DVD. Hull Museums and Heritage Volunteers.
Pegg, Nicholas. 2011. *The Complete David Bowie*, 6th edn. London: Titan Books.
Roth, Martin. 2013. 'David Bowie is What Follows'. In *David Bowie Is*, ed. Victoria Broakes and Geoffrey Marsh, 16–17. London: V&A Publishing.
Taylor, Ian, and Dave Wall. 1976. 'Beyond the Skinheads: Comments on the Emergence and Significance of the Glamrock Cult'. In *Working Class Youth Culture*, ed. Geoff Mungham and Geoff Pearson, 105–123. London: Routledge and Kegan Paul.
Thompson, E. 2004. *The Soundscape of Modernity: Architectural Acoustics and the Culture of Listening in America, 1900–1933*. Cambridge, MA: MIT Press.
Victoria and Albert Museum. www.vam.ac.uk (accessed 30 June 2016).
Waldrep, Shelton. 2015. *Future Nostalgia: Performing David Bowie*. London: Bloomsbury Academic.
Weird and Gilly. 2009. *Mick Ronson: The Spider with Platinum Hair*. London: John Blake.

# 6 Hard Floors, Harsh Sounds and the Northern Anti-Festival: Futurama 1979–1983

Ian Trowell

In 1979 the Leeds-based music promoter John F. Keenan announced the launch of 'Futurama: The World's First Science Fiction Music Festival'. This event would take place in Keenan's home city, at the disintegrating Leeds Queens Hall. The venue had been constructed as the Swinegate Depot for Leeds City Tramways in the early 1900s and extended for more vehicle capacity in 1914. Following what appeared to be a minimal makeover, it was switched to general entertainment use in May 1961 with the hosting of an Ideal Homes Exhibition. As the final decades of the century played out, Queens Hall witnessed indoor Christmas fun fairs in the 1960s, large-scale concerts by rock and pop bands, northern soul all-nighters in the 1970s and giant flea markets. The building was recalled as being makeshift and unsuitable at many levels regarding its conversion of use from transport depot to venue; it had poor acoustics, shoddy facilities and suffered from dreadful climatic conditions (see Figure 1).[1]

Futurama was an ambitious event that strived to bring a showcase of the genres of punk and its immediate offspring—post-punk—to this Yorkshire outpost. At the time, Leeds was a city that was at a standstill, struggling under a cloud of gritty northern poverty and a pervasive psychological curfew made real through the brutal series of murders by Peter Sutcliffe, dubbed as the

---

1. 'Motörhead complained about the acoustics, and it was absolutely freezing in winter, with ice forming on the retained tramlines' from https://en.wikipedia.org/wiki/Queens_Hall,_Leeds or 'The Queens Hall, supposedly a top venue... a converted tram shed, with the appalling acoustics, a floor of rock solid concrete, appalling climatic conditions, stinking toilets & terrible catering set in those days the most dismal part of the city!' from http://secretleeds.com/viewtopic.php?t=668.

**Figure 1:** Interior view of Queens Hall showing floor details—photograph Helma Hellinga.

Yorkshire Ripper, carried out in a relentless and monotonic rhythm.² Thus, Futurama enjoys something of a conflicted history. It can be read as an event that invites readings of trauma, disorder and negativity at the cultural and social levels; however it must be emphasized that it was seen at the time (and

---

2. Peter William Sutcliffe is an English serial killer who was dubbed the 'Yorkshire Ripper' by the press. Sutcliffe murdered thirteen women between 1975 and 1980, initially targeting prostitutes in the Leeds and Bradford area. He was captured and convicted in 1981.

is still remembered by many) as an important event and a brave attempt to create both a scene in Leeds and a fusion point for the various other city-based post-punk scenes.[3]

The 1979 event formed the first of a series of five festivals under the umbrella title of Futurama, the event running over an autumn weekend for each year until 1983.[4] Though these events featured national bands, there was a strong northern English post-punk presence, mirroring the city-based scenes that had started to coagulate following the initial fireball of punk rock. Furthermore, Futurama was pitched in a specific way and played out in an equally specific, but unpredictable, manner. The scope for uncertainty and deviation was high from the start, with the elements of the music itself, its manifestation in the North in both location and geographic nexus of bands, the strange nature of the venue, and a hostile music press reaction that paradoxically fed the scene around the festival year after year.

The countervailing factor in the hopes for Futurama concerned the specifics of the genres of punk and post-punk, most notably that these were genres of music that eschewed a festival atmosphere and mode of consumption, preferring to dwell in niches of both sonic and existential difficulty, introspection and awkwardness. They demanded a degree of attention and proximity in both the *filtering in* of the anxiety and angst within the sound and lyrical structures, as well as a space to embody and express emotion and uptight-ness. Narratives of spoken (or voice sampled) content, sonic ambience and musical style moved towards themes drawn from industrial and technological claustrophobia and futuristic ambiguity, a brittle and spittle of deviant punk in grim cities. The traditional festival ambience, formulated through the counter-cultural drifts of the 1960s and 1970s, with its embrace of positivity, unity and hope, its correlation with fresh air to

---

3. The promoter John F. Keenan has been supporting the Leeds music scene since 1977, and still continues to promote gigs in the city—see http://www.liveinleeds.com. A retrospective roundtable talk featured Keenan and other key musicians and activists from the Leeds scene in November 2015. There was general agreement that Futurama was a key event and a good thing for the city at the time—see https://www.youtube.com/watch?v=_3sTeMFQHNI.

4. The name Futurama was then taken up for a festival in Deinze, Belgium. A final Futurama 6 was put on by original promoter Kennan in 1989 utilizing the Palace venue at Bradford. This event, due to it occurring after the fracturing of the post-punk scene, is not considered in this chapter. A 'rival' event called 'Daze of Future Past' occurred in 1981 due to a London promoter booking Leeds Queens Hall and putting on a direct copy of the two-day Futurama format. It was this event that forced Keenan to temporarily move Futurama 3 out of Leeds.

carry both the sound-in-itself and the vibe associated with the sound, its shared space of letting go and becoming 'as one', were antithetical to punk and post-punk. Futurama, and its space of the cavernous, dark and dank Queens Hall, inadvertently formulated itself as a kind of *anti-festival*. It was outdoors in a sense, in that it brought a version of the outdoors as a kind of eternal wet, cold and distinctly northern night into the indoors. Being a depot and not a public station, the building utilized a basic build of internal girders and repeating triangular roof sections, as opposed to grand ferrovitreous structures associated with turn-of-the-century passenger terminals and arcades (Schivelbusch 1986: 49). This meant that a sublime experience of light, an 'impressionistic dissolution of the object' (Reynolds 1995: 204), would not be facilitated. Instead the Queens Hall offered something more akin to Joy Division's 'Shadowplay'—darkened spaces with objects as shadows-in-themselves as opposed to object and associated shadows—a perfect ambience for the event. Futurama would take place over a weekend in September, with punters allowed to blend with the industrial palimpsest and simply sleep on the dirty, concrete floor between each day. There were no festival codes followed, no invitation or opportunity to get in touch with nature, with spirits, with yourself.

With the academic milieu seeing a new interest in the general historification of the UK festival scene,[5] Futurama has continuously evaded discussion, mimicking perhaps its original circumstances (if not premise) of never quite being a festival. It presents an uncomfortable fit and resides as an outlier to narrative, eluding inclusion in various lists of key events and timelines.[6] This chapter redresses this imbalance, whilst at the same time working within the antagonistic constellation that surrounded the original series of events, therefore I propose to consider Futurama historically as an anti-festival in the fullest sense of the term. Firstly I will situate the 1979 Futurama festival at the junction of various cultural and social trends leading in to the moment of the event; secondly I will examine the dynamics of these trends over the five years of the festival's duration with particular regard as to how Futurama became a cipher for reading a direction of music and northern identity, emphasizing the post-punk lacuna in Leeds at the end of the 1970s. Finally I will develop a new series of narratives and contexts for understanding the Futurama phenomenon as anti-festival. With academic consideration and accessible resources of Futurama at a bare minimum, my work will be partly autoethnographic,

---

5. See McKay (2015) as the most recent example.
6. Both Clarke (1982) and McKay (2000) have chronologies, as does the UK Festivals website, http://www.ukrockfestivals.com/index.html.

drawing on my own recollections of attending these events, and partly developed through testimony mined from deeper enclaves of the internet such as specialist music discussion forums and responses to hosted videos on sharing sites such as YouTube.[7]

## Towards Futurama 1: The Context of 1979

I will now situate the occurrence of the 1979 Futurama within five overlapping themes: a timeline of festival culture leading up to 1979, the cultural dynamics of post-punk within the UK, the spatial dynamics of post-punk and the notion of northern enclaves of stylistic differentiation, the concept of sci-fi, and a wider concept of the cultural representation of the North.

Festival culture in the UK is generally acknowledged as starting with the 1956 Beaulieu Jazz Festival, with the 1960 edition of the same event also providing first evidence of subcultural factionalist scuffles.[8] This early incident of disharmony within the micro-worlds of post-war subcultures sets out the first media marker of festival-induced errant behaviour. Alongside this, a second contour is set out with the reporting of the Aldermaston CND marches as an organized form of getting together using music and dance, forging a countercultural festivity-within-activity. The final 'folk-devil' associated with festival culture emerges within the Richmond and Windsor festivals organized by Harold Pendleton, with the 1965 event bringing nomadism and dirt (McKay 2000: 6) alongside a general squalor (Clarke 1982: 27) to the foreground of public attention. This notion of dirt and squalor would re-emerge in a different context within Futurama.

The 1960s saw festivals gather force despite these media portrayals, with the counter-culture of the decade seizing upon the opportunities opened up through the festival format. This extended into outdoor spaces (Flower Children at Woburn Abbey in 1967, Isle of Wight from 1968, Hyde Park in 1969, Phun City at Worthing in 1970), all-night club events (such as the UFO club at the Roundhouse), and indoor events at hired spaces (Psychedelicamania at Camden Roundhouse for New Year's Eve in 1966, Christmas on Earth at Olympia in 1967 and the 14 Hour Technicolor Dream at Alexandra Palace in

---

7. Futurama 2 (1980) was recorded in its entirety and edited down for a short television programme. Residual recordings have emerged over the years and have been added to YouTube to evoke various responses. Futurama 1 was not recorded as a film event but various sound recordings exist. The inclusion of Joy Division in the line-up has meant that recordings of their set have populated YouTube.

8. An internecine dispute between modernist and trad jazz fans; see McKay (2000: 4) and Hewison (1986: 186).

1967).⁹ Throughout this period festivals began to define the decades and their music scenes.¹⁰

Depictions of dirt, disorder and anarchy aside, the festivals also worked a vein of positivity and hedonism, embodying what McKay (2000) originally framed as 'vital spaces, vital moments of cultural difference', and then expanded to 'utopian desire ... temporary heightened space-time having the fundamental purpose of envisioning and crafting another, better world' (McKay 2015: 4). Clarke (1982: 25) emphasizes the fusing of festival culture and counter-culture, with regard to the transformation of society and the bohemian retreat, an Edenic and holistic reading that persists into the present.¹¹ At the same time, the 1970s saw music genres shift more towards powerful rock and glam-rock performances with an emphasis on volume and spectacle, creating a new breed of festival that celebrated the communal appreciation of the music as a priority. The music and this open-air mode of communal listening seemed to symbiotically entwine, leading to mega-events such as the Donington Monsters of Rock Festival starting in 1980.

The dawning of punk in the second half of the 1970s would square up to this sense of festivity, optimism and lyrical and sonic allegiance to communal listening. Wicke (1990: 94) describes the old regime of rock as an 'immediacy of the musical experience and the highly personalised relationship between artist and audience', and such a nested and mediated set of modes of operation would be questioned as part of punk's critique and continual self-examination.¹² Whilst Malcolm McLaren devised an initial festival *of a sort* to both launch and claim the punk movement with his event at the 100 Club in September 1976, the fit between the festival and punk rock suddenly seemed out of joint.¹³ This situation proved itself with the disastrous attempt to hold a punk festival at Chelmsford Football Club in 1977—punk rock and festival culture would not make good bedfellows.¹⁴

---

9. See Miles (2010: 217) for extensive details of the 14 Hour Technicolour Dream event.

10. Sounes (2006: 42) describes the riot at the 1970 Isle of Wight Festival as a 'semi-colon between the music scene of the 1960s and the new decade', whilst McKay (2000: 17) uses the 1969 USA festivals at Altamont and Woodstock (both beset with controversy) as signalling 'the end of not just the decade but the sense of the decade, the idea of the sixties'.

11. Recent work looking at a Lefebvre derived 'rhythmanalysis' approach to the festival (Tjora 2016) documents a leisurely drift around a sanitized festival environment.

12. A clear example of this is provided by Laing (1985: 27) who dissects a sample of punk rock lyrical themes set against popular music genres.

13. Buzzcocks manager Richard Boon, quoted in Haslam (2015: 241), described the 100 Club event as 'a shop-floor window for things that hadn't yet been produced'.

14. The event billed as Chelmsford City Rock failed to attract any crowd and quickly descended into a farce. Clarke (1982: 152) has brief details, though a more comprehen-

My second theme to explore regarding Futurama 1979 is a brief contouring of the post-punk scene with specific regard to the line-up for the event. Reynolds (2006) provides the clearest and most extensive introduction to post-punk, and I will use his work as an overarching guide. He takes the symbolic impetus point of post-punk to be the implosion of the Sex Pistols in January 1978 and then suggests the period 1978–84 as the post-punk years (neatly encapsulating the five Futurama events). The key releases occur through 1979 with the Public Image Limited (PiL) single 'Death Disco' (June), Joy Division's album *Unknown Pleasures* and finally the PiL album *Metal Box* (December)—these releases signalling a clear break from a hackneyed punk sound but plunging deeper into disconcerting moods and cross-genre infections (dub, disco, funk-noir). By featuring both Joy Division and PiL, Futurama was certainly up to date with the pulse of post-punk, and these bands featured most prominently in the reviews of the event. The appearance of PiL and their vocalist John Lydon was a typically fraught affair. They performed in the early hours of the morning and offered what would be the first airing of tracks from *Metal Box*. The band were quoted as having a 'horrible time' with Lydon reacting by playing with his back to the audience. The sound was poor, the crowd were exhausted, and the tracks previewed from the pending album were described as 'bewildering and indecipherable'.[15]

My third theme concerns post-punk's heterogeneous region-specific rooting of sound across northern England. A staggered temporal take-up of music on a geographic basis pre-dates punk with the complex dispersal of the mod scene in the 1960s renegotiating sounds and codes to form the northern soul scene.[16] Post-punk's centrifugalism is predominantly unpacked through bands, labels, city-scenes and nuanced stylistic coagulations—with many of these divisions often lining up in parallel sequence (for example a label may crop up to represent a city with a particular sound). Of the approximately 30 bands that played Futurama 1 we can group around half of them as being attached to the cities of Leeds, Manchester, Liverpool and Sheffield, cities that were associated with a specific sound within the variegated post-punk milieu. Reynolds (2006: xxiv) turns his attention to these cities and, speaking of Manchester and Sheffield,[17] tries to pin down the underlying ethos and motivation to the sound and lyrical structures as 'the problems and the possibilities

---

sive report can be found at http://www.ukrockfestivals.com/city-rock-chelmsford-1977.html.

15. See http://www.fodderstompf.com/GIG%20LIST/leeds79.html.
16. See Anderson (2013) and Beesley (2014) for good overviews.
17. Manchester would be the dominant city represented in Futurama 1; however Sheffield would dominate Futurama 2 in 1980.

of human existence in an increasingly technological world ... pondering the dilemma of alienation vs adaptation in a machine age ... aestheticising panoramas of decay'. In his recent network-sociological approach to post-punk, Crossley (2015) works back across similar ground to Reynolds and etches out the socio-economic and cultural specifics of the North that forged both a nuanced and unified set of differences[18] regarding the sound and style of the music, seeing a common factor as being rooted in industrial decline and the opportunities opened up by cheap and accessible warehouse space. Crossley's work focuses on the modelling of networks, but it is possible to expand on this idea of desolate and semi-derelict industrial space as configuring an orientation to the genre influenced by the bleak hopelessness embodied in the aesthetics of the space.[19] There is also the emergence of a nascent club scene specific to the post-punk expressions in each of the four cities, with Haslam (2015: 286) suggesting that the Limit (Sheffield), Factory (as a venue in Manchester that predated the label), Eric's (Liverpool) and the F-Club (founded by Keenan in Leeds) all provided a creative hub and refuge within each city.

Other factors created specific dynamics and I can briefly cover these on a city-by-city basis. Manchester post-punk was forged by a strong core of individuals who brought in a wider palette of skills with individuals such as Martin Hannett (experimental producer) and Peter Saville (designer) uniting with Tony Wilson to craft a very strategic sound and identity for Factory Records. Wilson is described in Crossley (2015: 170) as someone who 'loved the transgressive nature of punk, he loved the North West of England, and he cherished the opportunity to bring the two together', pinpointing the nature of Factory's ambition to create their own sound within post-punk as a regional thing. There was even a semi-ironic attempt to curate an open-air festival at Leigh, with Factory organizing a kind of ceasing of (mock) hostilities between Manchester and Liverpool, but reports suggest that this event was woefully attended and has slipped into a historical grey zone.[20] Reynolds (2006: 174) in

---

18. By this I mean that northern cities were unified in creating something different to punk, even if that unified difference in sound and style then manifested itself as contrasts and diversity between cities.

19. See Edensor (2005) for a detailed study of the extended aesthetics of industrial ruin, with particular regard to ruin as representing a prefiguration of future degeneration.

20. The festival ran for three days—25, 26 and 27 August 1979—with Factory (Manchester) and Zoo (Liverpool) providing what is now considered as something of a classic line-up of bands with an official Factory number (FAC 15). In the end it is reported that between 200 and 500 people attended. Documentation of the event is listed at http://www.cerysmaticfactory.info/fac15.php.

turn emphasizes the urban landscape of Manchester that fed into the music, such that a 'desolate denatured environment persisted'.

Whilst Manchester post-punk seems to have been catalysed by a Sex Pistols gig that has achieved near-mythical status, Crossley (2015: 174) suggests a similar event in May 1977 by a different London punk band, the Clash, catalysed the Liverpool scene. This led to a loose consortium of individuals gathered together as a kind of *super-group* (Big in Japan) that only existed as a kind of agency to facilitate the formation of other bands who went on to define the Liverpool post-punk scene. Again there is a regional factor dictating both the coming-to-be and in-itself of the scene, the decline in the once busy docks of Liverpool creating cold and cavernous spaces of opportunity for bands to practice.

In Sheffield there was already a post-punk sound emerging with Cabaret Voltaire in the pre-punk era, setting out as early as 1973 and then using the punk boom to 'rise to prominence in a nexus of DIY musical activism inspired and triggered by punk' (Crossley 2015: 164). The Sheffield post-punk look and sound was very specific and based heavily on synthesizers and electronic machinery. Mallinder (2007: 304–305) situates the northern-ness of this in both an economic context: 'with a drum machine, sequencer or Super-8 projector, frequently cheaper or more available than a guitar amp or drum kit, access and affordability gave modernity an ironic appeal' and also a sociocultural context as a 'sonic nexus of electronic technology and regional dysfunction'. The Sheffield electronic sound was etched out in a very different way to the strategic and style-oriented approach in Manchester, utilizing ephemeral space opened up at the University (Lilleker 2005: 7). The brutal industrial landscape—both a brutality past of metronomic steel forges and a brutal present of dereliction—seeps into the music, bleeding into the wider theme of dystopian science fiction that Futurama touched upon. Martyn Ware of the Human League is quoted in Reynolds (2006: 150) as 'growing up in a science fiction noisescape'.

The Leeds scene is harder to pinpoint, without a local record label to bring together a possible sound or direction within the city's post-punk milieu.[21] Music seems to be centred around the University, Polytechnic and Art College with bands such as Gang of Four, the Mekons, Delta 5 and Scritti Politti developing an anxious, edgy and introverted-agitational sense of (dis)achievement looked over by art-activist tutors such as T. J. Clark (ex-British situationist)

---

21. The small print for the flyer for Futurama states that the event is hoping 'to establish a new record label and possibly a rock magazine for this part of the North' such that 'to the musicians/artists of this area it could mean the difference between success and obscurity'.

and Terry Atkinson (Art and Language). This connection to academia extending from contiguity to collusion could be considered as a barrier to a coherent identity as exemplified in other northern cities, leaving Leeds as a lacuna in the North. A recent move to celebrate and historify the Leeds scene via a film about the Mekons saw some critical reflection on how the scene developed within the strictures of the city, and there is a focus here *away* from ghosts of industrial past (Sheffield and Manchester) and more towards a very real horrific presence at the time with the grip of fear put upon the city by Peter Sutcliffe. This extreme cloak of psychological dread merged with more diffuse forces around racial tension and a culture of violence made prominent with the reputation of the large 'firm' attached to the city's football team.[22] Thus, the Leeds sound is not defined as reflecting and reacting against nuanced conditions of the city, but is defined in terms of its existence in spite of the totality of its surroundings. It emerged, survived and grew through a sense of preparedness to create music and a stubbornness to keep going.[23]

My fourth theme to situate Futurama concerns its claim to be a sci-fi festival, though this is often a misnomer as the wider effects of the festival as a series have played out in history. However, the flyer for the first event labels it as 'the world's first science fiction music festival' and advertises a constant flow of films including *The Man Who Fell to Earth*, *Freaks* and *Barbarella*, with supporting side-shows, slide shows, laser displays, street theatre and artwork. It is possible to semantically deconstruct the statement as being a declaration of the music itself being science fiction, a kind of grouped branding of the genres within the city-specific scenes. Certainly a key British author such as J.G. Ballard would be a possible unifying theme between the Sheffield and Manchester scenes; the lyrics of Joy Division drawing heavily on Ballard's works whilst the synth-based sounds of artists such as Cabaret Voltaire and Human League emerging directly from within a Ballardian post-industrial cityscape.[24]

My final theme concerns the wider context of the North represented in the media and popular culture around the time of Futurama in 1979.[25] This crosses over into the other themes, for example the simple historical fact that ascendant festival culture and the North were not coterminous: the chronol-

---

22. A firm is the vernacular term for an aggressive gang or aggregation of hooligans.
23. O'Brien (2012) documents the specifics of a gendered post-punk identity within the aggressive male culture of early 1980s Leeds.
24. Ian Curtis' reading of Ballard is explored by Jon Savage in his *Guardian* column: https://www.theguardian.com/books/2008/may/10/popandrock.joydivision.
25. Davidson (2005: 209) identified the North as starting at Sheffield, marked by the feeling of 'an arrival on the other side of the frontier'.

ogy of festival culture outlined above has the North as a conspicuous absence.[26] Another clue to the cultural annexing of the North occurs on the Futurama flyer, giving the location of Leeds as being 'at the other end of the M1 from London', the original multi-lane and complete motorway built in England and therefore in itself an icon of modernity. This gives substance to the fine differentiation between suggesting the M1 goes to Leeds or ends at Leeds, the latter terminology prioritizing the road itself against the destination. The M1 played a significant part in Leeds claiming an identity: firstly it became synonymous with 'The North' due to signs on the motorway always stating this as the final destination (Moran 2009: 71), and secondly it branded itself as the 'motorway city of the seventies' with all mail from the city employing this proud franking mark (Moran 2009: 204). Both of these instances can clearly be interpreted in an ironic manner, dovetailing back into the previous theme of sci-fi and the Ballardian investigations of motorway culture.

At the sociological level Taylor *et al.* (1996) offer a comparison of Manchester and Sheffield using testimony gathered in the early 1990s, and this enquiry provides strong evidence of the intra-region differences of cities in the North by working with the idea of structures of feeling.[27] Russell (2004) gives the historical overview of the North within the national imagination, though his critical eye loses focus as he brings his work into the late 1970s. Cultural readings of the region can be difficult to disentangle between a blanket North (versus South)[28] and place-specific representations, though Barry Hines television screenplay for *Threads* (1984) was a key moment even if it falls just the wrong side of the Futurama years. This disconcerting BBC drama depicts the nuclear apocalypse played out in Sheffield, and the theme of nuclear annihilation was a key signature in the lyrics of many punk and post-punk songs. Finally, it would be the work of novelist David Peace who would create the strongest images of life in the North at the time around 1979, particularly the Leeds area under the grip of fear from Peter Sutcliffe. Peace's writing relentlessly disrupts harmony, understanding and nostalgia with his attempts to 'establish alternative relationships between time frames ... Peace does not

---

26. Clarke (1982: 43) details the Krumlin Festival, 14-16 August 1970 as the first festival in the North, taking place on farmland in West Yorkshire. The event was beset by atrocious weather and photographs of the event resemble a humanitarian relief action. See http://www.ukrockfestivals.com/Krumlin-festival-1970.html.

27. The work attempts to redress the dominance of a realist political economy approach (such that the assumed economic poverty of the North provides a blanket way of understanding the region, its cities and its people), opting instead for a 'perspective of cultural sociology' (Taylor *et al.* 1996: 8).

28. Shields (1991: 207–51) provides an overview of the North as cultural representation.

turn to the past neutrally or offer history as consensus' (Shaw 2011: 3), thus leading to a sense of the North as both 'in an obstinate state of marginality' and 'a fractured peremptory of conflicted and conflicting space' (Shaw 2011: 11).

## Convergence of phenomenology and affect

> Asylums with doors open wide,
> Where people had paid to see inside,
> For entertainment they watch his body twist,
> Behind his eyes he says, 'I still exist.'[29]

> September 8 1979 and the glittering hi tech sci-fi Futurama festival, billed as cutting edge science show with futuristic music, restaurants and sleeping facilities …what a load of bullshit !!!!!! the conditions could not have been worse or more opposite the promised paradise, a huge dark dirty old bus depot with concrete floor, no restaurant or food, no drinking water, the toilets were six inches under water, and there were ever growing piles of puke, bottles and cans in the back two thirds of the cavernous bus depot. The accommodation was … sleep on the concrete floor!!!!!! That was a fucking hard night on that concrete with no bedding or blanket except my jacket!! Numerous fights broke out during the day as foolish 'entertainers' tried to put on a show in the side 'stalls' around the edges, this was attempted in almost complete darkness. One by one they were bottled off within seconds, some of them running for their lives!!!!!!! Psycho bouncers circled looking for the slightest excuse … all in all the conditions would be unacceptable in a concentration camp … enter Joy Division.[30]

> That floor—yes, I managed to find bit of cardboard to lay on and my leather did a good job and getting up early to find a warm drink. Remember the films shown about 1am—the Dali film repeating the razor blade through a woman's eye—over and over then some idjit screeching a guitar meaninglessly on the stage till threatened off it.[31]

> You felt momentarily what it was like to be homeless, to sleep on a concrete floor, like in a bus station, to just lie down in the midst of whatever chaos had ensued through the day.[32]

29. Joy Division 'Atrocity Exhibition'.
30. Testimony of event from https://www.youtube.com/watch?v=0cQT5qTyqCs.
31. Ibid.
32. From conversation with Sheffield musicians who attended Futurama 1.

> All i can remember about the Queens hall ones were all the bodies all over the floor in a right state and the smell. It looked like a hospital casualty ward with no lights.[33]

Crossley (2015: 222) considers Futurama 1 as a hub within his wider scheme of sociologically mapping subcultural networks: the festival 'contributing to the formation of both a national post-punk identity and concrete ties which lent that identity substance'. But the festival worked for many of those attending on a different level, due to the quick deterioration of the conditions within what was a difficult environment to start with. It was at this point that the affective themes of dystopian sci-fi and post-punk explorations of totalitarianism and brutal tests of endurance and discipline converged into an actual experience. As the *NME* review pointedly remarked in what it headlined as 'the Squalor of Leeds', Cabaret Voltaire's 'No Escape' and Joy Division's 'Atrocity Exhibition' took on a rather ironic meaning (see Figure 2).

**Figure 2:** Interior view of 1981 punk festival 'Christmas on Earth' at Leeds Queens Hall showing deterioration of venue and attempts to sleep (photograph by Helma Hellinga)

33. Ibid.

This concordance of musical and lyrical affect with phenomenological actuality formed a mental scar on many of those attending the event. The post-punk *habitus* of attending gigs, seeking out obscure and adventurous records and consuming music in a thinking space was interrupted with the forced conditions of the festival—bands performing relentlessly one after the other[34] within deteriorating conditions, the sense of an eternal gloom as night-time was sensed (but no one was quite sure) and the only option was to lie down on the floor and try to go to sleep. *Guardian* music journalist Dave Simpson attended the 1979 event and amidst the great bands he witnessed he recalls that

> the Queens Hall venue floor came off on your clothing: by the end of the Saturday everyone was a uniform bleak grey ... 27 years later, I can instantly remember that unmistakable, echoey atmosphere, the smell of glue and the desperate feeling of trying to get to sleep at 2am while a man onstage plays electric guitar in front of a film of earthworms.[35]

The contemporaneous review of the event in *NME* provides a good insight into the wider themes I outlined which feed into the understanding of Futurama and post-punk 1979, inadvertently providing a cut-off between the current and the futures to come. In reviewing the first day Andy Gill tries to align Futurama with the Isle of Wight Festival, both events bookending 1970s festival culture. Gill states he attended the Isle of Wight event and suggests the squalor that unites the two events somehow signals the sense of the end of an era. Gill as a professional journalist would have moved through the decade being paid to proclaim and promote the next big things to an *NME* readership eager to be instructed in the latest trends,[36] but he fails to remark on how post-punk (and punk) had escaped and critiqued the festival format as the 1970s played out. The squalor of the original 1970s festival culture can be understood as part of a wider *celebration* of a hedonistic other of transcendent politics and living, rooted to the earth and outside of a politics of authority. The squalor of Futurama is not embraced as a glimpse of a way forward; it emerges as the forced physical embodiment of the affective dystopia of post-punk. Taken together, the two festivals suggest a mirroring cultural mutation

---

34. Keenan devised a twin stage set-up such that as one band performed, the next band could be setting up ready to play straight after.
35. See http://www.theguardian.com/music/musicblog/2006/oct/25/themusicfestivalthatchange1.
36. Co-reviewer Ian Penman, covering the second day of Futurama, resorts to talking about bands not appearing but who are, in his account, fashionable.

of what Giorgio Agamben might classify as 'bare life' as formulated through the work of Hegarty (2007: 146), who takes his noise subject as 'subjectivity as a coming undone of subjectivity replaced by existing as the sole purpose of existing'.

## Futurama Unfolds: Distaste and Displace

The chastening review in *NME* did not deter the festival from moving on to a second event in 1980 even though the situation of the Queens Hall had not improved from the squalor it was accused of bringing about. Futurama 2 quickly accrued an equally impressive roster of bands and was much anticipated by the fans of post-punk in the North (and beyond), suggesting that the conditions of experiencing the event and their congruence with the music was seen as part of the thing itself, an ironic holism. Fans still bedded down on a cold floor stained with 50 years' worth of petrol, diesel and engine oil. However, what marks out Futurama 2 as particularly interesting is the shift of dynamics in the music scene of the time (see Figure 3). Both *The Face* and *i-D* magazines launched in 1980, and it was clear that post-punk was fracturing along a diverse number of lines of style and commercialism that would eventually overrule discernible stylistic delineation based upon region. These magazines promoted a barrage of tightly manicured and stylized images—either of a band or an evanescent and miniscule subcultural expression—with an aim to stake out commercial ground and make an impact on the mainstream music scene. The years 1981 and 1982 would see the charts shaken up with many of the obscure acts from these events, artists rising from wilful (and possibly woeful) obscurity to appear on key music television programme *Top of the Pops* within a matter of months. The line-up of Futurama 2, and to a lesser extent Futurama 3, resides as a kind of tipping point of such opportunism, with many artists about to go on to carve out wider success as pop-punk (Siouxsie and the Banshees, Altered Images), guitar pop (Echo and the Bunnymen, U2, Simple Minds) and synth-pop (Soft Cell).[37] Other included bands would quickly re-group and re-format after 1980 and seek out commercial success (Vice Versa became ABC, Frantic Elevators became Simply Red).

At the same time, a second strand of subcultural formation grew outside of this toying with commercial potential, with groups asserting a harder sound mixed with tailored identities encouraging loyal followings. This is initially evident with Futurama 3 which features the first shoots of a tightly

---

37. Soft Cell appeared at Futurama 2 as an unknown band; however 1981 saw the breakthrough of the synth-pop scene and by the end of the year the band had a number one hit with 'Tainted Love'.

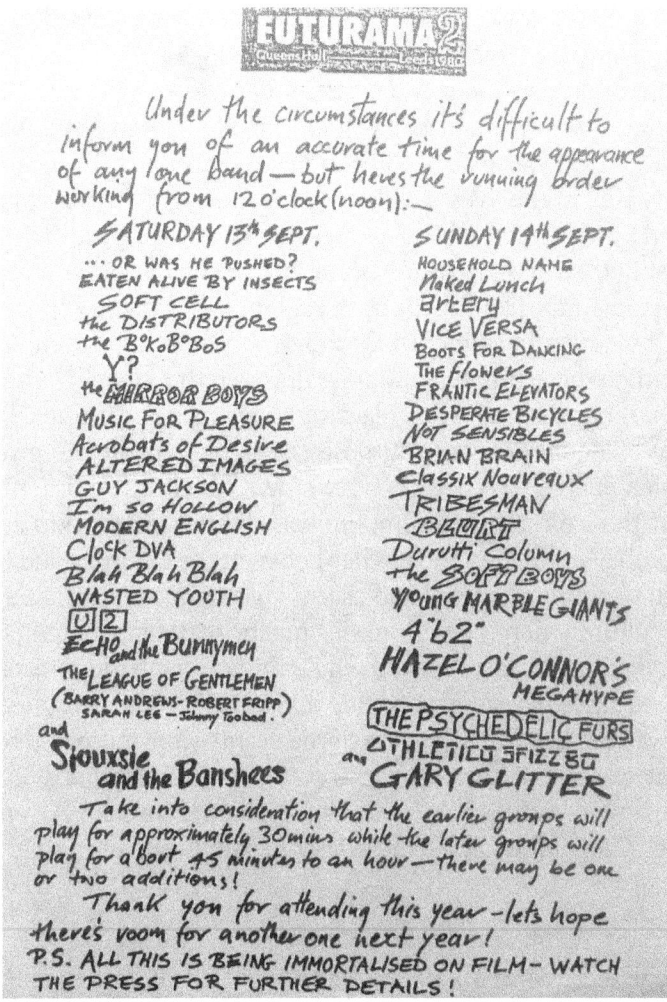

**Figure 3:** Flyer for Futurama 2, Leeds Queens Hall, September 1980

packaged goth image and sound (Bauhaus, UK Decay and Sisters of Mercy performing their first major gig) as well as Theatre of Hate who were developing a hard punk-rockabilly blend. Whilst three of the four aforementioned bands are from the South, they would have a substantial impact on the music scenes in the North. Futurama 4 would see a second day made up predominantly from northern goth bands (Southern Death Cult, Danse Society, Dead or Alive, March Violets) with horror-punk godfathers the Damned and newer artists Gene Loves Jezebel and Sex Gang Children contributing to the goth aura. Futurama 5, held at the end of 1983, consisted almost entirely of goth and 'Theatre of Hate style' bands, most of whom were resigned to ploughing a furrow in a difficult career satisfying a niche audience.

The sense of displacement and disarray that was engendered with Queens Hall to enmesh with the music itself continued through Futurama 3 and 4 as the festival itself was displaced from Leeds. Futurama 3 was held at Stafford Bingley Hall in the West Midlands, described as a '10,000-plus capacity shed owned by the Staffordshire Agricultural Society, purpose-built to accommodate penned farm animals' (Haslam 2015: 213).[38] Conditions here were equally dystopian as, like the Queens Hall, it was designed to be a one-off event place where a headline act was experienced without time or motivation to examine the actual surroundings. It is said that sleeping arrangements here became more surreal with black bin bags being given out.[39] Futurama 4 moved to an equally obscure outpost, the Deeside Leisure Centre in North Wales, which enabled a 4,000 capacity crowd to witness music through the covering of the ice rink. Free camping was offered nearby and an all-night game of football ensued on the pitches between the Saturday and Sunday.

It was this continued spatial and psychological squalor and the evidence of a new subculture emerging within the squalor that contributed to the *NME* generating a strong distaste for the whole thing. Seeing themselves as something beyond tastemakers, embodying a kind of Bourdieu-inspired mode of post-punk distinction, the reviewers of the events were tempered by both the flowing out of some Futurama bands to unlikely success in the charts and the honing down of other bands into what would form the goth and positive punk scenes.[40] Reynolds (2006: 270) describes the *NME* reaction to Futurama

---

38. See also http://www.last.fm/venue/8864379+Stafford+Bingley+Hall.

39. 'I'm surprised it had electricity and it smelt bad. The only other facilities were some porter-loos and a little club-house pavilion thing bar that wouldn't have been out of place beside a village cricket green. We also had the draconian licensing laws in 81 so it only opened 12-2pm and 7-10pm. Nowhere else to buy food/drink and we were probably about six miles outside Stafford but there was an infrequent bus service back into town. Everyone was kicked out of the shed at the end of the night as we weren't even allowed to sleep with the beer cans. However there was a cattle parade ring outside and they did allow us to sleep in the little grandstand that overlooked it. The organisers even handed out black bin liners to kip in. A thoughtful gesture.' https://www.myheartland.co.uk/viewtopic.php?p=89253.

40. The origins of goth as a formulated genre tend to drift backwards, though surprisingly early Factory Records publicity used the term to describe some of their artists. At the same time the comic-horror strand of punk would be developing a goth mode without referring to goth itself. The moniker of positive punk was a short-lived scene that ironically came to be in an *NME* feature in what must have been a slow news week. Most of the bands labelled positive punk, if not just an evanescent operation to catch a trend, would

2 as 'Castle Donington for the angst-rock brigade', further quoting *NME* journalist Adrian Thrills describing the crowd as 'post-punk's new hippies' and Paul Morley signalling 'the unwelcome rise of a new underground ... playing to the fans who are not so much the converted as the contained'.

## Batcave or Batley? A New Northern Cult

The persistence of the goth scene in heavily stylized and easily recognizable subcultural forms into the current era of 'neo-tribes' means that critical work on the goth phenomenon permeates contemporary research into youth subcultures (see Haenfler 2010 and Gunn 1999). Thus it is possible to understand goth as emerging from and travelling through certain distinct, and sometimes contradictory, formulations and clusters of moments, and at the same time lose a sense of the actual history of the scene. I assert here the historical imperative of Futurama and Leeds (and the North) as an important foundation in the goth identity.

Firstly, it is useful to look at a couple of British cultural histories other than Reynolds' post-punk magnum opus that document the possible beginnings of goth in the UK. Carpenter (2012) focuses upon the August 1979 release of the Bauhaus single 'Bela Lugosi's Dead' to mark out what he calls a stylistic 'ground zero', whilst at the same time acknowledging a more nebulous but prolific 'second-wave of gothic rock' (p. 31) emerging with bands such as Sisters of Mercy. Michael Bracewell attempts to plot the contour of pop delinquency in Albion and positions goth predominantly at its later stage, as it has pervaded into wider geographical realms, such that it can be classed as a 'suburban and provincial cult' dominated by a 'style indurate to the capriciousness of either fashion or pop' (Bracewell 1997: 119). In the same way that Bracewell writes his understanding of goth into the wider theme of his work, Haslam initially offers a version of goth instigated in the London club scene with the opening of the Batcave club in 1982. The Batcave was part of a sequence of fast-changing subcultural makeovers that permeated the tight London club scene in the same era as post-punk, seeing the birth of the New Romantic scene as a particularly London-centric phenomenon. Numerous histories of this New Romantic scene are evident in our nostalgia-heavy times, and the brief flowering of goth within this milieu is often taken as something more than what it amounts to. A couple of bands were specifically promoted with the Batcave, emerging overnight and disappearing just as quickly when

become part of the goth scene. The best history of the goth incunabulum is at http://www.historyofgoth.com or goth journalist Mick Mercer's archives at http://www.mickmercer.com/index.html.

the next trend was ushered in. However, Haslam almost confesses to fudging the issue, and immediately backtracks on his words by including notes from a discussion with West Yorkshire-based author David Peace (discussed above) where Peace squarely places goth in the West Yorkshire outlands of Leeds and its associated satellite towns: 'It wasn't showbiz. Being cut off from London gave it an endearing insularity' (Haslam 2015: 274). Haslam looks to be out of his comfort zone here, away from the cool and hip world of rare-groove and proto-funk clubs that were part of the early to mid-1980s, but Peace's words put us back into the true heartland of goth culture.

Peace talks of his experience at Wakefield's Hellfire club, a small club that supported a goth scene in one of the many West Yorkshire towns in the early 80s. Wakefield is a typical town within the region that shared a sense of poverty and disillusionment amidst a botched and stifling urban stricture. Davidson (2005: 207) documents a socio-spatial experience of a typically similar town at the same period in time when looking at the novelist Angela Carter's reflections on Doncaster, itself in South Yorkshire but bordering onto Wakefield, describing these places as 'newly built town centres, already failing to function as the genuine centre of anything'. West Yorkshire consists of a labyrinth of such places, sprawling endlessly sideways and diagonally, making progress through the region convoluted and laden, allaying any optimism derived from a misconstrued hyperboreanism.

A remarkable cultural document of the West Yorkshire nurturing of goth was made in the form of a bizarre one-off project around the Xclusiv nightclub in Batley, the film beginning with a trawl around this town that would be a million miles away from the thoughts or cares of the ephemeral goth fashionistas congregating around London's Batcave.[41] The film is essentially a two-hour documentation of a night at the club which stylistically can be read as a marker between Andy Warhol's tedium endurance films and a modern artwork in the participative genre such as Phil Collins' 2004 work *They Shoot Horses*. The soundtrack is diegetic so that the many jump cuts between shots mean that the music is stuttering and striated.[42] It is easy to lose sight of the landmark cultural documentation the film affords through its strange hybrid

---

41. The documentary was made seemingly as a private work and then sold to local fans of the scene. Footage survives at https://www.youtube.com/watch?v=A9sMZ_5NjM8, whilst details of the film's history and its survival is detailed at https://ilegality.wordpress.com/2015/01/01/the-height-of-goth/.

42. Alexis Petridis documents the film in a *Guardian* article, describing it with much compassion as a 'moment of transcendence' even though at the same time as being 'unwittingly hilarious, fascinating and incredibly boring'. See http://www.theguardian.com/culture/2012/may/13/alexis-petridis-height-of-goth.

of amateur-professional production values, but the entire work perfectly captures how this scene took root in the nexus of West Yorkshire towns that would have been absent from any pop cultural history.

The Futurama festival gave this region a specific post-punk direction with the goth sound and style. It instantly took hold in these smaller towns, supporting local autonomous scenes whilst feeding into a perceived goth stronghold in Leeds. The brutal nature of the spatial experience of Futurama itself, whether in Queens Hall, Bingley Hall or Deeside, energized a kind of other-directedness that spread from Futurama itself into the smaller enclave towns such as Wakefield, Bradford and Doncaster. The concept of other-directedness is theorized by Sandvoss (2005: 58) in regard to spatial experience as part of the consumption pattern of fans, itself drawing on work by Relph (1976: 92). Other-directedness is a stronger term than the more fashionable psychogeography; the experience of the space is determined in a forced, awkward and disconcerting sense, rather than the privileged drifting or 'deriving' psychogeographer being able to play with the codes of the space for their own subversive pleasure. Leeds Queens Hall was not open to such a psychogeographic reading; it remained a cold tram shed etched with an industrial palimpsest, repurposed as an entertainment space, and then stretched beyond the limits of this fragile and flimsy repurposing by submitting the audience to an extended duration bleeding over into a temporary regime of dwelling. The nuanced codes of northern post-punk lyrics and sonic readings were then 'unconcealed' in the Heideggerian sense, the cipher removed in the other-directedness of the brutal space.

## Conclusion: The Ghost Dance

Whilst goth emerged as an identity to choose from within what cultural critics such as Polhemus (1994: 131) call the 'supermarket of style', I also maintain that it emerged as a distinct subculture forged through a historical sequence of cultural and spatial negations. It involved a choice of engagement but then developed a direction towards a cultural vortex. Post-punk spoke a certain message to a subset of youth; and the Futurama festivals, and their staging in the city of Leeds, catalysed and fused a certain articulation of blankness and other-directedness. Leeds was the only city in the North to not have a post-punk difference and identity, and so the brutal tactility and sensoriality of Futurama gave birth to this new northern cult of goth. The elements of the space itself, the mix of dystopian sounds coming in from other cities, the warning sign pre-cursors of attaching the notion of festival to both punk and the North, created a kind of self-seeding counter-flow. It would not be London bands such as the Clash and the Sex Pistols that catalysed the Leeds scene, but a mix of pre-established northern scenes meeting in the cavernous other-directedness of the Queens Hall.

The venue was demolished at the end of the 1980s, and now functions as an emptied space in the role of a car park. Whilst the building as an external monument can be recalled and revisited through archive images, it is the brutality of the interior that lingers in the memory. The memorialization of interior space is dramatically configured in the idea of artistic negative space as developed by artist Rachel Whiteread and her work *House*, using a brutalist grey concrete cast of the interior presented as an exterior facing object of contemplation. A casting of the interior of Queens Hall can be imagined as set out in a dense and dark material somehow other than grey concrete, while the artistic negative space of the interior was experienced as darkness, noise and squalor, a more quotidian understanding of the word negative in both the moral and ontological context.

The haunting presence of the space of Queens Hall is subsumed by the haunting presence of the music of Futurama, and the transition between post-punk and early goth, bleeding out into unremarkable and indistinct suburbs of Leeds and satellite towns within the West Yorkshire conurbation. If punk appropriates and rejoices in the phrase—out of context, amphibological, or otherwise—from Shakespeare's *Macbeth* as 'signifying nothing' then post-punk can perhaps be understood as signifying nothingness. That is, leaving behind the detailed context of the original quote, signifying a something that is nothing, rather than not signifying anything. Derrida (1994: 24) speaks of the haunting presence of the past as a 'disjuncture in the very presence of the present, [a] sort of non-contemporaneity of present time with itself'. His notion of hauntology runs into a complex and derelict terrain with the haunting past of a 'no future' brought to bear in the present. The presence of the present cannot be avoided, but the no future of the sonic and lyrical nihilism and dystopia of both Joy Division and PiL becomes trapped in the empty space of the no longer Queens Hall and the re-rendered grain of a YouTube video.

## About the Author

Ian Trowell is a PhD candidate in the School of Architecture at the University of Sheffield. He is researching the travelling fairground in the UK as a historical and cultural phenomenon. His work focuses on spaces of amusement, visual economies of the fairground, sonic realms of legitimized noise, and the technological imperative of the fairground machine. He previously produced the music and culture fanzine *Autotoxicity*.

## References

Anderson, Paul. 2013. *Mods: The New Religion*. London: Omnibus.
Beesley, Tony. 2014. *Sawdust Caesars: Original Mod Voices*. Peterborough: Fastprint.
Bracewell, Michael. 1997. *England is Mine: Pop Life in Albion from Wilde to Goldie Harper*. London: Collins.
Carpenter, Andrew. 2012. 'The "Ground Zero" of Goth: Bauhaus, "Bela Lugosi's Dead" and the Origins of Gothic Rock'. *Popular Music and Society* 35/1: 25–52.
Clarke, Michael. 1982. *The Politics of Pop Festivals*. London: Junction Books.
Crossley, Nick. 2015. *Networks of Sound, Style and Subversion: The Punk and Post-Punk Worlds of Manchester, London, Liverpool and Sheffield, 1975–80*. Manchester: Manchester University Press.
Davidson, Peter. 2005. *The Idea of North*. London: Reaktion.
Derrida, Jacques. 1994. *Spectres of Marx: The State of Debt, the Work of Mourning, and the New International*. London: Routledge.
Edensor, Tim. 2005. *Industrial Ruins: Spaces, Aesthetics and Materiality*. Oxford: Berg.
Gunn, Joshua. 1999. 'Gothic Music and the Inevitability of Genre'. *Popular Music and Society* 23/1: 31–50.
Haenfler, Ross. 2010. *Goths, Gamers, and Grrrls: Deviance and Youth Subcultures*. New York: Oxford University Press.
Haslam, Dave. 2015. *Life After Dark: A History of British Nightclubs and Music Venues*. London: Simon and Schuster.
Hegarty, Paul. 2007. *Noise/Music: A History*. London: Continuum.
Hewison, Robert. 1986. *Too Much: Art and Society in the Sixties 1960–75*. London: Methuen.
Laing, Dave. 1985. *One Chord Wonders: Power and Meaning in Punk Rock*. Milton Keynes: Open University Press.
Lilleker, Martin. 2005. *Beats Working for a Living*. Sheffield: Juma.
Mallinder, Stephen. 2007. 'Sheffield is Not Sexy'. *Nebula* 4/3: 292–321.
McKay, George. 2000. *Glastonbury: A Very English Fair*. London: Victor Gollancz.
—2015. *The Pop Festival: History, Music, Media, Culture*. New York: Bloomsbury Academic.
Miles, Barry. 2010. *London Calling*. London: Atlantic Books.
Moran, Joe. 2009. *On Roads: A Hidden History*. London: Profile Books.
O'Brien, Lucy. 2012. 'Can I Have a Taste of Your Ice Cream'. *Punk & Post-Punk* 1/1: 27–40.
Polhemus, Ted. 1994. *Streetstyle*. New York: Thames and Hudson.
Relph, Edward. 1976. *Place and Placelessness*. London: Pion.
Reynolds, Dee. 1995. *Symbolist Aesthetics and Early Abstract Art: Sites of Imaginary Space*. Cambridge: Cambridge University Press.
Reynolds, Simon. 2006. *Rip it Up and Start Again: Post-Punk 1978–84*. London: Faber and Faber.
Russell, David. 2004. *Looking North: Northern England and the National Imagination*. Manchester: Manchester University Press.
Sandvoss, Cornel. 2005. *Fans: The Mirror of Consumption*. Cambridge: Polity Press.
Schivelbusch, Wolfgang. 1986. *The Railway Journey: The Industrialization of Time and Space in the 19th Century*. Leamington Spa: Berg.
Shaw, Katy. 2011. *David Peace: Texts and Contexts*. Eastbourne: Sussex Academic Press.

Shields, Rob. 1991. *Places on the Margin: Alternative Geographies of Modernity*. London: Routledge.
Sounes, Howard. 2006. *Seventies: The Sights, Sounds and Ideas of a Brilliant Decade*. London: Simon and Schuster.
Taylor, Ian, Karen Evans and Penny Fraser. 1996. *A Tale of Two Cities: Global Change, Local Feeling and Everyday Life in the North of England. A Study in Manchester and Sheffield*. London: Routledge.
Tjora, Aksel. 2016. 'The Social Rhythm of the Rock Music Festival'. *Popular Music* 35/1: 64–83.
Wicke, Peter. 1990. *Rock Music: Culture, Aesthetics and Sociology*. Cambridge: Cambridge University Press.

# 7 Scrap Value: Sleaford Mods, *Invisible Britain* and the Edge of the North

Brian Baker

In this chapter I will consider the music of the Sleaford Mods, a punk/hip-hop band whose most recent album, *English Tapas* (Rough Trade, 2017), continues their dramatization and interrogation of contemporary life in England. I will use the work of Imogen Tyler and her text *Revolting Subjects* (2013) to conceptualize working-class subjectivity and language as it is presented in their songs. The language of abjection, of revulsion and loathing, is crucial to the discursive patterning of their songs across their five albums released so far. Singer Jason Williamson's language is full of obscenity, recurrently focused on piss and shit and bodies, on anger and abuse, on aggression and violence and fear. I will pay close attention to these lyrics as well as situating the music, and the film *Invisible Britain* (2015) in which they appear, in terms of a cultural politics of marginalization and invisibility, which both the music and the film challenge.

## With a Z

In his review of the 2014 Sleaford Mods album *Divide and Exit*, the late Mark Fisher, writing in the magazine *The Wire*, begins by asserting the particular East Midlands quality of Williamson's voice, one shared by Fisher himself:

> Lacking any urban glamour, lilting lyricism or rustic romanticism, the East Midlands accent is one of the most unloved in England. It is heard so rarely in popular media that it isn't recognised enough even to be disdained. I must confess that I have a dog in this fight. I grew up in the East Midlands, and when I left university, I was described by a sympathetic lecturer as having a 'speech and accent problem'. The accent 'problem' gradually disappeared, as I learned to suppress the lazy Leicestershire consonants and articulate my

speech in something closer to so-called received pronunciation—an 'achievement' loaded with ambivalence and shame ... Sleaford Mods' Jason Williamson makes no such accommodation to metropolitan manners, and he's disgusted at those who speak in fake accents, whether they're imitating someone from Shoreditch or '*Lou Reed, GG Allin...*' (Fisher 2015).

There is a clear politics of subjectivity at work here (and of masculinity, to which I will return later in the article), and even though Williamson self-identifies not as working class but as lower-middle class in an interview published in *The Quietus*: 'And you know, if you really want to talk about it, I've probably been lower middle class since I was about 15 anyway, so fuck it...' (Parkes 2015), the assumption of a specifically located voice (in terms of class and geographic markers) takes on a particular rhetorical and political dimension.

Sleaford is a town in Lincolnshire, between the east coast of England and the city of Nottingham. The Lincolnshire area in which it is located returned one of the strongest 'Leave' votes in the 2016 British referendum on whether to leave or remain in the European Union. An economically deprived area, far from the metropolis and even from the culture of major cities (the nearest being Leicester, Nottingham or, up the coast, Hull), Boston in Lincolnshire and its surrounding areas have moved towards the anti-immigration rhetoric of the 'Eurosceptic' British political Right through economic isolation and neglect, and the presence of immigrant workers (often employed for exploitative wages and treated in dehumanizing fashion by gang-bosses). In a January 2015 report in *The Independent* newspaper, Boston was cited as the 'worst-integrated' town in Britain, 'home to a higher proportion of eastern European immigrants than anywhere else in England and Wales: 10.6 per cent of the town's population of 65,000 comes from one of the "new" EU countries such as Poland, Lithuania, Latvia or Romania' (Gallagher 2016). The combination of economic deprivation, and the social and community hollowing-out caused by neoliberal/austerity economics, white working-class resentment (and in some cases racism), and a sense of distance from the metropolitan centre and thereby power and influence, conjoins in a powerful and disruptive upwelling of alienation and disenfranchisement. Sleaford's (and Boston's) proximity to the coast and to the fens of Lincolnshire and Norfolk, to tourist-oriented images of rural England, provide no kind of cultural or economic salve to the conditions of late-capitalist life.

The opening shots of the film *Invisible Britain* (directed by Nathan Hannawin and Paul Sng) counterpose this visual and cultural fabric. The film begins with the English countryside, lush green under blue sunny skies; a montage of a medieval market town follows, with narrow streets thronged

**Figure 1:** *Invisible Britain* (Nathan Hannawin and Paul Sng, 2016)

by happy shoppers and visitors, intercut with the Union flag. There is here what Raphael Samuel diagnosed as '[a]n age which has made a fetish of the cottage garden and the village green, and which has promoted the Cotswolds as England's imaginary heart' (Samuel 1998: 161), a landscape symbolizing the South of England. There is then a fade to black, and a different sequence of shots: run-down housing estates; young people walking past an 'invisible' homeless sleeper; the decaying fabric of post-industrial cities in the North, crowds taking to the streets in protest. A highly polemical male voice-over asserts: '2015, Britain—a country on the verge of a nervous breakdown'. Filmed during and after the 2015 general election (but before the 2016 Brexit vote) *Invisible Britain* presents itself as a record of the Sleafords and Bostons of Britain rather than tourist-brochure promotions of heritage England. Although publicity material for the film suggested an inheritance of the filmmaker Patrick Keiller (director of the essay-films *London* (1994), *Robinson in Space* (1997) and *Robinson in Ruins* (2010)), the relation between voice-over and image is much less oblique in *Invisible Britain* than it is in Keiller's work. It is, in essence, a tour film, with footage of live performances filmed at a range of venues across Britain, intercut with interviews with fans and gig-goers, but also to-camera pieces by socially-active people in Colchester and Barnsley and other smaller towns that used to form the circuit for bands in the late 1970s and early 1980s. Williamson suggests that the Sleaford Mods tour was intended to take in 'places The Jam used to play'. I will return to the influence of Paul Weller's post-punk/Mod band in the next section, but it is useful here to note the model articulated between band and audience suggested by emulating Weller. The Jam were determined to downplay the trappings of rock 'stardom' and allow as much access to the band as possible, allowing fans into soundchecks and playing early enough so that fans could use public transport to get home. They were also a band with a particularly masculine following, left-leaning and socially conscious but whose sensibility can be revealed in the decision to leave 'English Rose', a gentle acoustic love song on 1978's *All Mod Cons*, off the track listing on the album cover entirely. The Jam's sound, with Bruce Foxton's bass increasingly high in the mix, and Rick Buckler's drums extremely powerful and loud, also has a strong influence upon that of the Sleaford Mods. In the footage from the film, the proximity of Williamson as stage performer to the crowd, and his interactions with them, visually indicate a strategy of proximity: 'stripping all that big band bollocks back', as the film alliteratively pronounces. What we are presented with is not stardom, but Williamson and Andrew Fearn as representatives of the audience themselves: 'they speak for the working man', says one fan.

Although the band's name refers to a small Lincolnshire town, Sleaford Mods are most associated with the city of Nottingham. Their single from 2014, also on the *Divide and Exit* album, 'Tied Up in Nottz' is, in some ways, a template for the developing Sleaford Mods sound. The video for the single begins before the music, with a shot of the city, then a low-level hand-held camera filming Williamson in a shop, which then cuts to Williamson and Fearn waiting at a bus-stop, listening to a tinny drum-beat on a mobile phone. As the video cuts to a shot filmed from the top deck of the bus, the drum pattern begins in rigid 4/4 time, and then the bassline kicks in, a simple two-note riff with a third note completing the phrase at the end of four bars. Fearn (vaping nicotine and texting) and Williamson sit at the back of the bus, 'performing' to camera in a parody of a 'live' video, but there is little sense of lip-syncing, let alone the appearance that this is in any sense 'live'. The lyrics are confrontational from the start: 'The smell of piss is so strong it smells like decent bacon / Kevin's getting footloose on the overspill / Under the piss station / Two pints, Destroyer, on the cobbled floors / No amount of whatever is going to chirp the chip up / 'The Final Countdown' by fucking Journey / I woke up with shit in my sock outside the Polish off-licence' ('Tied Up in Nottz', 2014).[1] In the video, the bus winds a way through the suburban streets of Nottingham, and the last minute of the film is performed with the bus parked at the end of the line, next to a playing field.

---

1. All song lyrics by Jason Williamson, reproduced with the permission of Wipe Out Music Ltd.

**Figure 2:** The edge of the city in 'Tied Up in Nottz'

The video enacts alienation and displacement: it begins in the city centre, and ends somewhere else, nowhere, an unnamed place at the end of the line. In miniature, the video presents the Sleaford Mods project: to articulate the experience of the edge of the city, a city that is itself provincial and far from the metropolis. That we can see concrete, railings and a playing field outside of the bus window indicates that we have entered what Paul Farley and Michael Symmons Roberts called the 'edgelands', the unknown and unrecognized and unvalued spaces of contemporary Britain: car parks, scrub, broken-down industrial estates, concrete and broken brick and grass. These 'undeveloped' terrains at the margins of urban or suburban conurbations signify the economic marginality of the 'edgeland'. This is pointed out by Farley and Symmons Roberts from the very first chapter, 'Cars'. While 'cars are a defining characteristic of the edgelands', in part because you need to be auto-mobile to arrive there, this geographical zone is 'also a graveyard for cars ... [M]aybe we see our own demise foreshadowed in theirs, our own future, cannibalised for parts, broken open, cast aside' (Farley and Symmons Roberts 2013: 11). These scrap yards, like post-industrial edgelands awaiting 'regeneration', have become part of the symbolic economy of the North, how it is produced in the imaginary of popular culture: a place of waste, the end of a working economy, a landscape of ruins and emptiness. I will return to the scrap yard later in this chapter, but here I would like to suggest that the music of the Sleaford Mods, and the *Invisible Britain* film, articulate a plurality of edgelands, edges that multiply and proliferate, creating ever more distance between the contemporary subject of capitalism and the receding centres of power. Williamson speaks *from* and *of* the edges—social, cultural, economic—but the practice of the band, in terms of how they make and release their records, how and where they tour, is in a continuum with a punk ethos of DIY, of operating outside of mainstream distribution channels (and production channels: *Invisible Britain* was crowdfunded).

If Williamson's accent locates the Sleaford Mods in a particular East Midlands context, this is not only distinct from the metropole but also from other cities of the North in which post-punk bands and movements have taken particular shape: from the Crucial Three (Julian Cope, Ian McCulloch and Pete Wylie) and Zoo Records to the Cream superclub in Liverpool; electronic music from Sheffield, from the Human League and Heaven 17 to Cabaret Voltaire to Pulp; gothic rock (The Cult, The Mission) in Leeds; and of course Factory Records, The Haçienda, Joy Division and New Order, The Fall and the Happy Mondays from Salford and Manchester. Although one can discuss the Sleaford Mods in terms of punk and post-punk, musically they take their bearings from outside the cultural centres of the North. Where the aforementioned groups were located in specific urban and working-class cultures, and whose identities are part constructed through their difference and independence from and antipathy to the metropolis, the Sleaford Mods have no such alternative centre in which to locate themselves. If the North of England is subject to a visual and socio-economic rhetoric which places it at the margins or edges of life in late-capitalist England, then the Sleaford Mods are from the margins of the margins, the edge of the North.

What I will go on to describe, using the work of Imogen Tyler, as the relation of the Sleaford Mods' music to social abjection, can be traced in specific discourses that concern the imagination and representation of the North and South of England over the second half of the twentieth century. Raphael Samuel, the British left-wing cultural historian and author of *Theatres of Memory* (1996), which interrogated the intersection of history and popular cultural forms, wrote in *Island Stories: Unravelling Britain* (1998) that in the sub-genre of the 'journey through ruins, the explorations of geographical and social wastelands ... the North of England is apt to fare badly' (Samuel 1998: 160). Although he has Mark Hudson's *Coming Back Brockens* (1994) in his sights rather than the work of Patrick Keiller or Patrick Wright's *A Journey through Ruins* (1991), Samuel is acute in his diagnosis of the rhetoric of exclusion and denigration at work in representations of the North, from postwar town planning to health to what food people eat. He anticipated Tyler's approach when he wrote:

> In the current denigration of the North, whether at the hand of writers or avant-garde photographers, it is difficult not to notice the play of ancient tropes. At the simplest level there is an Arnoldian contempt for the narrowness of provincial life and a corresponding

certainty that the culture of the metropolis—defined, these days, in terms of lifestyle rather than Classical education—is a very emblem of sweetness and light ... In the vilification of 'sink' estates one can sometimes hear echoes of that old Communist Party and Marxist fear of the *lumpenproletariat*—the supposedly animal-like lower depths—while the so-called 'underclass' has remarkable resemblances to those whom Charles Booth, in his multi-volume *London Life and Labour*, labeled as 'vicious'. Under any of these optics, the people become objects of disgust, at best yokels and buffoons, at worst hooligans and wreckers (Samuel 1998: 161).

In the post-'Brexit' vote analysis in 2016, the binary discourses of the 'progressive', pro-EU metropolis against the 'xenophobic' or 'racist' white working-class North again received a full airing, a reading that deeper analysis did not fully bear out. (Middle-class inhabitants of the Cotswolds, England's 'imaginary heart', also voted to leave the EU.) The Britain that the Sleaford Mods and *Invisible Britain* presents, marginalized and voiceless people living precarious lives, is particularly identified with the towns of the North of England rather than its cities—Rotherham and Oldham, for example, rather than Sheffield and Manchester; but as well as having cultural and geographical specificity, their work articulates a *condition of marginality*, the edge of the North, the edge of austerity, the edge of any hope for a better future.

## Mods, Punk and Hip-hop

Why Sleaford *Mods*? In his interview in *The Quietus*, Williamson responds to Taylor Parkes' suggestions about Mod (and in particular the 1979 'Mod Revival'):

> You'd have been a Mod in the early 80s, right?
> 'Yeah, yeah. Thought I was, anyway. Whatever my idea of a Mod was'.
> I don't think very many of us really grasped the concept at that age.
> 'No', scowls Jason, 'and a lot of people never did. It ended up as a kind of consumerist trap, really. Quite patriotic too, quite right-wing. And still is, in a lot of respects' ...
> Once an escape from that kind of doltish Brit parochialism—an assimilation of European and black American influences—Mod soon became a reinforcing loop for hard-knock lads, a peacetime uniform (Parkes 2015).

In *Invisible Britain*, Williamson suggests that he was 'a Jam nut for five years and refused to listen to anything else' as a teenager. I would suggest that, despite the clear hip-hop dynamics in the Sleaford Mods' music, it is The

Jam who retain the strongest influence, and on 2015's *Key Markets*, 'Giddy on the Ciggies' contains the line 'Subway / We're going to take you down to the Subway / At midnight', an unambiguous reference to The Jam's 1978 song 'Down in the Tube Station at Midnight' (from the *All Mod Cons* album Williamson referred to in *The Quietus* interview). The Jam, and Paul Weller himself, were themselves from the suburbs, from Woking in Surrey rather than London (like The Clash or the Sex Pistols). Mod, as a subculture that partook of the city but was notable for its adherents in the inner suburbs of London, articulates a masculine subjectivity that enunciates the tensions of the edge, the relations to the cultural, social and economic centre. Mod was also notably a *working-class* male performance. In 'The Meaning of Mod', from *Resistance through Rituals* (1976), Dick Hebdige makes a tentative connection between the 'Italianate style' of 'working class dandies ... who were dedicated to clothes and lived in London' of the 1950s and the successor youth subculture of the early 1960s, 'Mod' (Hebdige 2006: 71). Hebdige goes on to suggest further elements of the Mod style: 'to consciously invert the values associated with smart dress'; 'a desire to do justice to the mysterious complexity of the metropolis in his personal demeanour'; and a 'unique and subversive attitude towards the commodities he habitually consumed' (Hebdige 2006: 72). Hebdige's understanding of Mod is of a performative obsession with style: 'Mod was pure, unadulterated STYLE, the essence of style', a style constructed through appropriated commodities whose codings were altered through relocation to a different context (Italian motor scooters, Italian suits, even amphetamines) (Hebdige 2006: 76). Hebdige's reading of Mod is as a mode of resistance, a performance of working-class masculinity that stylized and appropriated the work uniform of the suit and turned it into an index of subcultural difference. The later 'Mod Revival', of which Williamson was a part, has a different set of connotations, more aligned with the nostalgia and problematic political connotations Williamson identifies in his interview. The Jam were a key band in the 'Mod Revival', precipitating it and in some senses curating it; but the revival was as much informed by the rise of Two-Tone (the deliberately multi-cultural label which focused on ska music) and the influence of skinhead/suedehead styles as of 1960s Mod. Simon Reynolds, in *Rip It Up and Start Again* (2006), notes that by 'the late sixties mods who hadn't followed the psychedelic path turned into ska-loving skinheads ... the 2-Tone bands and the new mod groups made seven-inch music: brisk and punchy, near mono, and designed for transistor radios' (Reynolds 2006: 288). It is worth noting that one of the reference points made by Sleaford Mods fans in *Invisible Britain* are The Specials, a ska band whose 1980 hit 'Ghost Town' articulated much of the popular anger and resistance to Thatcherism in that year. While Williamson says of The Jam that he 'never saw them as a political band', the same concern with social issues, with the fabric of contemporary Britain, connects all three bands.

In 'Face to Faces' on 2015's *Key Markets*, Williamson sings: 'this daylight robbery is now so fucking hateful it's completely accepted by the vast majority / in chains', and then 'we have lost the sight / and in the loss of sight / we have lost our fucking minds / all right?'. Hebdige, in 'The Meaning of Mod', suggests that '[t]he mod's cry of triumph, quoted above, was for a romantic victory, a victory of the imagination' (2006: 76). Mod is thereby directly invested in *imagination* as a means of resistance to power, even if that imagination is largely at the service of re-presenting the self. This seems to directly echo the lyrical approach used by Weller in The Jam's 1980 album *Sound Affects*. In 'Set the House Ablaze', the rhythm of the verses is martial, the sound of marching feet. Lyrically, it begins with a report that a mutual friend has 'seen you in the uniform' and the leather belt and black boots suggests not the Army, but the police or Nazi stormtroopers. The lyric then explores a theme of self-betrayal, of buckling under power, of becoming an instrument of 'indoctrination'. The final word is 'mechanical', and the construction of the song enforces this through its coiling guitar figure and tight rhythm section. Opposed to power is *vision*. A consistent use is made of metaphors of vision: the uniformed friend is as if 'by someone blinded', and a middle section makes the idea overt. There's no collapse to cynicism. Instead, the lyrical keynote, reflecting Percy Bysshe Shelley's call for lions to awaken from slumber and to cast off their chains quoted from *The Mask of Anarchy* on the back cover, is a kind of Romantic revolution, one in which *vision* is crucial.

The Sleaford Mods are Mods, I would suggest, in the sense of a performance of a masculine subjectivity that resists articulations of power and exclusion through enactments of explosive *vision*. That the film is called *Invisible Britain* is therefore in a continuum with the Sleaford Mods' project: to make visible what is invisible, to speak what is unheard. As I will discuss in the conclusion, there is not an unproblematic dynamic at work here with regard to expressions of masculinity, but first I would like to turn to the influence of punk and hip-hop in terms of the Sleaford Mods' musical practice.

In *Invisible Britain*, one of the interviewed fans says that watching the Sleaford Mods live is 'what it must have felt like to watch the Sex Pistols'. For an audience of 30- and 40-something men who, like myself, were too young to participate in punk, the chaotic and formative Sex Pistols gigs of 1977 are now framed by nostalgia for a moment of radical energy that we were born too late to experience. Musically, the Sleaford Mods have little to do with the Sex Pistols besides a driving 4/4 rock beat: there are very few guitars, for instance. Williamson's lyrics do make the odd allusion, as in 'Tweet Tweet Tweet' (issued as a single, then re-recorded for *Divide and Exit* in 2014), where he sneers 'I don't care'; more pointedly, *Invisible Britain*'s first sequence ends with the phrase, in voice-over: 'Ever get the feeling you've been cheated?', which were, of course, the last words spoken by Johnny Rotten as the lead singer of the Sex Pistols, in their final concert at the Winterland Ballroom in San Francisco in January 1978. Johnny Rotten's parting shot, one that deliberately undermined the entirety of the Pistols' career, is re-purposed here as a general marker of cynicism and alienation, for another generation and community who feel that they have 'No Future'. The connection the audience members make to the Pistols is probably not a matter of musical similarity but more to do with the aggression and confrontation of lyrical performance on the part of Williamson and Lydon, the anger at the state of contemporary Britain that the lyrics and performance express.

If the Pistols' streamlined and powerful rock and roll is very different to the musical fabric of the Sleaford Mods, there are other punk and post-punk precursors in which to situate their work. Salford's The Fall have often been mentioned, again mainly because of the singer and lyricist Mark E. Smith, whose surreal and acerbic stories of the North are presumed to have influenced Williamson's lyrical approach. As a duo, however, who rely on a laptop to create and perform their beats, whose stage performance feature no live instrumentation, and whose drum and bass guitar work are clearly *sequenced* rather than *played* in the majority of their songs, the Sleaford Mods are much more like electronic duos that combine a charismatic singer with a 'backroom' colleague who creates the beats but is much less present in interviews or media, from Sparks to the Pet Shop Boys. (It is noteworthy in this context that Taylor Parkes' interview with the band in *The Quietus* only features Williamson.) Perhaps the most interesting comparison, however, is to the electro-punk duo Suicide, whose rudimentary electronic beats and confrontational performances, particularly by singer Alan Vega, epitomized a punk sensibility that refused the gestures of rock and roll authenticity offered by the Pistols or The Clash. In working without guitars, but only a cheap rhythm box and keyboards and a bank of effects pedals, Suicide's live performances were 'as infamous as they were infrequent', according to Simon Reynolds, who suggests that '[y]ou could see Suicide's confrontational shows and physical altercations with the audience … as performance art' in which 'ideas from minimalism, auto-destructive art, living theatre and Pop Art clashed' (Reynolds 2006: 54). The most 'infamous' of these shows, '23 minutes over Brussels', was recorded while Suicide were supporting Elvis Costello and the Attractions, and in which a confrontation between singer and audience ends in a near-riot. Williamson's relationship to his audience, as *Invisible Britain* attests, is far less confrontational, even though it seems to call up the energies of punk; dialogue between Williamson and the crowd could be described as 'banter', a circulation of (very homosocial) verbal and physical gestures which are inclusive rather than aggressive. Where punk's shows directly manifested the aggression and violence that they saw directed at themselves and other marginalized groups in society, the Sleaford Mods shows instead attempt to form a communal bond against what is perceived to be outside the boundaries of the gig, the economic and social system which enforces privation and misery. The chant of 'Sleaford Mods, Sleaford Mods' that begins 2015's *Key Markets* (followed by the song 'Live Tonight'), one that is rhythmically based on the Mod chant 'We Are The Mods', is then a kind of tribal or communal sense of belonging: *us* versus *them*.

In *England's Dreaming* (1991/2005), Jon Savage describes punk in precisely these terms:

> Punk was an international outsider aesthetic: dark, tribal, alienated, full of black humour. It spread from the US through the UK and France and through Europe, Japan and Australia in the years following 1975. For anyone in the UK who at that point felt cast out because of class, sexuality, gender, or even choice, who felt useless, unworthy, ashamed, the Sex Pistols were an attraction/repulsion machine of, as Paul Morley notes, 'infernal' power that offered the chance of action, even surrender—to something larger than you— and thus possible transcendence. In becoming a nightmare, you could find your dreams (Savage 2005: xiv).

Note the echo of the language of dreams and vision, the Romantic inheritance of Mod, that we saw above in relation to The Jam's *Sound Affects*. To think of the Sleaford Mods as a 'punk band' is correct in some senses, because their music and lyrics enunciate precisely, in a twenty-first-century context, what Savage proposes about punk in the quotation above. On their 2015 tour to promote *Key Markets*, I attended the opening gig at the Manchester Ritz (a much larger venue than the ones they play in *Invisible Britain*); supporting them was Steve Ignorant, once lead singer and founder member of Crass. This is an interesting conjunction, because Crass, 'a band/label based in a communal farmhouse [in Essex], [were a key part of] the anarcho-punk movement [which] was more ideological and idealistic, spewing out vinyl tracts denouncing the unholy trinity of state/church/military, while extolling pacifism and self-rule' (Reynolds 2006: 424). Crass were crucial in organizing the means or production and distribution of their music outside of the mainstream, the system controlled by the 'major' record labels. Their centrality to the 'DIY' ethos mapped out on the sleeves of punk singles by the Desperate Bicycles or Scritti Politti—information about how to press up your own vinyl single and how much it cost— places Sleaford Mods in a cultural and economic circuit deliberately counter to the mainstream: their early work was self-released, and their recent albums have been made available through the small Harbinger Sound label. (A single released in the autumn of 2016, 'TCR', and the 2017 album *English Tapas* were on the classic 'independent' label Rough Trade.) In a sense, this is a different form of punk's insistence on 'authenticity': Williamson and Fearn are just two 'ordinary blokes' who seized the opportunity to do it themselves, and thereby offer both a different vision of contemporary Britain and a socio-economic model of how activism can work. *Invisible Britain*'s purpose is, implicitly, to connect the Sleaford Mods project with social and cultural activists working to improve the lives of those who live in the 'invisible' towns, from community coffee-shops and performance spaces in Hartlepool to branches of the Unite union in Barnsley. To connect one with the other is to short-circuit ideas of 'stardom' or the 'big band bollocks' derided in the film itself. It is also to insist that we can, like them, 'do it ourselves'.

The final musical connection is to hip-hop, and Williamson's 'spoken' word delivery and the breakbeat dynamics of some of the Sleaford Mods' songs certainly place their work as a particularly British, punk-inflected variant of hip-hop. In *Invisible Britain* Williamson mentions the influence of the Beastie Boys and Public Enemy, though the very locatedness of his voice and Fearn's beats, which rarely use funk rhythms (and tend to use drum programming rather than samples), tend to separate the sound and dynamic of the Sleaford Mod songs from American hip-hop in particular. In fact, there is not a very strong inflection of black music on the Sleaford Mods' music in general, much unlike hip-hop; and in performance, also much unlike standard hip-hop strategies, Williamson is very self-contained during the songs, with no call-and-response or embedded audience participation. What Fearn takes from hip-hop is sparseness of instrumentation, with drum and bass guitar dominating, and occasional leitmotifs introduced via synthesizer programming. What the spare musical fabric allows, of course, is for Williamson's performances to take centre stage, even though missed cues and errors are often incorporated into the tracks themselves, another of the ways in which the sheen of professionalism, 'big band bollocks', is undermined. As we shall see in the following section, one of the tracks that begins with a fluffed take is 'Liveable Shit' from *Divide and Exit*.

## Liveable Shit

'Liveable Shit' begins with a circular drum pattern dominated by a ticking hi-hat and synthesized crash alternating with a natural snare on the second and fourth beats. A bass guitar figure, played high in its range, make a busier and less spacious sound-stage than is often the case. Williamson then begins:

'So I go in this morning and I walk, oh duh, shit, boom-boom, keep it going...'. The vocal flub, the incapacity to do the job, plays humorously against the subject matter. The first 'verse' (there is no verse/chorus structure here, just the repeating drum and bass guitar line) then begins properly:

> So I got in this morning and I went to the loo / He walked out the cubical, and it fucking stunk. / Every morning I get in and it's / The same time / same trap / same stink / and it glides through the air / and by the time it's hit yer / it's been pacified by 10 yards of fresh air ('Liveable Shit', *Divide and Exit*, 2014).

The refrain, in which Williamson doubles his own voice with a backing track, runs 'Liveable Shit / you put up with it'. This scatological vignette repeats a crucial motif in Williamson's lyrics: smells, stink, shit, piss. In one sense, this is part of the materiality of Williamson's word-pictures of contemporary Britain, an attempt to render it in as direct and visceral a way as possible. If you remember, 'Tied Up in Nottz' begins 'The smell of piss is so strong / it smells like decent bacon', and later in that song the lyric runs, 'release the stench of shit grub like a giant toilet cracking'. In lyrics such as these, life *is shit* and is *filled with shit*, literally. However, there is a politics to Williamson's insistence on the smells and sights of piss and shit. In 'Urine Mate', the first track on 2013's *Austerity Dogs*, a scenario which plays out at the local betting shop begins: 'I seen Roxy Rob putting his bin out at nine o'clock this morning / And all the people from Mapperley Park point and laugh / cause he's pissed and he stinks of urine / Urine, mate / Welcome to the club'; the idea that the alcoholic man is pointed at and made the butt of jokes is crucial, as David Bell points out in his review of the album for *The Quietus*: 'tabloid hate figures (the poor, immigrants, Roma, single mums, etc) aren't simply "abject" but are produced as such: forced to live in squalor and then, as that squalor takes effect, demonised by the press and bourgeois small-mindedness/self-interest' (Bell 2013). Bell also invokes Tyler's investigation of 'social abjection' in contemporary Britain, *Revolting Subjects* (2013), which I will examine here in more detail to frame Williamson's presentation of the poor and the marginalized.

Tyler draws upon the work of Julia Kristeva, most notably in *Powers of Horror* (1982), to theorize the production of socially marginalized and excluded subjects through what is called 'social abjection'. Tyler writes:

> Julia Kristeva's (1982) seminal psychoanalytic account of abjection has had a considerable influence in arts and humanities disciplines for over two decades. However, there has been no sustained account of objection as a lived social process, and abjection has received little sustained academic attention within the social sciences ... *Revolting*

> *Subjects* argues for a more thoroughly social and political account of objection through a consideration of the consequences of being our project within specific social and political locales (Tyler 2013: 4).

While critical of Kristeva's national and (French) Republican imperatives in her conception of abjection, Tyler fruitfully opens up both an approach to the everyday lives of the marginalized and disproved in contemporary Britain, but also their representations in the media. 'The poor are those whose autonomous modes of speech and cultural production are devalued, marginalised and/or silenced', Tyler writes (2013: 173), implicating social marginality with the assumption or denial of the potential to speak or be seen, the very kind of cultural production that the Sleaford Mods enunciate in their work (as discussed in the last section). By *speaking shit*, Williamson presents the marginalized (the poor, the asylum seeker, the workless, the traveller) in terms that reveal the abjection of their everyday lives but also the processes that do the work of abjection: most notably, reactions of disgust. In 'McFlurry', also from *Austerity Dogs*, Williamson reveals a Britain 'where the cuts make people stink / You smell'. In performance, this has become '*we smell*' or '*we all fucking smell*' to avoid the impression that Williamson himself is disgusted by others, but that his initial lyric is a kind of ventriloquism of those who would 'point and laugh'. As Tyler suggests, 'Disgust is political'. 'Through the act of being disgusted', she suggests, 'the subject constitutes the disgusting object' (Tyler 2013: 24). In the references to smell, stink, toilets, piss and shit Williamson exposes the mechanisms of abjection and disgust, mechanisms that have a political purpose. As Tyler notes, 'The poor are the abject, those were both excluded from intelligible categories of being but included through their exclusion, securing, constituting and legitimising the hegemonic politics of the state' (Tyler 2013: 174).

To return to 'Liveable Shit', the stoicism or fatalism of the speaking subject is revealed in the final section, in which Williamson states 'So now I don't dream of anything / I just wait for it to turn up'. Life becomes a matter of endurance, of seeing it through, rather than enjoyment or even of anger, still less of hope for change. In a sense, however, it is the very act of Williamson's *storytelling* that provides the means for resistance to the ideological mechanisms that he reveals. As Tyler suggests:

> It is the vitalization and proliferation of political protests and acts of resistance within their many documentary afterlives that allows for the weaving of alternate political imaginaries with which to perceive differently the state we are in ... using the *mediation* of resistance, the reframing of events and the capacity of the aesthetic practices of counter mediation to fracture the neoliberal consensus (2013: 13; original emphasis).

Tyler's insistence on the possibility of the *cultural work* that can be done by music or art or poetry or other kinds of artistic practice, to *remediate* and re-present resistant or marginalized lives and experiences, is clearly central to the Sleaford Mods and their politics. It is this, then, that provides some light of hope among the abjection.

**Conclusion: Scrap Value**

Two or three years ago, driving home on the M6, my old car started to attract attention from other drivers. I saw a couple of flashes in my rear-view mirror, and then a car drew alongside and the passenger pointed to the back of the car, mouthing the word 'exhaust'. I pulled on to the hard shoulder, got out carefully, and had a look. The exhaust pipe was dragging along the floor.

In truth, I'd known the exhaust was blown from the start of my journey back from work, but I'd thought, I'd hoped, that I'd be able to nurse it home. I hadn't realized the whole system was about to drag sparks down the motorway. So that was it. It was knackered. I took it to the scrap yard. This is something with which my Dad would have been perfectly at home. He (like his father before him) had spent much of his working life as a van and lorry driver, and did so in a time when you could get the bonnet of a car or van up and tinker with it mechanically yourself, rather than having to plug in a computer to run diagnostics on the engine management system. Overalls, oily hands, road dirt and soot from the exhaust were part of that time and world, part of my Dad's masculinity as I was growing up. I was never that interested in tinkering with machines, and didn't learn to drive until my late thirties. I came to adult masculinity outside of that world, outside of those codes. Going to the breaker's yard was to enter a world-outside-the-world, a world with which I was deeply unfamiliar and uncomfortable.

Scrap is of course the re-working of unwanted, no longer utile material into something of monetary value. A few years ago, if you wanted to scrap a car, you'd have to pay to do so; now, with the prices for materials rising (along with the market for second-hand parts for older cars), the scrap merchant would pay you for the vehicle. But I had no idea how much my old car was 'worth'.

The boss, unmistakably the fief of this zone of half-stripped automobiles, came striding along in a few minutes. Yes, he said, they'd take it. How much was I looking for? I named a pretty low figure. He hesitated for a moment, then nodded, and stuck out his hand. After shaking on the deal, he pulled out a roll of ten-pound notes and counted off the amount. Cheers. This world-behind-the-world was also half-in, half-out of the economic world I knew: it interfaced with it to process the documentation to scrap a car, but the financial transaction was done with a roll of tenners, no receipt, nothing. Clearly this was the semi-official edge of the black economy, a circulation that avoided the eye of the Exchequer and in which money travelled from hand to hand, pocket to pocket, without the government taking a tithe.

I walked out of the yard back to the main road, where my wife and daughter would pick me up. I stood there in a great wash of relief. I'd done it, got away with it. He hadn't laughed at the amount I suggested, hadn't sneered at my obvious and entire lack of knowledge about the process. Perhaps I'd got a fair price, perhaps he'd done me up like a kipper. But I didn't care. The interview was finished, the transaction complete. I'd escaped from a space in which the codes of masculinity were entirely separate from the ones I had learned, in school and work; the codes of masculine behaviour, physical bearing and speech that I had internalized to be able to operate successfully in the university system were alien to the scrap yard. In being the first of my family to go to university, I'd translated myself out of one kind of subjectivity and into another, and here was the physical embodiment of the working-class masculinity that my Dad and Grandfather would have recognized and been comfortable with, but which I now found deeply discomfiting. For me, the scrap yard was about recognition, of the bits of the performance of masculinity—to do with class, in particular— that I consciously left behind, to fit in to societal and institutional expectations. It's not a metaphor for me 'scrapping' bits of myself or the traditional working-class masculinity of London and Essex that I'm no longer part of. It's not even that one man's trash is another man's treasure. Rather, it's a moment that stays with me because I was not at home, I was not comfortable there. Perhaps more importantly, I was not comfortable with *myself*. In that estranging moment, I could recognize the dislocations of very different 'man's worlds'.

As you might have noted, in this final section I have carefully re-modulated my own discourses, my own language, just as Mark Fisher confessed to at the beginning of this chapter. The colloquialisms, the local markers of language ('knackered', 'tenners', 'done me up like a kipper') that are excluded from academic discourse have been deliberately re-inserted into my sentences. My own negotiations with codes of masculinity, with class, and with language, frame my own responses to the music and lyrics of the Sleaford Mods. The aggression of Williamson's delivery, the very masculine homosocial community of reception for their music (the gig I saw was full of 30- and 40-something white men), the insistence on obscenity (not only piss and shit, but 'fuck' and 'cunt') makes me uncomfortable; not nearly as uncomfortable as I was in the breaker's yard, but a version of it. In their work I can understand my own negotiations with and fear of abjection, of being exposed within the academic environment as not belonging, an imposter, a fraud. While I feel all of those things, Williamson's performance disrupts as well as inhabits the kinds of marginalized, excluded working-class masculinities that discomfited me so much. The final song the Sleaford Mods played in the Manchester Ritz gig I attended in 2015 was 'Jobseeker', one of their earliest but best-known songs. In it, Williamson takes on the persona of 'Mr Williamson', a 'jobseeker' coming to an interview at the Department of Work and Pensions and playing his own unemployability: 'Can of Strongbow. I'm a mess / Desperately clutching on to a leaflet on depression / Supplied to me by the NHS / It's anyone's guess how I got here / It's anyone's guess how I'll go / I suck on a roll-up / 'Pull Your Jeans Up' / Fuck off – I'm going home'; but then he switches persona to become the interviewer: 'Mr Williamson! / Your employment history looks quite impressive / I'm looking at three managerial positions you've previously held with quite reputable companies / Isn't this something you'd like to go back to?' 'Nah!'. The switching between subject-positions and speakers, the doubling of jobseeker and advisor (who soon could become a jobseeker himself), the elements of performance and exaggeration, the humour of the lyrics, leaven the bleak picture that both the Sleaford Mods albums and the film *Invisible Britain* paint of the contemporary United Kingdom, and in particular its forgotten, disenfranchised and post-industrial towns of the North of England.

In the middle section of 'Liveable Shit', Williamson notices those whose voices no longer bear the traces of 'localism': 'Just fake accents nicked from someone posh they might have met in Shoreditch / A vegetarian vet / Lou fucking Reed / whoever'. From the East Midlands, a 'nowhere' at the edge of the North, peripheral to metropolitan cultures and power as well as the social and cultural communities of the major cities of the North of England, Sleaford Mods articulate in their music and Williamson's particular voice a *condition* of marginality, the position of the 'national abject'. This placelessness is itself a consequence of the deterritorializing forces of neoliberalism, the dislocations and alienations that form the place from which the Sleaford Mods speak. It is in the act of speaking, doing it yourself, that they offer the potential for something else.

## About the Author

Brian Baker is a Senior Lecturer in English and Creative Writing at Lancaster University, UK. He has published, among other books, *Masculinities in Fiction and Film* (Continuum, 2006), *Contemporary Masculinities in Fiction, Film and Television* (Bloomsbury Academic, 2015) and *The Reader's Guide to Essential Criticism: Science Fiction* (Palgrave Macmillan, 2014). He is currently making films, writing on 1960s science fiction, and developing a collaborative project on sound, music and literature.

## References

Bell, David. 2013. 'Sleaford Mods, *Austerity Dogs*'. *The Quietus* 26 (November). http://thequietus.com/articles/13987-sleaford-mods-austerity-dogs-review (accessed 21 June 2016).

Farley, Paul, and Michael Symmons Roberts. 2013. *Edgelands: Journeys into England's True Wilderness*. London: Vintage.

Fisher, Mark. 2015. 'Review of *Divide and Exit*'. *The Wire* 362 (April). https://reader.exact-editions.com/issues/38497/page/58 (accessed 3 July 2017).

Gallagher, Paul. 2016. 'Boston: How a Lincolnshire Town became "the Most Divided Place in Britain"'. *The Independent*, 28 January. https://tinyurl.com/a6838041 (accessed 20 July 2016).

Hebdige, Dick. 2006. 'The Meaning of Mod'. In *Resistance through Rituals: Youth Subcultures in Post-war Britain*, 2nd edn, ed. Stuart Hall and Tony Jefferson, 71–79. London: Routledge.

Hudson, Mark. 1994. *Coming Back Brockens: A Year in a Mining Village*. London: Cape.

Keiller, Patrick. 1991. *A Journey through Ruins*. London: Radius.

Parkes, Taylor. 2015. 'Life in Hell: Sleaford Mods Interviewed'. *The Quietus*, 15 July 2015. http://thequietus.com/articles/18327-sleaford-mods-interview-2 (accessed 10 February 2016).

Reynolds, Simon. 2006. *Rip It Up and Start Again: Postpunk 1978–1984*. London: Faber.

Samuel, Raphael. 1996. *Theatres of Memory: Past and Present in Contemporary Culture*. London: Verso.

—1998. *Island Stories: Unravelling Britain, Theatres of Memory Volume II*. London: Verso.

Savage, John. 2005. *England's Dreaming: The Sex Pistols and Punk Rock*. London: Faber [1991].

Tyler, Imogen. 2013. *Revolting Subjects: Social Abjection and Resistance in Neoliberal Britain*. London: Zed Books.

*Discography*

The Jam. 1978. *All Mod Cons*. Polydor.
—1980. *Sound Affects*. Polydor.
Sleaford Mods. 2013. *Austerity Dogs*. Harbinger Sound.
—2014. *Chubbed Up*. Ipecac.
—2014. *Divide and Exit*. Harbinger Sound.
—2015. *Key Markets*. Harbinger Sound.
—2017. *English Tapas*. Rough Trade.
Suicide. 1977. *Suicide*. Red Star.

*Filmography*

Hannawin, Nathan, and Paul Sng (dirs.). 2015. *Invisible Britain*. Velvet Joy Productions.

# Part 3
Hip Hop and Grime

# 8 From Broken Glass to Ruf Diamonds: Manchester Hip Hop

## Adam de Paor-Evans

When one considers music culture in Manchester during the 1980s and 1990s, hip hop is not an obvious cultural arena for discussion. However, amidst the spectacle of The Haçienda, the pop boom of Factory Records and the evolution of rave subculture and form of dance music which produced the pop cultural phenomenon of Madchester, and in the space of music between The Fall and The Charlatans where brief stardom was found by Inspiral Carpets, Northside and Candy Flip, Mancunian hip hop was evolving a cultural position of its own. During the decade between 1984 and 1994, the year the Stone Roses formed and the year *Definitely Maybe* by Oasis was released, hip hop in Manchester established itself as an organic and flexible counter-narrative to two cultural positions—firstly the very local yet nationally explosive position of The Haçienda and the Madchester spectacle, and secondly the position of hip hop in London which was growing an international presence with seriousness, professionalism and rigour. To the rest of the UK, the Manchester indie scene and the London hip hop scene overshadowed Mancunian hip hop largely via the contemporary national music press and media coverage of the time. There were music press articles about Manchester hip hop artists such as Broken Glass, MC Buzz B, Krispy 3 and Ruthless Rap Assassins; however, despite MC Buzz B and Ruthless Rap Assassins being signed to major labels after their initial independent releases (Polydor and EMI respectively), hip hop groups from London were being represented strongly in the media—for example MC Duke, Derek B and Demon Boyz all featured on the front cover of early issues of *Hip Hop Connection* (HHC).[1]

---

1. *Hip Hop Connection* (HHC) was a monthly publication and considered by the UK hip hop community to be the gospel of British hip hop and the UK's version of *The Source* mag-

Towards the late 1980s London-based artists were also gathering much more momentum as challengers to American hip hop crews, and the buzz surrounding groups such as London Posse and Hijack was reaching a feverous state in the UK and also made a solid impact stateside. As London Posse toured the US in 1986 supporting post-punk band Big Audio Dynamite, Hijack caught the attention of Ice-T who subsequently signed them to Rhyme $yndicate Records in 1989. This signing led to Hijack's seminal debut album *The Horns Of Jericho* being released worldwide on Warner Bros. Records in 1990, regarded by a majority of hip hop fans as one of the strongest albums ever produced by a British crew. To outsiders of both Manchester and London, the perception was that a critical mass was building in London that was not apparent in Manchester. Concurrent to the media representations of London-centric hip hop, a continuing portrayal of Mancunian culture was promoted to the rest of the UK through the spectacle of Tony Wilson's Factory Records and The Haçienda, Madchester and rave subculture which seduced two generations of youth. Interesting, then, that Tony Wilson was a lover and advocate of Mancunian music culture, which he celebrated through his Granada Television shows *So It Goes* (1976–77) and *The Other Side of Midnight* (1989) as well as *Granada Reports*. While these regional programmes explored and presented new music culture from the Manchester area, nationally the spectacle of Madchester and the baggy scene was conveniently appropriated by national music journalism, hence offering a cultural package to its consumers in much the same way as the London hip hop scene was handled.

## Contextual Framing of Mancunian Hip Hop

Understanding the context of both London-centric hip hop culture and Manchester's Factory and Madchester indie scenes is central to the subject of this chapter, which begs the question: what is Mancunian hip hop? What follows is an investigation of the key developments of hip hop culture during a significant decade in Manchester and, starting in 1984 with Broken Glass (formed in the summer of 1983) and concluding with Ruf Beats and the Jeep Beat Collective in 1994, explores the cultural triggers responsible for underground hip hop in the locale and wider territories. Three interrelated sub-questions are framed and examined here: To what extent did the evolution of Mancunian hip hop coexist, complement or oppose the cultural dynamics of The Haçienda, Madchester and rave subculture? What was the relationship between hip hop in Manchester and London in terms of regional, national and international

azine. It ran between 1998 and 2009. ('Hip-hop and It Don't Stop: What Does the Future Hold for Hip-Hop', *The Independent*, 23 October 2011).

cultural representation, identity and value; and finally, are there particular cultural qualities in Mancunian hip hop that differentiate from the gravity of London hip hop and the spectacle of Madchester?

In order to support the interrogation of these questions, this chapter draws on three semi-structured interviews conducted during December 2016 with The Ruf—owner of Ruf Beats record label and front man of Jeep Beat Collective; Lady Tame—Manchester's first female emcee to gain a recording contract; and Jojo Mavrakis—Mancunian, hip hop champion and radio DJ, first engaged in the culture during the formative days of the Broken Glass breakdance crew. Broken Glass are important not only as the pioneers of breakdancing in Manchester but also as the first established Manchester crew who released their only record on Morgan Khan's London-based Streetwave label ('Style of the Street', 1984). Lady Tame and Krispy 3 also had recording deals with well-regarded London independent labels Music of Life (1990) and Kold Sweat (1993–94) respectively, subsequent to their debut records being released on Manchester-based private presses. Finally, The Ruf's later contribution during the early to mid-1990s extends past the sole artist vinyl release, and under the guise of Jeep Beat Collective he released compilation albums, mixtapes, promoted and performed at club nights and mini-festivals as far afield as Germany and also ran a mail order record shop. The material drawn upon from these interviews provides a series of critical moments of lived experiences and cultural contexts through time, as participants involved in hip hop as artists and performers, but first and foremost as lovers of hip hop culture.

These interviews are framed within a theoretical context by means of Pierre Bourdieu's cultural positioning within his seminal text *Distinction* (2010 edition). Bourdieu critiques the notion of value, taste and practice, primarily through the lens of the bourgeoisie, and it is these concepts that ground the exploration of the questions posed here. The investigation into the hypothesis that a Mancunian grassroots and self-critical approach to hip hop provided an original and sustainable underground counter-culture requires careful handling, and care is taken to draw on Bourdieu in a manner relevant to the cultural context of this inquiry. Bourdieu's subject for his ethnographic study, bourgeoisie France during the 1960s and 1970s, of course differs greatly to the conditions of Manchester hip hop culture from 1984–94; however certain strategies of pretension, evaluations of taste, and critique and acquisition of cultural value enable a distinguishing from what is 'other', and in this case the 'other' appears as the mainstream and dominant socio-cultural forces.

In conclusion, this chapter affirms the position that whilst Mancunian hip hop culture did not achieve the reverence of its counter-part in London or the financial success of Madchester, it bred a rich culture of artists, practitioners, producers and consumers that has led to a regional stability and sustainability of hip hop culture, through counter-actions, reframing, and reflexive and reflective evaluation.

**Style of the Street**

During the summer of 1983, one decade after Wigan Casino opened for its first ever northern soul all-nighter and Kool DJ Herc threw the first ever hip hop party in The Bronx;[2] a few months ahead of the UK miner's strike and during the depths of Thatcher's Britain, a breakdance crew were formed in Manchester called Broken Glass. Through busking in Piccadilly Gardens, the group evolved which included Kermit, Benji, Dave the Wave and Swanny among several others.[3] In addition to the well-documented independent scene, Manchester also had a thriving electro-funk scene,[4] and further to their daytime busking practices, Broken Glass triggered the development of b-boying[5] at Greg Wilson's club nights at The Pier in Wigan and at Legend and The Haçienda in Manchester on Friday nights.[6] Already at this point, it begins to become evident that a relationship between hip hop and the alternative scene existed. Greg Wilson also played an hour each Saturday night at The Haçienda where the profile of electro-funk was raised by introducing this sound to the regular crowd.[7] The impact of these club nights on what was to become the Madchester explosion is crucial to understanding the narrative of Manchester hip hop.

Electro-funk is by nature up-tempo, and the up-tempo approach to music is critical here as first and foremost Broken Glass were a breakdance crew, and

2. It is widely acknowledged by the hip hop community that the marker for the birth of hip hop is a party thrown by Kool DJ Herc on 11 August 1973 at 1520 Sedgwick Ave., The Bronx, NYC (KRS ONE 2009).
3. Greg Wilson's detailed description of the early days of Broken Glass and other formative moments in UK hip hop can be found at http://www.electrofunkroots.co.uk.
4. Electro-funk was the formative style of hip hop music championed in the UK at this time which was a natural progression from jazz-funk culture. Although the extended musical heritage rooted in the origins of NYC hip hop that included soul, rock, disco and reggae was also inherent in UK hip hop, the influence of these genres was less evident within pioneering UK hip hop records.
5. B-boying is the adjective to describe the practices of b-boys and b-girls. The 'b' derives from 'break', usually the drum pattern(s) in a piece of music's breakdown where dancers would breakdance. B-boying is recognized as one of the four major practices of hip hop along with graffiti writing, emceeing and DJing.
6. Detailed narratives of Greg Wilson's experiences at Legend can be found at http://blog.gregwilson.co.uk/2011/08/legend-manchesters-other-club.
7. See http://www.electrofunkroots.co.uk/articles/broken_glass.html for detailed accounts.

up-tempo music is most desirable to dance to. The same dynamics of the up-tempo sound of electro-funk is evident a decade prior to the electro-funk era, when the northern soul scene was rife in Lancashire. Both the up-tempo pace of electro-funk and northern soul are paralleled with the physical dynamics of breakdancing and northern soul dancing, with both styles producing comparable dance moves. When the northern scene began to fade, the search for the up-tempo post-northern soul sound led some consumers to jazz-funk, electro-funk and rap music, as Jojo Mavrakis recounts:

> It was all about up-tempo in Manchester and growing up in the north-west, the DJs would always have up-tempo and high energy tunes; it didn't matter where it was from and who did it. Of course our parents were still buying up-tempo tunes from their love of northern soul, so records like 'Rapper's Delight' (1979) and the electro sound was the same thing. Breakdancing isn't that far removed from northern soul dancing and there is a huge connection there (Interview with Jojo Mavrakis, 19 December 2016).

This may be exactly why crews like Broken Glass evolved in the manner in which they did, when the nation had been exposed to hip hop's breakdancing element through television via Jeffrey Daniel's backslide dance move[8] and Malcolm McLaren's 'Buffalo Gals' video in 1982.[9] Manchester youth already had a primary heritage in similar dancing through the lived experience of the northern soul scene, which provided the hip hop generation with a first-hand platform to explore breakdancing. This would explain their fast evolution of skills, which by the end of the same year as McLaren's *Duck Rock* album saw Broken Glass performing choreographed dance moves; these breakdancers already had a perception of similar spatial and rhythmic aesthetics which had been constructed socially and experientially. Subsequently the execution of certain dance moves signalled particular emergent qualities within these formative hip hop practices. Bourdieu discusses 'the aesthetic disposition, understood as the aptitude for perceiving and deciphering specifically stylistic characteristics' (Bourdieu 2010: 43), which when applied to this context shows these dance moves as intentional representations of hip hop, distinguishing actions, execution and taste; informing a regionally pioneering practice.

---

8. 'The backslide' was soon to become known as 'the moonwalk' by the mid-1980s, appropriated by Michael Jackson.
9. The 'Buffalo Gals' video is commonly referenced as the point of arrival for hip hop culture in the UK. See *The World Hip Hop News*, BBC4 (2016). DJ Semtex attests that 'Buffalo Gals' and its associated LP *Duck Rock* brought hip hop to the mainstream. See DJ Semtex (2016).

The buzz surrounding Broken Glass led to them performing at club nights at various locations in the UK and short television magazine programmes, although what certainly anchored them as pioneers of UK hip hop is evidenced by the sole record they released in 1984. 'Style of the Street' was a perfect fusion of electro and rap featuring vocals by Kermit (who later joined Black Grape), remixed by Greg Wilson and released on Morgan Khan's formidable Streetwave label. It featured on the Street Sounds electro edition *UK Electro* (reaching number 60 in the UK album charts),[10] which at the time was the champion compilation series that brought electro and hip hop to the majority of UK youth, and as such positioned Broken Glass as peers of American electro-rap pioneers such as Newcleus and Captain Rock. Morgan Khan's Streetwave/Street Sounds empire was heavily anchored in the London scene and provided the cornerstone of electro-funk and hip hop in the UK. By the time of the release of *UK Electro* in 1984, Street Sounds had released five well-received compilations of American electro and hip hop.[11] However, many consumers of *UK Electro* outside the North-West were unknowledgeable about the engagement of Manchester artists Broken Glass and in particular Greg Wilson, assuming the artists were London based, a forgivable conclusion to reach as the only graphic clue on the sleeve design was a Union Jack which consumed almost the entire front cover.

What was presented through the *Electro* series was both 'systematic product' and generator of a new kind of national yet subcultural habitus (Bourdieu 2010: 168). The *Electro* series represented good taste in the tracks it compiled following a process of classification. As an artist, to become represented on an *Electro* album was to be propelled to immediate reverence, as judged by the lovers and consumers of *Electro*, those that constructed their habitus by incorporating this dimension of lifestyle (Bourdieu 2010: 169).

What is critical here is to substantiate two versions of habitus operating concurrently: the tasteful product as previously described, and the social space of the Broken Glass context, the actions of which were a production of spatial language, or a 'reproduction of space' as discussed in Evans (2014: 194). Broken Glass developed their breakdancing and subsequent music styles from direct spatial exploration within a Mancunian context, yet to the outsider it was the release of the product and more significantly the manner in which it was received that resulted in the affirmation of their position as pioneers of UK hip hop. Bourdieu discusses the principle of selection as something

---

10. It is important here to point out that Greg Wilson was responsible for the remixes of six of the seven tracks from UK Electro, with the exception of 'Hip Hop Beat' by The Rapologists.

11. The compilations produced prior to *UK Electro* were in order of release: *Electro 1* (1983), *Electro 2* (1983), *Electro 3* (1984), *Electro 4* (1984) and *Crucial Electro* (1984).

**Figure 1:** 'Style of the Street', Side A, label detail, Cat. No. MKHAN 17 (1984)

that is 'socially constituted and acquired', and the graphic and audio package of the Streetwave release 'Style of the Street' and the *UK Electro* compilation respectively as the mode of representation informs us that this is proper to the period (Bourdieu 2010: 42).

The reification of this practice through the material product is important to attest the value of the work of Broken Glass and Greg Wilson, but also to demonstrate the broader ramifications of the 'Style of the Street' product as both a conduit and anchor point for the spatio-dynamics of Broken Glass and Greg Wilson's respective regional engagement within The Haçienda phenomenon, and the perception of high-quality hip hop practice by consumers across the breadth of the UK.

### Unleashing the Talent, Taming the Gap

In the years that followed 'Style of the Street' many independent Manchester artists released records, but two North-West artists of some importance signed record deals with esteemed London-based hip hop labels Music of Life and Kold Sweat. Chorley's Krispy 3 released two albums and three 12-inch singles on Kold Sweat between 1993 and 1994, while Lady Tame released one track on a Music of Life 12" (with Doc Savage appearing on the other side) in 1990. Interestingly enough, both artists had previously released records on local independent labels. Lady Tame's debut 'Loud Ladies' was the only release on 061 Records (named after the Manchester telephone area code at the time). Unlike Ruthless Rap Assassins and MC Buzz B who signed to major labels after initial independent success, Lady Tame and Krispy 3 are a crucial link between the indie label worlds of Manchester and London, as both Music of Life and Kold Sweat were independently owned labels with direct distribution deals and no major label stakeholders. This is important in exploring the regional, national and international cultural representation, identity and value of underground hip hop between London and Manchester. Music of Life was quickly established as a solid representation of London hip hop, so how was Lady Tame perceived as a newly signed artist from Tameside?

Lady Tame's debut release 'Loud Ladies' was produced by Piccadilly Radio and Key 103 radio DJ Stu Allan after hearing her rapping on a home-recorded freestyle. The record was received well on the underground Manchester scene upon its release in 1989, and subsequently Lady Tame was invited to perform at the various regional DMC mixing heats which were gathering huge momentum around the UK with London peer Monie Love. These performances plus her regional reputation from freestyling live in the studio on Stu Allan's *Bus Diss* radio show led her to being signed by London's Music of Life label. One wonders where the spatial thresholds of the city's edges are, as according to Morra, 'despite Manchester's celebrated regeneration, just beyond the city remains a landscape of authenticating bleakness' (2014: 99); both Lady Tame and Krispy 3 hail from these geographical zones. Lady Tame's pride in her Manchester heritage runs deep, her chosen name referring to her home place Tameside, in the Metropolitan Borough of Greater Manchester to the east of the city; this may not have connected with Londoners and the southern audience received Lady Tame with some incredulity:

> The Capital was always unsure of me and I often met with skeptical comments and crowds. Their female rapper was Monie (Love) and they rightly supported her but I proved I could break down postcode barriers by proving I could spit (rap), and spit articulate and with relevance and with ease. The respect came my way by me proving I could hold my own miles away from my hometown (Email correspondence, Lady Tame, 29 November 2016).

The cultural distance between Manchester and London has been apparent in literature since Elizabeth Gaskell's nineteenth-century novel *North and South*, and the term increased in usage and application during the 1980s when the chasm between North and South economically, culturally and socially became blatant (Smith 1989: 1). Hylton maintains that 'outside its thriving central core, there is a very different Manchester' and continues:

> As at November 1996, an estimated 161,600 of Manchester's citizens were dependent upon Income Support or other income based allowances. This represented some 37.5 per cent. The city as a whole had over twice the national average for unemployment and its inner areas more than three times. Almost 100,000 jobs were lost to the city between 1971 and 1995 (Hylton 2003: 231).

Krispy 3's hometown of Chorley also suffered similar decline: 'at the close of the twentieth century Chorley faces a future in which the traditional industries which fuelled its growth and prosperity have receded and died' (Heyes 1994: 1). Heyes affirms that although the harsh industrial landscape was shocking to strangers, 'many revised their opinions when they had time to appreciate the community' (Heyes 1994: 1). By the time of Lady Tame's Music of Life signing and Krispy 3's debut release, Thatcher had been in office as Prime Minister for eleven years. Following a one-day visit to the North-West, Thatcher stated in a public statement from 1979 that the people there needed to 'work for wealth' (David 1979). Rhys David recorded in the *Financial Times*: 'Britain would be able to afford German levels of wages and public expenditure when it matched German levels of work, the Prime Minister said yesterday' and concludes: 'The Prime Minister also defended the Government's changes in regional policy, one effect of which will be to reduce the levels of grant aid available to large parts of the North-West' (David 1979). Thatcher's flippancy which translated as work harder for less, affirmed a long-term loathing for Thatcher's government by many in this region. The impact of Thatcherism in mainstream culture has been clearly documented elsewhere, but within hip hop culture, the divide is less obvious and explored here based on tangential yet related factors to those of Thatcherism. It could be argued that despite Thatcherism, wider opportunities presented themselves in London through labels like Kold Sweat and Music of Life, and those opportunities had to be seized as they were not presenting themselves in the North-West. According to Lady Tame:

> The North/South divide was prevalent even in the hip hop movement. We were always seen as secondary and irrelevant which is why I was so proud to represent my city as the only female from Manchester with a [record] deal back then.

This sense of pride is a quality often associated with working-class life, and on the subject of working-class pride versus the privileged classes, Lady Tame suggests:

**Figure 2:** Lady Tame in London after signing to Music of Life (1989)

> A middle-class or rich artist that hasn't come from nothing will not have the same passion, fight or emotion as a working-class artist will. When you fight for the basics in life as a people, you have an inbuilt strength that replicates in your delivery and lyrics.

Additionally, there is something connected to representational distancing at play. Pocock and Hudson imply that the way in which the North is perceived by southerners is the result of continual production and packaging through various forms of media, which gather momentum as a collective attitude: 'for the past hundred and fifty years [literary works] have projected a consistent image of "the north" in sharp contrast, overt or implied, to that of the south' (Pocock and Hudson 1978: 111–12). The emergent stereotypes represent low socio-economics and the North as a place of bleakness to southerners, and it may be this misunderstood imagined habitus that resulted in Lady Tame releasing only one record with Music of Life, despite her eloquent rap style which delivered with precision and intelligence. Lady Tame's reflection on why there is not a larger discography is thus:

> In all honesty I think my postcode, the fact I was white in a black dominated scene and the fact I was female meant record companies didn't know what to do with me back then.

Bourdieu discusses 'distinctive power in terms of cultural possessions or practices' which 'tends to decline with the growth in the number of people able to appropriate them' (Bourdieu 2010: 227). So what if the cultural value of a record as artefact is constructed around a set of pretentions such as geographic origin of the artist? If the geographic origin of the artist is not what is presented through the artefact, does the artefact lose its value? What the industry desired was to present Lady Tame as a more accessible, constructed representation for the mainstream:

> The industry I found wanted to box me in a Betty Boo style appearance, sound and package which I firmly refused to do.[12] I had several big auditions at major companies like Jive [Records] who would have signed me in a heartbeat if I would have switched to crossover pop, wearing a short skirt and heels. That was NOT me. I only wanted to deliver hardcore underground rawness NOT pop hence I refused many deals. I would rather be known for a short career representing truth, reason and authenticity than someone who sold her soul to the industry for exposure.

The commercial record industry made a series of presumptions regarding taste and value to commercialize Lady Tame by presenting her within a different social construct. By reconstructing her habitus and image, and by retaining what it considered tasteful tropes such as specific items of clothing, accessories, sounds and lyrics, the industry intended to remove Lady Tame from both her northern roots and the artistic social space of the underground hip hop scene for capital gain. Bourdieu suggests that situations of this nature can only be dissatisfactory, and the 'very relationship to temporal power and to the associated profits which defines the "bourgeois" intellectual or artist compromises the "disinterestedness" which, even in the eyes of the dominant fraction, specifically defines intellectuals and artists' (Bourdieu 2010: 316).

## Collective Gravity, Resistance and Pressure

In 1993, The Ruf released the white-label 'Ruf & Rugged Megamix' which contained 15 minutes of classic hip hop on a limited private pressing of 500 copies. In many ways, this vinyl release epitomized all things good about hip hop culture: its originality, chaos, dynamism, energy, and most importantly its con-

---

12. Betty Boo became a pop act after working with Music of Life artists She Rockers.

tinuing counter-narrative to all things mainstream, and could be considered a seminal release to the extensive Ruf Beats catalogue that was to follow. Under the various other guises of Jeep Beat Collective, Mind Bomb, The Godfather of Weird and D.J. Davies, The Ruf's discography is almost as extensive as the Ruf Beats label's output. With almost 50 releases between 1993 and 2003, countless shows, collaborations and networks Europe-wide, The Ruf's experience provides a critical insight to the issues of cultural representation, identity and value within Mancunian hip hop. As we sat amongst boxes of records at his shop Planet Rock in creative focal point Wellington House, Ancoats, discussing The Ruf's early engagement with hip hop, three primary areas of concern arose. The first related to the issue of representation and the facets that form the habitus, and it became clear that the relationship between Madchester and hip hop was not so dialectical:

> With hip hop and other black music, I can hear it a lot within baggy music—The Charlatans, Stone Roses, all used banging beats and basslines. There was a lot more going on that crossed through genres.

The influences of hip hop on the Madchester sound was not critically explored at the time, and as a result, the belief was that Madchester had purely been born out of some Mancunian passion alone; however The Ruf recalls that:

> If it had not been for DJs like Hewan Clarke, Leaky Fresh and Stu Allan in the mid to late 80s, these DJs were playing very varied records that went on to influence baggy and the music was very open.[13] A lot of those bands—Stone Roses, Happy Mondays—were influenced by hip hop and stuff being played in Manchester. You'd listen to the radio and you'd hear the baggy stuff, but it wasn't defined, it was just all music, and things were wide open. People would listen to all different things, and we all did ok out of it. There was definitely a thriving independent sector right up until about '92 or '93.

Media representations of the Madchester phenomenon conveniently described the scene largely in isolation from other cultural influences, which was not the case. The Ruf explains:

> The problem sometimes is when you look back at scenes that were media driven, the actual reality is a lot more eclectic, wider, and a lot of stuff happening at the same time. There's a tendency within journalism to say this is a certain thing, and that is a certain thing.

---

13. 'Baggy Scene' is an interchangeable term with Madchester, so named after the baggy sweatshirts and jeans worn by its followers.

Interestingly, McKay acknowledges a connection between northern soul and the Madchester rave scene, promoting Steve Redhead's argument that both the northern and rave scenes are part of a long, complex history associated with youth style, although the discussion is devoid of any mention of hip hop culture (McKay 1996: 106). The Ruf affirms the importance of hip hop in the construction of The Haçienda and the Madchester scene:

> International 1 and 2, and Tropicana which were originally hip hop venues, and they would put on Jungle Brothers and then the next night The Charlatans for example.[14] These venues and clubs get forgotten about and they weren't just programming one kind of music, and The Haçienda too was playing hip hop.

What starts to become clear is that a multiplicity was in operation within the scope of the city. Although one club might become known for a certain experience, hip hop transcended the spatial enclosures of the clubs, its presence having a transferable impact onto other scenes. The Ruf contextualizes this multiplicity further:

> I don't think that Factory Records were influenced by hip hop or the other way around, but maybe what it did give was the DIY mentality and illustrated to others that you could put your music out, and I'd say that there were somewhere between 50 and 100 independently released records from the mid-80s to the early 90s in Manchester. Tony Wilson was very aware and supportive of Manchester musicians, whoever they were and whatever they were doing; he supported independence and also he was passionate about bringing large events to the North, arguing against having to always go to the South (Interview with The Ruf, 6 December 2016).

By the late 1980s, the London accent had become accepted as it carved a place in hip hop; there was a particular slant that was influenced by both Cockney dialect and the Jamaican vernacular which also appropriated certain colloquialisms, became acceptable and represented quality and taste. Whilst London artists such as London Posse, Demon Boyz, Hardnoise, MC Mell 'O' and Gunshot capitalized on this dialect, artists practising outside this dialect became more distanced from the emerging identity of UK hip hop. With newer art-

---

14. Jungle Brothers are a crew from NYC and part of the Native Tongues (including Tribe Called Quest and De La Soul) who were renowned for working across genres, and in particular house music, as illustrated by their record *I'll House You* (1988), a rework of house anthem *Can You Party?* by Royal House of the same year, and both records released by Idler's Records Inc.

ists aspiring to the success of these artists, false dialects became more evident through the UK hip hop community, and these false accents were soon delivering false references, stories and contexts.

**Figure 3:** The Ruf behind the decks/counter at Planet Rock (2016)

On the difficult subject of honesty and truth, a solid representation of raw views can be heard throughout The Ruf's 'Westwood is a Tw*t (Allegedly)', released under the name Mind Bomb Vs. Jeep Beat Collective on double pack 12" in 1996. London-based hip hop DJ Tim Westwood had gained a national reputation in the late 1980s for his hip hop radio shows on Kiss FM and fortnightly television presentations under N-Sign Radio on ITV's Night Network.

Although the latter were short broadcasts, Westwood was responsible for bringing a strong visual to growing hip hop culture in the UK via the music video, and these shows presented for the first time in the UK music videos by underground US hip hop artists of the time such as EPMD, MC Lyte, Schoolly D and K-9 Posse. Westwood was, to many original UK hip hop lovers, a national institution, someone who was a key part of the hip hop habitus and respected as such. His support for underground US hip hop as well as the growing UK scene (albeit London biased) through his representations in *Open Space, Bad Meaning Good*, a 1987 documentary by the BBC, verifies his engagement in hip hop culture, although by 1994 when Westwood joined BBC Radio 1 to host the UK's first national rap show, faith from the underground community in his agenda had begun to fade. He rarely played any homegrown talent, and it seemed his acquired fake accent became more comedic on a weekly basis, almost self-parodying as an extreme social construct and 'stylization of life' through material acquisition and more ephemeral aesthetic disposition (Bourdieu 2010: 377).

'Westwood is a Tw*t (Allegedly)' is more lament than diss,[15] a representation of the frustration that artists experienced in Westwood's trajectory, and disappointment in his lack of bringing UK hip hop to a wider audience. Two key sections of lyrics deal with these points, firstly in verse one:

> Ahhhhhh...let's fuck it up now...
> Cos enough is enough
> Hear the lyrical assault from the brother called Ruf!
> Shakin' up the scene cos no other would dare
> Fuck Westwood!!!
> We said it and meant it, now where's your DJ skills, man?
> Your accent, for real man?
> You don't slam, man
> With your U.S. jams, man
> Hip-hop forgotten as you follow your trends
> Swingin' in the Jungle, where will it end?
> Deny your culture with sad fake slang
> And cling on, on American arses you hang
> You don't impress me
> You cannot test me
> I'm runnin' round defences like I was George Best, see?

---

15. To 'diss' in hip hop vernacular is to disrespect, usually with intention. There have been hundreds of diss records produced since the 1980s, perhaps the most famous of these being the 'Roxanne saga' in 1984 where diss records were exchanged between U.T.F.O. and The Real Roxanne, both produced by Full Force.

Verse two opens with a tongue in cheek plea in the style of Ol' Dirty Bastard's *Shimmy Shimmy Ya* (Elektra, 1995):

> Timmy Timmy Ha Timmy Ho I say,
> Please will you please play my records today?

Verse two then continues with reference to the issue of fake accents:

> Blade cuts deeper[16]
> Slowly bleedin'
> UK rap dyin', nobody's heedin'
> The truths, the youth who put on voices
> Actin' American

The song itself is not presented in an aggressive manner, but is very much comedic and brings an almost farcical angle to the work. The use of the words 'tw*t' and 'allegedly' in the title owes more than just a little to northern humour; the potential brashness of the words are tempered by their delivery which enables the listener to sympathize and 'connect with these characters on an emotional level' (Jarski and Maconie 2009: xvii) and at the same time considering 'The North in the national imagination could be warm and witty' (Russell 2004: 163). The Ruf's northernism is fully apparent here, epitomizing his natural vernacular and colloquial approach to the context of hip hop.

## Conclusions: Future Habitus of Hip Hop

In answering the questions this chapter set out to address, it is becoming clear that coexistence is present between the changing nature of the music spectacle and hip hop culture in Manchester. The spatio-cultural presence of The Haçienda and the cultural explosion that followed during the later Madchester years were continually underpinned by the subtle, morphing company of hip hop, occupying the liminal spaces between club nights, gigs, fashion statements and other constructs of the habitus. While The Ruf recalls 'you had people wearing Joe Bloggs who'd never even been to Manchester' as an explosive Madchester fashion phenomenon, he also recollects that after a night raving, you might 'go home and listen to some nice chilled hip hop'. Mancunian hip hop continually evolved through a necessity to survive, and each time a portion was consumed by a commercial entity, it re-evaluated and reframed its position to continue to live. It is these re-evaluations and reframing that demand further work, and this requires particular investigation through the

---

16. This is a metaphorical reference to UK artist Blade, who is widely regarded as remaining true to the artform of UK hip hop.

vast range of independent Manchester hip hop artists that produced diverse music and work in subaltern and multiple natures. One particular moment which certainly deserves future investigation is where Kermit Leveridge of Broken Glass and Ruthless Rap Assassins joined ex-Happy Mondays front man Sean Ryder in the group Black Grape.

The passion and richness within Manchester hip hop culture is undoubtable. A heritage spanning four decades which is still vibrant through the spatio-cultural dynamics of the record shop, the event and club nights, and the consistent and original record releases of contemporary Manchester-based artists such as Spye with his fluid, intricate flow and wordplay, Chalk's personal honesty and The Mouse Outfit's full live band, indicate that Manchester hip hop continues to innovate and offer something of a counter-narrative to the mainstream of UK hip hop. It is resistant to the stylization of life through accepted tropes and habitus, resistant of that which 'expresses itself in the specifically stylized way of life to which all aspiring members are expected to adhere' (Weber 1994: 114). Writing in *The Wire* in 1996, Simon Reynolds describes a two-fold sense of what is 'real' in terms of hip hop, the most relevant here being: 'First, it means authentic, uncompromised music that refuses to sell out to the music industry and soften its message for crossover' (Reynolds 1996). Whilst the notion of the authentic is important, this definition of 'real' omits a critical component of the cultural phenomenon of realness in hip hop that extends beyond the edges of music through identity. A broader sense of realness encompasses attitude, actions and the way in which one presents and displays oneself, often using material things as support mechanisms. In other words, a habitus is created based on the material culture of hip hop to reinforce one's realness and propagate what is deemed tasteful. Often though, this imagined realness is a constructed fabrication and not a contextual reality of one's self. Striving to be real, results in the unreal. Through striving not to 'be real', in a sense, independent Mancunian hip hop has evolved to become more real, and it is the many facets of its individuality that breathes life. To 'be real', is to be tasteful, to operate in a genuine social construct and with distinctive qualities. The originality found in representations of Manchester hip hop is something that was first apparent in the music of the pioneers MC Buzz B and Ruthless Rap Assassins, yet it is also this distinctive approach to hip hop that positioned Mancunian hip hop in a narrative juxtaposed somewhere between the Madchester scene and the London hip hop community.

Much of Manchester now exists in a material vacuum, or as Hatherley states, a 'mausoleum of Blairism' where the result of many millennium building projects did nothing more than further distance the city's people from the government (Hatherley 2010: 156). But it is here where the future of Mancunian hip hop is to thrive, where it must continue to critically reflect on its cultural context, continue to socially comment and re-imagine its hip hop habitus through a multiplicity of the regional, local and individual. It needs to continue to operate within the 'liminal zones' and socio-spatial constructs 'to provide a necessary escape from "normal" work-a-day life' in order to thrive, but also continue to develop its own sense of everyday (Shields 1991: 86). The future of Manchester hip hop is dependent on embracing its shifting socio-spatial identity, its audible gravity, its variable representations and the palimpsest of the city in true DIY northern style.

## About the Author

Adam de Paor-Evans is School Lead for Research and Innovation at the School of Art, Design and Fashion, UCLAN. He is a cultural theorist and his work explores the tensions, actions and practices of subculture, identity and the liminal with reference to their broader social and political contexts. He has published work ranging from the relationship between the urban condition and hip hop culture to the temporal and identity of global housing. He is also a multi-media artist working as Project CEE: Cultural Exploration + Engagement which explores various subcultural practices. His publications include the chapter 'On the Origins of Hip Hop: Appropriation and Territorial Control of Urban Space' in the 2014 Routledge book *Consuming Architecture.*

## References

Allan, Stu. 2009a. *Stu Allan – Bus Diss.* https://manchesterradio.files.wordpress.com/2011/05/stu-allan-bus-diss-mixes.mp3 (accessed 22 December 2016).

—2009b. *Stu Allan – Bus Diss.* https://manchesterradio.files.wordpress.com/2011/05/stu-allan-bus-diss-1987.mp3 (accessed 22 December 2016).

—2009c. *Stu Allan – Bus Diss.* https://manchesterradiomusic.com/91-2/ (accessed 22 December 2016).

Bourdieu, Pierre. 2010. *Distinction: A Social Critique of the Judgement of Taste.* London: Routledge.

David, Rhys. 1979. 'Margaret Thatcher. Remarks Visiting the North West (Defending Economic Policy)'. *Financial Times*, 1 September. http://www.margaretthatcher.org/document/104136 (accessed 8 January 2017).

DJ Semtex. 2016. *Hip Hop Raised Me.* London: Thames & Hudson.

Evans, Adam. 2014. 'On the Origins of Hip Hop: Appropriation and Territorial Control of Urban Space'. In *Consuming Architecture*, ed. Daniel Maudlin and Marcel Vellinga, 185–201. London: Routledge.

Hatherley, Owen. 2010. *A Guide to the New Ruins of Great Britain.* London: Verso.

Heyes, Jim. 1994. *A History of Chorley.* Preston: Lancashire County Books.

Hylton, Stuart. 2003. *A History of Manchester.* Chichester: Phillmore & Co.

Jarski, Rosemarie, and Stuart Maconie. 2009. *The Wit and Wisdom of the North.* London: Ebury Press.

KRS ONE. 2009. *The Gospel of Hip Hop.* New York: Powerhouse Books.
McKay, George. 1996. *Senseless Acts of Beauty: Cultures of Resistance.* London: Verso.
Morra, Irene. 2014. *Britishness, Popular Music, and National Identity: The Making of Modern Britain.* London: Routledge.
Pocock, Douglas, and Ray Hudson. 1978. *Images of the Urban Environment (Focal Problems in Geography).* London: Macmillan.
Reynolds, Simon. 1996. 'Slipping into Darkness'. *The Wire* 148 (June). https://tinyurl.com/techstep-1996 (accessed 7 January 2017).
Russell, Dave. 2004. *Looking North: Northern England and the National Imagination.* Manchester: Manchester University Press.
Shields, Rob. 1991. *Places on the Margin: Alternative Geographies of Modernity.* London: Routledge.
Smith, David. 1989. *North and South: Britain's Economic, Social and Political Divide.* London: Penguin.
Weber, Max. 1994. *Sociological Writings.* London: Bloomsbury Academic.
Wilson, Greg. 2006. *Broken Glass and the Birth of the British B Boy.* http://www.electrofunkroots.co.uk/articles/broken_glass.html (accessed 21 December 2016).
—2011. *Legend – Manchester's Other Club.* http://blog.gregwilson.co.uk/2011/08/legend-manchesters-other-club/ (accessed 4 January 2017).

*Films and documentaries*
Davidson, Sue. 1987. *Open Space, Bad Meaning Good.* London: BBC2.
D'Cruz, Jaimie. 2016. *The World Hip Hop News.* London: BBC4.

*Discography*
Broken Glass. 1984. 'Style of the Street'. London: Streetwave.
Lady Tame/Doc Savage. 1990. 'Tame 1 Unleashed' / 'Straight From The Underground'. London: Music of Life.
Mind Bomb vs Jeep Beat Collective. 1996. 'Metacosmic Dimensions' / 'Westwood Is A Tw*t (Allegedly)'. Manchester: The Ruf Label.
Ol' Dirty Bastard. 1995. 'Shimmy Shimmy Ya'. New York: Elektra.
The Ruf. 1993. 'Ruf & Rugged Megamix'. Manchester: The Ruf Label.

*Interviews*
Jojo Mavrakis, 19 December 2016. Skype interview.
Lady Tame, 29 November 2016. Email correspondence.
The Ruf, 6 December 2016. Planet Rock Records, Ancoats, Manchester, UK.

# 9 The Missing Star of MC Tunes

## Les Gillon and Ewa Mazierska

This chapter explores the case of MC Tunes, a rapper from Manchester. We try to answer typical homology questions[1]: how has his career and music reflected his cultural environment, especially his life in Manchester's Moss Side during the period when music from Manchester was thriving nationally and internationally, and how has his music affected his life and identity.

MC Tunes' input into the musical history of Manchester and the North of England is largely unacknowledged or relegated to a footnote, suggesting that he was at the periphery of the phenomena most important in the musical history of Manchester and the North West. Dave Haslam in his book *Manchester England: The Story of the Pop Cult City* mentions MC Tunes twice, first time as a collaborator of 808 State and the second time as an example of the success of Madchester (Haslam 1999: 170, 183). Nathan Wiseman-Trowse in his monograph *Performing Class in British Popular Music*, in the chapter 'Dream Pop and Madchester' writes briefly about 808 State and MC Tunes as an exception to the rule that guitar bands dominated the Madchester phenomenon (Wiseman-Trowse 2008: 159). Georgina Gregory, again in her examination of the Madchester phenomenon, mentions him in a footnote as an untypical representative of this wave due to being a rapper rather than a pop-rock musician (Gregory 2014: 147). C. P. Lee in *Shake, Rattle and Rain: Popular Music Making in Manchester 1955–1995* (2002) ignores

---

1. In this sense we follow a suggestion given by Simon Frith in his essay 'Music and Identity': 'The academic study of popular music has been limited by the assumption that the sounds must somehow "reflect" or "represent" the people. The analytic problem has been to trace the connections back, from the work (the score, the song, the beat) to the social groups who produce and consume it. What's been at issue in homology, some sort of *structural* relationship between material and musical forms' (original emphasis). Frith continues by claiming that music not only reflects people's histories and identities, but also produces them. 'Music, like identity, is both performance and story, describes the social in the individual and the individual in the social, the mind in the body and the body in the mind; identity, like music, is a matter of both ethics and aesthetics' (Frith 2007: 204). Following Stuart Hall, Frith argues that identity is mobile and music reflects and abets it (ibid.).

MC Tunes completely. What interests us here is why MC Tunes did not play a more central position in the Manchester music scene. Our research is based on interviews with MC Tunes, and his collaborators and friends, particularly music producer and impresario Johnny Jay, which we conducted in summer 2016. We also draw on interviews he gave previously, most importantly in *Nish Clish Banging: The MC Tunes Tapes* (1990–2011), a documentary by Howard Walmsley, textual analysis of his songs, as well as the cultural history of Manchester, the city where MC Tunes spent practically his entire life.

## MC Tunes' career

MC Tunes was born Nicholas William Dennis Hodgson in 1970 in Manchester's Moss Side into a working-class family, yet with interests in music and culture. His father was a small drug dealer with no stable occupation, a guitarist and avid music fan. His mother had a variety of mainly poorly paid and temporary jobs. She had a passion for music, as testified by her large collection of records. The family also had a history of problems with drug addiction, with both Nicky's father and uncle being heroin users. The difficulty in looking after a child in such circumstances was eased by the significant involvement of Nicky's grandmother in bringing up the boy. The formative years of Hodgson coincided with the rule of Margaret Thatcher, when the North–South divide widened, adding to the (already distinct) sense that the North lags behind and is mistreated by the metropolitan elites.

Nicky Hodgson first came to the attention of DJ and producer Johnny Jay when Jay was running dance events for young people in the 1980s. Jay recalls the 'skinny white kid' who impressed the largely black audience with his 'beat boxing', using microphone techniques to produce a vocal imitation of a drum track. The teenager returned a few weeks later and performed a rap that was equally skilful. It was the pairing of the young rapper, now renamed MC Tunes, with Johnny Jay that led to commercial success for both acts with chart singles and albums released on the London-based independent label ZTT. Hodgson signed up to a record contract by this company in 1990 and within that year he delivered two top twenty chart singles and a top thirty debut album. Yet, the following year, he was dropped by the label.

The story of MC Tunes' relationship with ZTT may appear to follow the familiar narrative of a young, northern working-class artist who is 'discovered' by the London-based music industry and then exploited commercially before being discarded. However, the story is more complex, involving issues of race, class, culture and taste. To reveal it, let us first look at the history of ZTT. The label was established in 1983, and of its three founders it was the musician and record producer Trevor Horn who was most involved with the creative process. Horn was arguably the most prominent British auteur producer of the 1980s. His pioneering use of digital sampling and sequencing, as featured on the worldwide hit singles of Frankie Goes to Hollywood, had a strong influence on the sound of pop music on both sides of the Atlantic. Horn had previously played keyboard in the British progressive rock band Yes, and his 1980 solo hit 'Video Killed the Radio Star' (released under the band name Buggles) incorporated many of the recording and arrangement techniques of progressive rock into the idiom of the mainstream commercial pop single (Warner 2003). Both in his solo releases and in his work with Yes, Horn's musical approach is informed by the distinctly European character of progressive rock, which melodically and harmonically tends to draw strongly from the European classical tradition, rather than from Afro-American music that underpins most US rock music. Horn embraced cutting-edge technologies, using devices such as the new sampling keyboard computer the Fairlight CMI, to create pop records in new ways and with new sounds. That said, in 1983 Horn produced Malcolm McLaren's seminal *Duck Rock* LP which is regarded as one of the moments of arrival for hip hop in the UK. Hence, he already had experience of bringing rap to a commercial realm.

Horn's co-founder Paul Morley was a journalist rather than a musician or producer, but he nonetheless played a key role in defining the creative direction of ZTT (Warner 2003: 75). In an interview with designers Declan & Garech Stone, Morley lists thirty-six influences, 'words and concepts and writers and dreamers' that he drew upon when Horn approached him about setting up the label. The list begins with the word 'Europe' and continues in an equally Eurocentric vein. Futurism is referenced and listed separately; entries include FT Marinetti, Baudrillard, Hugo Ball, Wyndham Lewis, Barthes and Adorno. Of the fifteen musicians or bands listed, five are German, and the list includes avant-garde and classical composers, as well as pop musicians (Stone 2010). There are only two females listed, but this lack of gender balance was not so unusual in 1980 when the list was compiled. What is perhaps more surprising is that no black artists were listed and the list shows virtually no evidence of any interest in music of Afro-American origin. The influence of Futurism went beyond the initial concept list. The label's name, ZTT, was taken from FT Marinetti's sound poem, *Zang Tuum Tumb*. The label's 'house band', The Art of Noise (led by Horn and later including Morley himself), was named after the Futurist essay 'The Art of Noises' by Luigi Russolo (Warner 2003: 75–76). Many of the musicians on Morley's list would have satisfied Russolo's manifesto demand for new sounds produced by new technologies. Brian Eno, Karlheinz Stockhausen and Steve Reich all produced music that took advantage of the new opportunities afforded by the latest music technology.

Clearly there was a mismatch between ZTT's Eurocentric aesthetic and the musical direction of MC Tunes, given Nicky Hodgson's passionate commitment to hip hop, funk and other forms of black US music. The signing came about as a result of Hodgson's involvement with pioneering electronic dance music producers 808 State and, by his own account, his record deal with ZTT came about as a by-product, almost an afterthought, of 808 State's deal with the label:

> 808 State had done a track called *Pacific State*, which was on a little independent album called *Quadrastate*, and it went really big and it was selling shitloads. So ZTT signed them through a guy called Ron Atkinson, who had a record shop in Manchester called Music Mania. They re-released *Pacific* and it got to No. 7 in the charts. I was doing demos with 808 State at the time and one of the people down at ZTT heard *The Only Rhyme That Bites* and said 'yeah, let's put it out' (Peel 2004).

Given the clearly defined technological, aesthetic and cultural tropes that ZTT embodied, it is not surprising that 808 State's cutting-edge use of music technology would appeal to Trevor Horn. Moreover, the decision to sign 808 State was made in the aftermath of a difficult period for the label, when legal disputes with artists meant that they needed to replenish their roster of artists. However, 808 State founder member Graham Massey indicates that it was not a straightforward decision for the band: 'It was considered a bit of a risk to go to ZTT. They were famous in the mid-80s for the Art of Noise and Frankie Goes to Hollywood, but it seemed like their time was passing. Everybody had left them, there was controversy over people taking them to court' (Seaman 2010).

The decision of 808 State to sign with a London-based label is perhaps surprising, given that 808 State was so deeply rooted in the Manchester music scene that was then at its high point. Indeed, 808 State were sampling contemporary Manchester artists and creating records to be played to Manchester audiences in the city's most important independent venue, The Haçienda. As early as 1983, they had produced an acid house remix of New Order's 'Blue Monday' which had been released on the Factory label earlier that year. On 'Tunes Splits the Atom' the band used a sample from the Stone Roses song 'I Am the Resurrection', which was also newly released. Band member Darren Partington captures the celebratory nature of this use of material sampled from their musical contemporaries:

> The students love *Tunes Splits the Atom* because of the Stone Roses sample. A lot of people were initially wary because you don't sample the Stone Roses, you just don't. It's one of those sacred things. Does

> it sound like we had fun when we made it? I think it still does. With MC Tunes it was nice to take the 808 hat off and just have a bit of fun, musically. It was a breath of fresh air to have a batch of lyrics to cover with music (Peel 2008).

Massey says that the band saw advantages to signing to ZTT rather than a Manchester-based label: 'One of the attractive things about them was we were a big fish in their pond. If we had gone to Factory we would have had to compete with New Order and the Happy Mondays' (ibid.). These words draw attention to one aspect of the history of music in Manchester, which is omitted or played down in the existing literature, namely the effect of the music taste of Tony Wilson and politics of Factory on those on the outside or the fringe of this phenomenon. While Factory managed to put on the map music produced in the North, it focused on punk and post-punk music and music which could appeal to (continental) European sensibility, rather than American. Also, although Wilson was known for his appreciation of good lyrics, famously describing the lyrics of Shaun Ryder as being 'on a par with W.B. Yeats', he showed little interest in or appreciation of texts created by rappers, whose poetry was of a different sort than that of modernist poets.

While 808 State stayed with ZTT, releasing their last studio album with the label in 1996, MC Tunes was dropped after just a year. The reasons for that decision are not clear cut, but one element was artistic differences between artist and label. The second MC Tunes album *Damage by Stereo* was nearing completion when the decision was made and Hodgson maintains that the label were unconvinced that the genre had any longevity: 'I was saying how rap was going to be around in 10 and 20 years-time and that it was the new rock and roll, but they just couldn't see it. They thought it was going to go the way of Showaddywaddy or glam rock' (Peel 2004). Ultimately, ZTT and Factory followed a similar ethos, revealing affinity to European high modernism, rather than to poetry fed on the working-class life, as articulated in hip hop. It is likely that if Hodgson's patrons saw potential in rap as the dominant genre of the upcoming generations, MC Tunes' career might have turned out differently. It shall also be emphasized that MC Tunes' success and failure took place at the time when the recording industry was the core of the music business. The failure of the first record had a more dramatic effect on the artists' career than now.

If the story of the rise and fall of MC Tunes invites us to consider it in the context of familiar narratives about the exploitative nature of the music industry, it also plays into another familiar narrative: that of the talented working-class outsider, unprepared for fame, unmanageable and unable to take advantage of opportunities because of a wild and chaotic lifestyle, as immortalized, for example, in the British New Wave films, such as *The Loneliness of the Long Distance Runner* (1962) by Tony Richardson. Before he was dropped from the label, Nicky Hodgson was involved in a violent incident that led to him facing serious charges. Most likely the incident did not directly contribute to the decision to drop MC Tunes from the label. ZTT was still commissioning videos for the second MC Tunes album even while Hodgson was on bail. Indeed filmmaker Howard Walmsley recalls that there was a sense of urgency on the part of the label to get the videos made in case Hodgson was convicted and received a custodial sentence. Although Hodgson was eventually cleared of those charges, the incident may have reinforced an impression of Hodgson as being aggressive and volatile, and his blunt, uncompromising demeanour, forged on the streets of Moss Side, made the label wary of dealing with him. In a 2012 interview, Terry Christian, who has known Hodgson throughout his career, argues that the fact that Hodgson was a Northerner whose work dealt with issues facing the working class, worked against him in his relations with the music industry. Christian also refers to Hodgson's increasing use of alcohol and drugs as a factor in the decline of his career (Christian 2012).

The removal of MC Tunes from the roster of ZTT artists was far from being the end of Hodgson's career. In 1995 he formed the Dust Junkys, a band that augmented a standard guitar, bass and drums rock band line-up with the addition of a turntablist, Ganiyu Pierre Gasper. The fusion of hard rock and hip hop reflected two apparently different tropes in Hodgson's early musical influences, uniting the rap of the Sugarhill Gang with the 'underground' rock music of his mother's record collection. In integrating these styles it is arguable that the Dust Junkys were breaking new ground on the UK music scene. During the early 1990s US bands such as the Red Hot Chilli Peppers were starting to incorporate elements of hip hop into the rock band format, but often these predominantly white bands tended only to incorporate the technical features of rap rather than the deeper cultural characteristics of hip hop. By contrast, the Dust Junkys were a multi-racial band, whose name signifies an addiction to the 'rare grooves' of the black dance music scene.

The major label Polydor released the band's first single, 'Living in the Pocket of a Drug Queen', in 1997. They released two further singles, including 'What Time Is It?', which reached the UK top 40 charts and an album over the next two years. The band also toured extensively and played at major music festivals such as Reading and Glastonbury, but despite this it failed to gain major success or to secure much coverage in the music press. Johnny Jay argues that both in the production and to an extent in the music arrangements on the band's debut album, *Done and Dusted* (1998), the unique qualities of the songs were not well served. He points out that ultimately the most commercially successful part of the project was 'Rinse (Beatbox Wash)', which was originally released as the B side of the band's first single. Unlike the rest of the band's recording this track features no instruments; the sounds on the record are all created by Hodgson using multitrack recordings of him 'beat-boxing', singing and rapping. The track refers back to the earliest forms of hip hop and to Hodgson's earliest practice as a teenager in Moss Side. It was a sample of this record that the DJ and producer Fatboy Slim used as the vocal hook line of his successful single, 'Gangster Trippin'', which reached number 3 in the UK Singles Chart.

Hodgson blames the racism of the rock music industry (and in particular the music press) for the failure of the band to achieve mainstream success, arguing that it was perceived at the time that the presence of non-white faces on the cover of a rock music publication such as *NME* would reduce sales. If such an attitude prevailed in London, it was even more the case in Manchester, where the rap scene was less developed. However, some of those who worked with Hodgson state that a major factor was the low work ethic on Hodgson's part which prevented this project from achieving greater success. It must be mentioned, however, that by this point the musician was raising his son as a single parent, which made it difficult for him to commit to the long days and nights in the studio needed to make a success of the project.

## MC Tunes and 'Real Manchester'

Spatial branding is an important aspect of every hip hop artist's identity. Murray Forman observes that rap's lyrical construction commonly displays a pronounced emphasis on place and locality.

> Whereas blues, rock and R&B have traditionally cited regions or cities,... contemporary rap is even more specific, with explicit references to particular streets, boulevards and neighbourhoods, telephone area codes, postal service zip codes, or other sociospatial information. Rap artists draw inspiration from their regional affiliations as well as from a keen sense of what I call the *extreme local*, upon which they base their construction of spatial imagery (Forman 2002: xvii; see also Evans 2014).

The black ghetto, and specifically the 'hood', from which the majority of hip hop stars originate, educates in both a social and musical sense. It teaches the youngsters about social hierarchies, places that are friendly and off-limits, rewarding them for knowing how to behave and punishing transgressions. There is also a certain paradox concerning hip hop artists. They are expected to remain rooted in their poverty-stricken area, but at the same time transcend it by becoming famous.

9 The Missing Star of MC Tunes **181**

**Figure 1:** MC Tunes DJ-ing in York, 2016. Courtesy Richard Alexander

As Steven Graves argues, spatial roots are even more important in the case of white rappers, with Eminem being the best-known example (Graves 2009: 252). This is because white rappers do not have the 'natural credibility' linked to their skin colour. On the contrary, they appear to be fake and must make up for it by showing that they belong to a specific milieu. Eminem achieved this goal by presenting himself as somebody with intimate links to Detroit. His songs to a large extent reflect the history of his city, including the period of its industrial and urban decline, with his track 'Beautiful' making reference to some of the well-known post-industrial ruins of this city. At the same time, Eminem presents himself as immersed in black culture, as demonstrated by the fact that he records and performs predominantly with black artists.

MC Tunes can be compared to Eminem as he also 'makes up' for being white by showing attachment to his place. In this case we can mention two places: Manchester as a whole and its district of Moss Side where Hodgson was raised. Let's begin with Moss Side. Its importance in the musical history of Manchester is recognized by Dave Haslam, who devotes one chapter to it in his book *Manchester England*. In it, he focuses on two aspects of Moss Side's history: being a traditional settlement of black communities and a site of unsuccessful projects of modernization. The first had to do with, on the one hand, the colonial history of Manchester, which resulted in many people from West Africa, Somalia and India settling in this city and, on the other hand, to the racism of its inhabitants, which led to the black community being hounded into just a few areas (Haslam 1999: 223–24), of which Moss Side was the main one.

Apropos modernization of this district of Manchester, Haslam writes eloquently: 'Moss Side is an area full of history rubbed out, the kind of place promises are postponed, good times fade and new beginnings are made every decade; hopes, like battered buildings, are regularly demolished' (1999: 221). He also notes that modernization projects were typically imposed on Moss Side by external actors, such as government agencies, which disrespected the views of the local population, leaving the locals suspicious and alienated. This was especially reflected in the Moss Side riots of 1981. The rioting started at the local police station and later moved into the surrounding streets over two days. The background to this event was institutional racism, particularly by the police (who routinely harassed black youths), recession and Thatcher government's hard-line approach to crime and unemployment, which by this point was seen by her government as a private rather than public problem (Evans 2013: 1–14; see also Adam de Paor-Evans' chapter in this collection). Unemployment was at this time high across the whole of Britain, but it affected particularly strongly the North, and such areas as Moss Side whose population's livelihood relied on manufacturing. The 1980s was also the time when heroin and crack cocaine replaced marijuana and alcohol as a favourite drug of the inhabitants, leading to turf wars between the gangs.

The future MC Tunes was only eleven when the riots took place, and was their observer rather than a participant, but they confirmed his perception that he lived on the wrong side of the social divide. In common with Eminem, he lived in what had been to a large extent a black ghetto, absorbing the local way of living, and musical influences. On his own account, there were only two viable career paths in Moss Side: that of crime, primarily dealing in drugs, and making music. As we already indicated, as is the case with many famous rappers, the future rapper tried both with a degree of success. In this respect he followed in his father's footsteps, who was both a heroin dealer and user, and a gifted guitarist. Hodgson claims that music was always around him.

Hodgson's musical sympathies reflect strongly on his Moss Side heritage. He mentions that in his life he always liked 'real music'. Quizzed on the meaning of this term, he admits that 'real music' is one that is grounded in reality and affects one's real life. Moreover, it foregrounds rhythm, rather than melody. The acts that affected the protagonist of this chapter most in the early days were 'Rapper's Delight' by the Sugarhill Gang and the work of dub's pioneer, Lee 'Scratch' Perry, although Hodgson watched them only on television, rather than attending their concerts. For MC Tunes the music of these artists was 'real', because stripped to the basics and upon hearing them, one wanted to jump, dance and imitate the sounds emitted by them. This was also popular music according to one of the definitions of 'popular music': it 'reflected or 'represented' ordinary people who tuned into it. Such music had a class dimension: it appealed to those with no formal training in listening to music. However, in the actual context of New York the productions of Sugarhill Gang were seen as fake as they were designed by the label. Moreover, Big Bank Hank from Sugarhill Gang stole Grandmaster Caz's raps.

MC Tunes' linking 'real' with hip hop also brings to mind the discourse on hip hop as 'real music' (as opposed to rock, which by this point, namely late 1980s to early 1990s, lost this quality). Simon Reynolds pointed out in an essay, published in *The Wire* magazine that

> 'real' has two meanings. First, it means authentic, uncompromised music that refuses to sell out to the music industry and soften its message for crossover. 'Real' also signifies that the music reflects a 'reality' constituted by late capitalist economic instability, institutionalized racism, and increased surveillance and harassment of youth by the police. 'Real' means the death of the social: it means

> corporations who respond to increased profits not by raising pay or improving benefits but by ... downsizing (the laying off the permanent workforce in order to create a floating employment pool of part-time and freelance workers without benefits or job security) (quoted in Fisher 2009: 10).

Although MC Tunes' favourite artists were not British, they were black, as also were many of MC Tunes' neighbours and friends, and eventually his collaborators, like the previously mentioned Johnny Jay. His preference for American music pointed to Britain lagging behind in hip hop, as his relation with ZTT and Factory demonstrates. His own work was meant to fill this gap: make 'real' music in both senses of the word.

In this context it is worth comparing MC Tunes to Morrissey. Morrissey epitomizes everything MC Tunes is not, despite living only several miles away. This is because rhythm plays a less important function in the work of the Smiths, and because Morrissey, despite his interest in the working-class life, offers a 'highly processed', poeticized and refined version of reality. Although what inspired MC Tunes might not be so different from what interested Morrisey, such as life full of drugs and crime, the events he referred to had to reach his lyrics directly and fast, before they faded from his memory. This was what made his music 'real' in Hodgson's own view. Smoking a joint, when writing the lyrics and melody, facilitated this process.

However, it is notable that for MC Tunes performing rap in a way that was 'real' did not preclude his adoption of an accent that was not his own. Rather than performing in the strong working-class Manchester accent that is his natural form of speech, he imitated the American accents of his musical heroes. If his music can be said to represent in any way the Moss Side that produced him, it is that it represents the musical soundtrack of the area, the sounds that his friends on the estate were listening to, rather than those they produced in conversation. MC Tunes admits to having been annoyed by critical comments about his Americanized vocal delivery. He cites the example of Mick Jagger adopting the vocal styles of black American rhythm and blues singers, and it is worth mentioning that in the 1960s a 'transatlantic style of singing' dominated British rock music. It is still relatively rare to hear in the UK an identifiable local, regional or even national accent in mainstream rock and pop. Arguably, in the UK grime scene, artists have found success using their British regional accents and street slang and those characteristics are seen as chief indicators of their authenticity. That said, as MC Tunes himself ruefully points out, sometimes even these local accents are fake, as Manchester-based grime artists tend to adopt South London accents. This comment also suggests that in hip hop Manchester has again lagged behind London.

MC Tunes uses his native accent only once on any of his records. The track 'My Own Worst Enemy' is a first-person narrative of a day in the life of a heroin addict, which is based on the life of Hodgson's uncle, who died at an early age as a result of drug addiction. The lyrics in the form of interior soliloquy are delivered for the most part using MC Tunes' usual American accent and there are no specifics that would identify any particular location for the story. However, there is a moment when the narrator is woken from a drug-induced semi-conscious state by an angry householder who threatens him and berates him as a 'dirty little smackhead'. For this interruption of the interior monologue Tunes drops into his own highly identifiable Manchester accent, as the imagined urban landscape of US hip hop is disrupted by the hard realities of Moss Side.

In common with Eminem whose work is inspired by the present day and history of Detroit, in Hodgson's other lyrics and even titles of his songs, such as 'Mancunian Blues', 'Primary Rhyming' and 'Tunes Splits the Atom', he refers to Manchester. However, both in his work and his off-screen pronouncements, MC Tunes draws on different aspects than Eminem. First of all, while Eminem is quite specific about Detroit; Manchester is less concrete in the lyrics of our protagonist. One has to know that its author is from Moss Side to link them to this part of Manchester.[2] The name of this district is not mentioned; neither do we learn about its landmarks or inhabitants. The lack of what Forman describes as the *extreme local* can be attributed to the different position of MC Tunes from those of American and even London hip hop artists within their local scenes. While his American and London counterparts were part of a developed or fast developing hip hop scene, MC Tunes was one of a small group of artists and hence he proclaimed his belonging to Manchester rather than a specific district or street.

Often Manchester appears in lyrics of songs that do not have much to do with Manchester, as in 'Tunes Splits the Atom', which is essentially about writing, performing and experiencing music or perhaps just rap. We find here such lines:

> Make it bang, combinating with slang
> Manchester the dance capital of England

We find no justification for such claims in any references to the musical history of the city. Rather the lyrics refer to a phenomenon that was unfolding as the song was being recorded and what would in retrospect be named

---

2. This might be a reason why Haslam does not mention MC Tunes in his chapter on Moss Side in *Manchester England*.

Madchester. The statement that Manchester was the 'dance capital of England' could simply be considered an extension of the tribal bragging of hip hop in which the expertise of the performer is used competitively, not only to assert their own verbal superiority but to champion the neighbourhood and local street culture within which their skills have been developed, except that, as mentioned earlier, on this occasion the entire city is praised. The way in which the line within 'Tunes Splits the Atom' is delivered seems to take the regional assertiveness further. The rhythm of the lyric places the word 'dance' on an unstressed upbeat so that the word is almost lost in the delivery; for a moment in 1990 it sounds as though MC Tunes is proclaiming a more fundamental northward shift in the seat of power. But the audacity of the claim derives from the context in which the London-based media and music industry were belatedly beginning to acknowledge the significance of the musical and cultural trends emerging from the Manchester music scene.

'Tunes Splits the Atom' both exemplifies and documents the musical syntheses that underpinned and characterized the developing Manchester music scene. Although the title of the song promises *fission*, the record itself represents *fusion*. That fusion between US hip hop and European electronic pop music is best illustrated by MC Tunes' 1990 appearance performing the song live on *The Word*, a youth-oriented Channel 4 television programme. *The Word* was broadcast from a London-based studio, but one of its main presenters was Terry Christian, a presenter and journalist whose attitudes and strong regional accent proclaimed his working-class Manchester origins. It was Christian who introduced the live performance of 'Tunes Splits the Atom' on the show, describing MC Tunes as 'one white boy who can certainly rap' and flagging up the fact that the performer was from Moss Side in Manchester.

Musically, MC Tunes is connecting to the funk rhythms of hip hop in a way that serves to humanize the techno of 808 State. The technology that made early 90s techno meant that while it was possible to create incredibly fast and complex rhythmic patterns, the slurring of beats or the use of small polymetric gestures was more difficult to achieve. In creating the instrumental track, 808 State have used various strategies to alleviate the unvarying regularity of the rhythm patterns, for example the bassline pushes the stressed beat forward an eighth-beat (quaver) on every second bar so that the stress falls at the beginning of bar one and at the end of bar two. This skip beat gives a forward momentum to the rhythm. But it is MC Tunes' vocal performance that adds the subtler syncopations associated with US funk and hip hop. This approach to dance music production was not new; electronic dance music of the kind pioneered by Georgio Moroder had adopted the strategy of the 'Diva' which undoubtedly helped early EDM records to achieve crossover appeal from the clubs and raves to the mainstream pop music charts. The Diva, often a female US female vocalist, overlaid the melodic, vocal decorations and rhythmic phrasing of the American soul song onto this essentially European form of electronic music. Donna Summer's 'I Feel Love' set the template for this kind of dance record.

In the live TV performance of 'Tunes Splits the Atom' the fusion between hip hop and techno is underlined in the visual aspects of the performance. MC Tunes and his two young black male dancers are dressed in versions of the urban street fashions so familiar from US rap videos. The musicians by contrast are depicted as 'boffins', perhaps even as caricatures of the mad scientist, dressed in white lab coats and safety googles. The contribution of 808 State is celebrated and perhaps even mythologized in the final verse, when MC Tunes name checks the band members Graham Massey, Darren Partington, Andrew Barker and Martin Price:

> Emphasize the nature of the beast
> With a musical compromise
> Between Darren, Price, Massey, and Barker
> Built like volcano, the talent's the lava.

As this example also shows, rather than denigrating Manchester as a hotbed of criminality, Manchester is here celebrated. Hodgson does not draw on what is known as 'ruin porn', namely gaining cultural and monetary capital from presenting something as a site of obscene poverty, which is a norm in American hip hop and, to an extent, British grime, as the very term 'grime' suggests. This reflects, in our view, MC Tunes' ambivalent attitude to Moss Side and Manchester at large. On the one hand, it was a place where he had a very hard life and which contributed to the premature deaths of his father and uncle. On the other hand, he could not live and create anywhere else.

## Conclusions

This chapter attempted to uncover a largely forgotten, but important figure in the Manchester music scene, arguing that MC Tunes was a highly gifted rapper and champion of Manchester as a music city. In particular, his claim that Manchester was 'the dance capital of England' highlighted that the new dance music was emerging from the clubs of Manchester.

We also tried to account for reasons why he did not achieve a popularity that in our view he deserved, drawing attention to factors such as the lack of a developed hip hop scene in Manchester, and the strong association of Manchester with a different type of music. Had Hodgson lived and worked in London, his career might have looked different. We also acknowledged certain personal traits of Hodgson, such as being fiercely independent, as well as somewhat rebellious and unruly, which might put off his patrons and collaborators. It is also true that as a white working-class artist from the North of England, who was championing the music of black America to a London-based label that looked to continental Europe for its inspiration, MC Tunes faced some unique challenges in his career. In conclusion, he can be described as an artist who missed his star largely because he missed his time.

## About the Authors

Les Gillon is an academic and musician based within the School of Journalism, Media and Performance at the University of Central Lancashire. In addition to his work in the field of aesthetics and the visual arts, he is involved in practice-based research in music composition and performance. His book on the Turner Prize, *The Uses of Reason in the Evaluation of Artworks*, is published by Palgrave Macmillan.

Ewa Mazierska is Professor of Film Studies at the University of Central Lancashire. She has written over twenty monographs and edited collections on film and popular music. They include *Relocating Popular Music* (Palgrave, 2015), edited with Georgina Gregory, *From Self- Fulfillment to Survival of the Fittest: Work in European Cinema from the 1960s to the Present* (Berghahn, 2015), *Falco and Beyond: Neo Nothing Post of All* (Equinox, 2014) and *European Cinema and Intertextuality: History, Memory, Politics* (Palgrave Macmillan, 2011). Mazierska's work has been translated into nearly twenty languages, including French, Italian, German, Chinese, Korean, Portuguese, Estonian and Serbian. She is principal editor of a Routledge journal, *Studies in Eastern European Cinema*.

## References

Christian, Terry. 2012. 'Q & A with MC Tunes. 15/11/2012'. https://www.youtube.com/watch?v=7ZlV562lr3M (accessed 23 April 2017).

Evans, Adam. 2014. 'On the Origins of Hip Hop: Appropriation and Territorial Control of Urban Space'. In *Consuming Architecture*, ed. Daniel Maudlin and Marcel Vellinga, 185–201. London: Routledge.

Evans, Eric J. 2013. *Thatcher and Thatcherism*, 3rd edn. London: Routledge.

Fisher, Mark. 2009. *Capitalist Realism: Is There No Alternative?* Winchester: Zero Books.

Forman, Murray. 2002. *The 'Hood Comes First: Race, Space, and Place in Rap and Hip-Hop*. Middletown, CT: Wesleyan University Press.

Frith, Simon. 2007. *Taking Popular Music Seriously*. Farnham: Ashgate.

Graves, Steven. 2009. 'Hip Hop: A Postmodern Folk Music'. In *Sound, Society and the Geography of Popular Music*, ed. Ola Johansson and Thomas L. Bell, 245–60. Farnham: Ashgate.

Gregory, Georgina. 2014. 'Madchester and the Representations of the North-South Divide in the 1980s and 1990s'. *Manchester Region History Review* 25: 93–149.

Haslam, Dave. 1999. *Manchester England: The Story of the Pop Cult City.* London: Fourth Estate.

Lee, C. P. 2002. *Shake, Rattle and Rain: Popular Music Making in Manchester 1955–1995.* Ottery St. Mary: Hardinge Simpole.

Peel, Ian. 2004. 'Warriors of Pop, 21 Years of ZTT'. *Record Collector* (September): 48–57.

—2008. *Zang Tuum Tumb* (box set sleeve notes). ZTT.

Seaman, Duncan. 2010. 'Graham Massey, 808 State'. *Yorkshire Evening Post*, 19 March.

Stone, Declan, and Garech Stone. 2010. 'An Interview with Paul Morley'. *The Stone Twins.* http://www.stonetwins.com (accessed 17 April 2017).

Walmsley, Howard. 2011. *Nish Clish Bangin: The MC Tunes Tapes* (documentary about MC Tunes).

Warner, Timothy. 2003. *Pop Music Technology and Creativity: Trevor Horn and the Digital Revolution.* Farnham: Ashgate.

Wiseman-Trowse, Nathan. 2008. *Performing Class in British Popular Music.* Houndmills: Palgrave.

# 10 Hashtag 0161: Did Bugzy Malone Put Manny on the Map?

## Kamila Rymajdo

*Walk With Me*, Bugzy Malone implores his listeners with the title of his debut EP, and they did. In July 2015 the record went in at number 8 on the British album chart, catapulting Bugzy to the position of highest charting grime artist that year, relegating the previous highest grime album entrant, JME, who went in at number 12 in May 2015 with his second album *Integrity>*. That Bugzy is not from grime's home of London is what made this even more momentous an event for the genre. Following that release Bugzy was nominated for two Music of Black Origin awards (MOBOs): 'Best Newcomer' and 'Best Grime Act', and although he did not win, the honours were huge if one takes into consideration that the artist was overwhelmed to even be mentioned by the awarding body on Twitter, only a few months before the nominations were announced. Such was the extent of his gratitude that his nemesis Chip chided him for it on his track 'Light Work' from the *Light Work EP* with the line 'gassed off a MOBO tweet'. This rapid rise to UK-wide recognition would suggest that Bugzy had a huge following, especially in his home town, which he repeatedly referenced during this period with the refrain '0161, Manny on the map'. But Bugzy's trajectory was altogether more complicated, as was his place on the Manchester music scene.

> Studies of the music industry often fall into one of two broad perspectives: those which emphasise corporate power, and those which, critiquing this, emphasise the active role of the consumers of music. More recently, a 'middle ground' has emerged, informed by critical political economy, which views the industry as in tension between these two polarities (Shuker 2001: 31).

My investigation of Bugzy Malone's place within the Manchester urban music scene and the wider grime scene during the year 2015 falls into this middle ground, especially in light of the rapidly changing landscape of the production and consumption of grime music in particular, and popular music at large. The urban landscape has also been changing, with cities increasingly becoming 'locations where knowledge, creativity and innovation flourish' (Hospers 2009: 354). It therefore makes sense that it is in cities such as Manchester and Bristol that grime's second wave has been breeding, even if Bugzy described where he is from as 'a little town' on 2015's 'Relegation Riddim'.

Moreover, the start of Bugzy's career is ripe for a dissection because

> [m]ost histories emphasise musical forms that at their moment of origin had small followings, and that were often produced on the margins of the record industry. ... The historians of popular culture, then, privilege forms of popular music and artists that were not dominant in popular music culture of the time. Rather, they emphasise new sounds and styles of artists. The historical story is that they are part of a new type of music that starts in the margins and moves into the mainstream (Wall 2003: 12–13).

Grime music, a relatively new genre, but one that has been creeping into the mainstream since the mid-2010s, has since its inception been mostly linked with London. However, it chose as one of its defining artists of 2015, a newcomer from the margins—from the North.

**Defining Grime**

Grime, in Bugzy's words on 2015's 'M.E.N' from the *Walk With Me* EP is 'English hip-hop' though the genre is more prevalently associated with UK garage, drum and bass and dancehall, emerging in the early 2000s on UK pirate radio stations such as Rinse FM, with key pioneers including Wiley, Dizzee Rascal, Kano, Jammer, Skepta, JME, Ghetts and Lethal Bizzle. 'Contrary to American hip-hop's rootsy rhetoric, about being "real" and knowing and respecting your history, grime is a year zero sound which asks only what's next and seeks to get there first' (Hancox 2013: 179). Prominent grime crews included Boy Better Know, So Solid Crew, Newham Generals and Roll Deep, with Boy Better Know's Skepta now an international superstar, backed by American hip-hop heavyweights such as Kanye West, A$AP Mob's Young Lord and A$AP Rocky and Canadian hip-hop superstar Drake.[1] Wiley is widely regarded as the 'God-

---

1. Skepta toured Europe and America extensively throughout 2015, with an appearance at Drake's OVO Fest, as well as being shouted out by Kanye West at the American rapper's 2015 Brit Awards performance, where West invited the whole Boy Better Know crew onto the stage, followed up by a gig where several artists from BBK warmed up for the star at a London gig at the KOKO venue the same week. A$AP Mob's Young Lord col-

father of grime' and invented his own sound, Eskibeat, while Dizzee Rascal won the Mercury Music Prize in 2003 for *Boy in da Corner*. The prize was awarded to Skepta in 2016 for his album *Konnichiwa*. Sonically, the genre began with tracks that were strictly 140 beats per minute and had low bassline frequencies, but as the genre evolved, so did its parameters. In 2005, *The New Yorker*'s Sasha Frere-Jones said 'grime sounds as if it had been made for a boxing gym, one where the fighters have a lot of punching to do but not much room to move' (Frere-Jones 2005).

A handful of major record deals for grime's mid-00s rising stars, such as Shystie's signing with Polydor and Lady Sovereign's signing with Roc-A-Fella, signalled grime's ascent into the mainstream. However, Form 696's creation in 2006[2] to target violence at music events caused many urban gigs to get cancelled, slowing down the commercialization of the genre (Thomas 2015). In spite of this, 2009 saw 'five number ones from different grime artists including: Dizzee Rascal, Tinchy Stryder and Chipmunk' (Thomas 2015), while in October 2014 Stormzy, fresh from winning a MOBO award for 'Best Grime Act', became the first unsigned MC to perform on the *Later...with Jools Holland* show, which is the most watched music show on mainstream TV in the UK. In 2015 he won 'Best International Act' at the BET Awards (Thomas 2015).

The genre is now widely accepted to be in its second wave, with sub-genres such as wonky grime and weightless, as championed by artists such as Mumdance and Logos (Fraser 2014). With instrumental grime on the rise, many now believe MCs are no longer essential for a piece of music to be defined as grime. However, the majority of grime tracks do still contain raps, which often take as their subject matter sends or disses, which are usually aimed at fellow grime artists.

It was through a diss that Bugzy came to prominence, with a widely praised appearance on Charlie Sloth's BBC 1Xtra 'Fire In The Booth' segment of his 'The Rap Show', which was the fastest 'Fire In The Booth' appearance to reach 1 million views on YouTube. In the freestyle Bugzy entered into a war of words with fellow grime artist Chip (formerly Chipmunk), culminating in the single 'Relegation Riddim', the video for which was filmed in Chip's home district of Tottenham, seen by many in the industry as a daring move by Bugzy. The beef was originally between Chip and Tinie Tempah, and Bugzy was later accused,

---

laborated with Skepta on 2014's 'It Ain't Safe' and A$AP Rocky has professed his love of grime in many interviews.

2. Introduced by the London Metropolitan Police, the risk assessment form requested promoters and licensees in 21 London boroughs to disclose the personal details of all performers listed on events, as well as the genre of music and likely ethnicities of target audiences.

especially by Chip, of jumping on it to further his own career, with Chip going as far as to say he 'birthed' Bugzy's career with the clash on his track '96 Bars of Revenge' featured on the *Believe & Achieve Episode 2* EP. With his battles appearing to be strategically chosen with an already famous, specifically London, grime MC, it seems Bugzy had little faith in the relevance of Manchester and Manchester-based grime artists aside from himself. Moreover, there are several implicit messages of alienating himself from the city's music scene on Bugzy's output as well as in his conduct, and these two factors, I will argue, are part of the reason Bugzy became so successful outside of Manchester.

**The North, the Music Industry and Grime**

> Attempts at defining the North are more frequently made than is the case for other English regions. This is clearly suggestive of its status as England's most important region, but it also underlines its essentially subordinate relationship to the 'South' (Russell 2004: 14).

This subordination, like in other areas structuring the cultural politics of a region, is evident in music, as far back as the mid-eighteenth century, when 'there were perhaps 1,500 musicians in the metropolis' while 'no other town managed to support more than about 50' (Russell 2004: 209). 'Over the twentieth century, London maintained its dominant position and, indeed, enhanced it from the 1920s as the establishment of the BBC, the largely south-eastern-based recording and film industries and a plethora of new dance halls and cafes added to its advantages' (Russell 2004: 209). This clear-cut way of producing and distributing music was 'carried out by people with a number of equally well-defined roles. A&R agents "discovered" the potential talent and signed them to the label' (Wikström 2013: 123). The fact that most record labels were based in London makes it easy to understand the city's dominance during the last century.

However, the music industry has changed in the last two decades, most importantly by moving its operations almost entirely online. The 'Internet makes it possible for the artists, musicians and technicians working together on a recording to be located in entirely different locations around the world' (Wikström 2013: 128). In turn, this creates musical scenes that are completely decentralized. And yet, despite such changes, Manchester's grime artists still failed to chart in the same way London artists did when the genre first burst onto the musical landscape. A possible reason for this is the way music began to be distributed during this specific time. With illegal downloading through sites such as Napster prevalent in the early 2000s, as well as the popularity of pirate radio stations, chart music was not truthfully reflecting what the younger generation was listening to. The grime artists that did chart were the ones with record deals, whose music came out legitimately, on CDs. Still, by the mid-00s, the Record Industry began its 'subtle reclamation of the word "download"' (Barfe 2005: 350). File-sharing technology was finally adopted by giants such as Apple and '[t]he advent of an official download chart, as happened in the UK in August 2004, is indicative of the industry's belated change of heart' (Barfe 2005: 350). With crackdowns on illegal downloading and the ascent of Apple's Music store, it seemed that what was in the charts would now more accurately reflect what people were actually listening to. And yet the grime music which began to chart after this shift was still London-centric. Therefore, when in 2011 the aforementioned BBC Radio 1Xtra DJ Charlie Sloth posed the question, why are there no big grime stars from the North of England, it seemed like a legitimate concern worth investigating.

In his documentary for the station, entitled *It's Grime Up North*, Sloth began his journey in search of the answer, by first interviewing several urban stars at a MOBO awards pre-party, where it soon became evident that many artists could not name even one MC from outside London. The situation was indeed very bad, which seems strange given that a Northerner by the very characteristics that are ascribed to Northerners would be a perfect candidate for a grime star: '[He] has "grit", he is grim, "dour" [and] plucky' (Kohl 2007: 111). Then, there is Manchester's rich musical past, ostensibly a perfect breeding ground for new generations of musicians. When discussing such a long history it is difficult to know where to start, but because grime is a genre that relies heavily on nightclubs, I will focus on Manchester's clubbing history to show how it created a blueprint for musicians beginning their careers in the city in the 2000s.

'Throughout the 1980s the student body in Manchester was increasing year by year, until in 1989 the university campus was the second largest in Europe' (Lee 2002: 211). Beneficiaries of this shift were places such as The Haçienda club, and its adjoining Factory Records, which kick-started the careers of some of Manchester's most famous bands. This business model is sure to have influenced Murkage, the Manchester club night, which emerged on the underground scene in the mid-00s. Championing urban genres such as dubstep and indeed grime, the club night eventually gave birth to a band of the same name, with their 2011 track 'Paperweight' described by the *Manchester Evening News* as 'the best record to come out of the city for 15 years' (Quinn 2014). However, despite appearances at BBC Introducing and BBC 1Xtra stages at Leeds and Reading festivals in 2011 and 2013 respectively, and airplay from BBC Radio 1 and 1Xtra, their 2014 debut album *Of Mystics & Misfits* failed to gain the kind of recognition their first releases did, and in spite of rising popularity in France, the band eventually disbanded in 2015. Although their career was relatively short, what the example of Murkage illustrates is that there definitely was a concurrent urban scene in the North to that in the South, and it was creating urban music artists of high calibre. So why the lack of grime stars?

Travelling to Liverpool, Manchester, Leeds, Sheffield and Newcastle, Sloth found several possible causes for the state of affairs: lack of local radio station backing; heavy indie and rock and roll musical history of cities such as Manchester and Liverpool, where grime or hip-hop have never been synonymous with the cities' identities; and a lack of local support networks for any up-and-coming stars. Also, unlike in London, in the North, according to the documentary at least, there seemed to be no crews.[3] There is no overt brotherly love amongst musicians like we see in Boy Better Know in any of the cities Sloth visits, a sentiment echoed by Bugzy himself during his 'Fire In The Booth' performance where he raps that Manchester is a city where 'nobody's impressed and don't wanna see nobody progress'. Of course every MC Sloth interviews in the film has his 'associates' with whom they posture, but they are usually not fellow artists, like in the London crews. However, the most poignant thing about Sloth's documentary is that none of the artists featured have since made it big. After showcasing his two favourite MCs from all those he met on his travels, at a 1Xtra Live event at Manchester's Apollo venue, the last scene shows us a relieved Sloth saying to camera, 'the roadtrip's over, I can go home', which seems to contradict his previous commitment to putting the North of England on the grime map. But, several years later, Sloth did come through for the North for real with his backing of Bugzy and eventual signing of him to his record label Grimey Limey, which is even more impressive given that Bugzy was not even on the local grime map at the time of the making of the film (as his absence from it testifies).

In his book *Manchester England: The Story of the Pop Cult City*, former Haçienda DJ, Dave Haslam, writes that

> In the long story of Manchester's urban popular culture there are creative booms and slumps, cycles of action and reaction. In some ways this pattern mirrors the economic cycle. As far back as the 1840s Friedrich Engels had observed that the British economy was locked into a cycle that gives rise to a crisis every five or six years; a 'perennial round' of 'prosperity, crisis, prosperity, crisis' (Haslam 2000: 162).

3. Collectives of artists, producers, DJs and other creative affiliates working under an umbrella name, often collaborating on joint projects or featuring on each other's tracks. An example is Boy Better Know.

The year 2011, when Sloth's film was made, was a year of continuing recession, and for the music industry, the year started with an especially bad downturn, due to HMV's announcement of the closure of 60 stores nationwide. Ironically, in Sloth's documentary we see hopeful MCs giving Charlie their CDs, which can be read as a sign that the North is, true to stereotype, always behind the forward-thinking South. Another reading of Sloth's receiving the countless CDs is the continued power of radio. It appears, too, that in 2015 Sloth's power had not diminished. At that year's Rated Awards, described by *VICE* magazine's online music imprint Noisey as 'the first proper attempt at an awards show that champions British urban music from the bottom to the top' (Zadeh 2015), the broadcaster won best DJ. Still, despite radio remaining relevant, and thus being a possible main cause for the lack of grime stars outside of London, there are now more ways of getting music to large numbers of audiences, and new grime releases are now more often than not premiered via YouTube music channels such as SB.TV, Link Up TV and GRM Daily (whose power was certified by its launch of the Rated Awards). The sheer amount of channels would make it seem that getting noticed should be getting easier than in the past. However, despite all the new, supposedly more democratic, means of distribution, within the grime genre music from London still ruled until 2015. I will now investigate exactly how Bugzy Malone broke through this glass ceiling.

**Who is Bugzy Malone?**

According to the track 'Childhood Memories' from his 2014 *The Journal of an Evil Genius* mixtape, Bugzy Malone aka Aaron Davis was born on 20 December 1990. He hails from Manchester suburb Cheetham Hill via Moss Side (the area of Manchester associated with gang warfare in the 90s and nicknamed 'Gunchester') and after a 2007 stint in prison which he describes in his 'Fire In The Booth', he began his musical journey in 2010 with a mixtape entitled *Swagga Man*, before going on to release *Why So Serious* in 2011, with *Lost in Meanwhile City* coming out in 2012. The year 2014 saw the release of the aforementioned *The Journal of an Evil Genius* and finally his debut EP *Walk With Me* came out in 2015. He has since released a handful of singles and 2016 EP *Facing Time*. Although thus far he has not revealed the inspiration behind his name, its origin is most likely the 1976 film *Bugsy Malone* by Alan Parker, where children play the roles of gangsters. This is in tandem with Bugzy's own life history, with the MC revealing on 'M.E.N' that he had 'already been stabbed by the time I was Year 9'.

Bugzy's sound changed dramatically during the five years that passed between his first release and *Walk With Me*. The 2010 'New Sound Remix' featuring fellow Mancunian Wrigley boasts a jazzy hip-hop beat and is noticeably more positive than his later work. In 2014 he featured on Manchester band Murkage's 'Officer Parker' remix with Star One (which also featured Manga and Fallacy); however, he did not collaborate with any other local artists thereafter (aside from producers who worked on his own music) making his intentions to go it alone clear with bars like 'I'm not here to make friends' on 2015's GRM Daily 'Daily Duppy Pt. 2' catalogued on *Daily Duppy: Best of Season 4*. In a rare interview with David Renshaw of *NME*, Bugzy says of Manchester bands Oasis and Stone Roses, 'I've not kept tabs on them. ... It's different genres of music innit? Grime music is still a young culture in itself. And my goal is to move it on to a more respected place' (Renshaw 2015). His August 2015 absence from Murkage Dave's mixtape for Noisey, where the former Murkage musician collaborated with a wide spectrum of Manchester artists to create a mixtape in 48 hours (a task also undertaken by London's JME), could not be a more clearer sign that if Bugzy's aim was to push grime to a more respected place, his fellow Manchester artists were not up to scratch to do that with him. This paradox of his apparent love for Manchester through his repeated '0161, Manny on the map' refrain and simultaneous signs of his turning his back on the city is highlighted by Chip, who, on 'Light Work', pulls Bugzy up on the fact he signed with a London record label, rather than one in his own city, and on October 2015 follow-up '96 Bars of Revenge', he pulls Bugzy up again, rapping 'You're screaming 0161, But for your city, you ain't doing too much', 'Man wanna ride off the 0161 ting, But share their shine with no one.' However, Chip's shouting out of another Manchester artist on the rise, Geko, shows that inadvertently at least, Bugzy is shining a light on other Manchester talent, even if it is through tracks that are dissing him.

Bugzy's insistence on painting himself as a lone figure is evident even in the artwork on his EP, where the MC appears in the centre of an area of white negative space, which is atypically large for a grime album cover. He seems to be saying, 'there is no one else here but me', which he echoes by performing alone through most of the video for his breakout track 'M.E.N', driving aimlessly as he recounts getting arrested for an altercation in a Manchester nightclub. Comparisons with lonesome comic book characters such as Batman or his adversary Bane also heavily feature throughout his tracks, such as the single 'Pain' where he says 'Emotionally scarred so bad I was wearing a mask like Bane'. Most importantly, there are no featured artists on the EP, which is atypical for the genre. A paranoia about his success pervades the album, with lyrics such as those on 'Ready To Blow' where he says, 'I got a taste of happiness, til I realised that people just wanna steal this', 'I got a million views, And it felt like a million people wanted this seat'.

**Figure 1:** Still from Bugzy's 'M.E.N' video

In conversation with the psychoanalyst Arabella Kurtz, J.M. Coetzee describes the group experience as 'an experience in which one's ego awareness is suppressed or dwindles away. The world seems all of a sudden uncomplicated' (Coetzee and Kurtz 2015: 106). But on the negative side, a group can also be understood as 'a mob, from *mobile vulgus*, the street rabble whose passions are mobile, easily stirred, unpredictable' (Coetzee and Kurtz 2015: 106). Perhaps Bugzy feels he has enough on his plate with his own mental instability, chronicled on *Walk With Me*, where feelings of disconnectedness and an inability to deal with his feelings pervade as the running themes of the EP. On 'Pain' Bugzy laments, 'I never contacted a counsellor to get rid of this pain, I walk with it and now I'm going insane, Losing control of my own brain', with the overriding message being that he has enough to deal with and is in no condition to take on the problems of others. Perhaps also, not unwisely, he is aware than being part of a gang or a crew could land him back in jail with the chances of betrayal increasing when more people know one's (possibly illegal) business. Rapping about drug dealing and 'being known to the police', in his 'Fire In The Booth' he traverses a fine line between gangster and grime star, again something his nemesis Chip picks up on and ridicules him for on 'Hat-Trick', where he uses the letter 'G' to signify 'gangster' in the lines, 'Back to you now my lion, you're getting more G, I dunno what drugs you sell, but buy more G'. However, most importantly to this discussion, the Manchester group closest to his musical output, Murkage, failed to have a long-term career, and it is perhaps because of this particular failure that Bugzy decided to go it alone for his stab at wider success.

Aside from his past history of crime, family dysfunction is also at the heart of Bugzy's music, both before *Walk With Me* and on this EP. With bad relationships with both his father and step-father, the MC laments on *Walk With Me*'s 'Pain', 'What about a kid that had to find his dad, Only to find that he didn't like him back', before going on to say that 'I watched the family break into pieces, I thought that adults could iron out creases, I thought that family was cousins and nephews and nieces, not arguments and police'. Going through his many mixtapes, listeners will learn that Bugzy's mother married a white man and Bugzy attended a suburban school where he felt he did not fit in, on account of being black and less well off than his fellow students. A meeting with his father in his teens led the artist down a path of drug dealing and robbery, and finally jail. 'Pain' is a culmination of a body of work that deals with the MC's domestic situation; however, it feels like the most honest and hard-hitting take on his family history. It also gives us more clues as to Bugzy's possible reasons for going it alone in his music career. If his own family failed to provide him with a support network, then it is possible he has no trust in a musical support network either.

Bugzy's insistence on flying solo was further accented by his lack of endorsement of other artists on his SoundCloud page up until and inclusive of October 2015. Therefore it is noteworthy that one of the three people he did follow during this period is arguably American's most successful rapper of all time, Eminem. Bugzy, by being a fan of Eminem, therefore subconsciously, if not consciously, saw similarities between them, not least their ability to 'paint pictures with words', a phrase Bugzy uses repeatedly through all his mixtapes and on the *Walk With Me* EP. With a tendency to play out complex violent narratives, Bugzy is indeed similar to the 'Guilty Conscience' rapper in that he is aware of his flaws, drawing out not only possible outcomes for violent acts he might commit, but also meditating on situations he has handled badly and people he has hurt. Moreover, with Eminem as a role model, it is clear why local success did not satisfy Bugzy.

The similarities between Bugzy and Eminem draw attention to the fact that Bugzy's early output certainly, and his later work arguably, lean more towards hip-hop than grime. After all, Bugzy was making music when Sloth's documentary was made, but if the DJ knew of Bugzy at that time, he either did not class him as a grime act or did not rate him. So how did the artist end up on the 2015 MOBO awards 'Best Grime Act' shortlist? The answer will no doubt have a lot to do with the evolution of grime as a genre and its incorporation of elements of other genres, such as hip-hop and pop. Another factor is the tastes of grime's new fans. This new generation's preferences are noted with much distaste by grime's older MCs, and importantly to this argument, Bugzy's main nemesis Chip, who repeatedly raps about the need for grime fans to learn about the genre's history. On 'School of Grime' from his *Believe & Achieve Episode 1* EP, which features old-timers D Double E and Jammer, Chip chides 'I went to a school of grime, I didn't see you that time', while D Double E spits 'Represent London, I represent grime' and Jammer adds 'D Double E, Chippy and the Murkle, Man are coming from the Lord of the Mics school', referencing the clash culture Jammer was at the heart of, where MCs would battle each other in front of live audiences at ticketed events filmed for DVDs. For the older MCs, London and clashes are still defining features of the genre. But for Bugzy, 'the headmaster of my time', as he describes himself on 'Relegation Riddim', there are new rules to follow. Indeed, despite calls from the culture's leaders and fans alike, the two MCs did not clash at any point during their beef, with Bugzy eventually abandoning it to focus on touring and making more music in 2016.

## Neoliberalism and the Mancunian Psycho

> [The] development of music has been profoundly influenced by the development of capitalism. ... To become a commodity—a thing that is exchanged for money on a systematic basis—individual musical constructions must be capable of being parceled up in ways that allow mass production and mass sale. ... Economists approach the music industry, like all industries, by looking separately at supply and demand (Lovering 1998: 33).

However, unlike in other industries, supply and demand are a lot more difficult to predict and so 'investment is shaped by highly subjective corporate projections regarding future consumption patterns' (Lovering 1998: 33). With the music industry changing rapidly and dramatically with the advent of peer-to-peer file sharing, digitalization and increased fan participation through social media, those predictions are ever harder to make. I believe that Bugzy's success was a culmination of a careful strategy of tapping into this chain of supply and demand and breaking away from certain cultural shackles. Manchester, a city associated with left-wing politics and a musical heritage that produced groups rather than solo artists, was ripe for change, as was the grime genre, focused too long on London-centric artists and crews. Having carefully bided his time, Bugzy entered the scene at just the right moment to ensure maximum profit and success, making sure his EP dropped before the long-awaited release of grime's biggest star Skepta, and in time for the MOBO nominations, a recognition that cemented Bugzy as a player in grime's top league. By painting himself as the only credible Manchester grime artist, Bugzy created a situation where the only supply was himself, while the demand for more varied embodiments of grime grew with grime's second wave.

That Bugzy concentrates on his own story is also typical of the neoliberal condition. It is an ideology focused on the individual, which is famously satirized by the character of Patrick Bateman in Bret Easton Ellis' seminal 1991 novel *American Psycho*. There are several comparisons to be drawn between the novel and its film adaptation, and Bugzy's music and image, and I believe it is this irony of being the perfect neoliberalist, whilst at the same time growing increasingly detached from the outside world, that was at the heart of his 2015 streak of success. Audiences who have grown up on talent shows such as the *X-Factor* want both, someone they can relate to, as well as someone to ridicule, and Bugzy embodies both sides of the coin. Whereas other artists have been one or the other, risen and fallen, then perhaps risen again, such as Bugzy's enemy Chip, Bugzy was able to symbolize opposing facets concurrently. Simultaneously representative of mainstream and underground music, with his careful strategy of giving very few interviews, he managed to be enigmatic, while being very open in his lyrics ensured optimal relatability. Utilizing these polarities in subtle ways, as opposed to his predecessors, who went from serious grime artists to comical pop stars, was integral to Bugzy's carefully constructed identity.

The artwork for *Walk With Me* is one of many features that legitimize the comparison between Bugzy's character and Patrick Bateman, the stockbroker and serial killer central to Ellis' novel. Bugzy's name is written in red in a style that connotes the letters etched with a finger dipped in blood. One of the most recognizable promotional images from the film version of *American Psycho* depict a crazed Bateman with his mouth open and blood splattered all over his face, against a background of white negative space. Although it is doubtful whether Bugzy was influenced by this particular image specifically, the similarities of the use of white negative space and blood are the first of many other aesthetic likenesses. Both Bateman and Bugzy are fond of wearing leather gloves, signifying violent acts about to be committed, and in the title track of Bugzy's 2014 mixtape, *The Journal Of An Evil Genius*, entitled 'Serial Killer', the rapper wears a coat that bears a striking resemblance to the one worn by Bateman in the film adaptation when he commits one of his murders. Moreover, much like the first-person *American Psycho*, Bugzy's mixtape is a confessional piece of work and each of the tracks is accompanied by a video, adding another layer of ominousness. In the opening of 'Serial Killer' Bugzy tells us how being depressed turned him to fantasize about killing everyone around him, and a similar disaffect plays a part in Bateman's story. On 'Unwelcome Guest' Bugzy talks of being visited by a demon, who teases him and questions his situation in life. In the video Bugzy plays the demon as well as himself; as the demon his eyes turn into black circles and the lighting becomes tinged with red. This slight change suggests that the demon is another version of Bugzy himself. On 'Childhood Memories' Bugzy spits bars to a fictional therapist about problems during his formative years, while 'Troubled & Tormented' sees Bugzy break into a house and rap that him and 'Luficer are similar, we're both outcasts' before going on to kill the man inside this house, who he tells his listeners, was a former friend. The mother of the victim turns out to be the therapist he was confiding in previously, and the story comes full circle as the woman's voiceover tells us that the killer preyed on victims' close ones in a calculated game of causing maximum pain and distress.

**Figure 2:** Still from Bugzy's 'Serial Killer' video

Like Bateman, Bugzy is an avid consumer, boasting on 'Daily Duppy Pt. 2' how he 'left with a backpack, came back with a suitcase full of brand new snapbacks in it'. Snapbacks, or hats, are not Bugzy's only weakness either. On *Walk With Me*'s 'Watch Your Mouth' he confesses, 'I just got the North Face with the black bits, I just got a self-portrait, that's sick, I just got a pair of trainers with my name on, All in the same day, that's a hat-trick', which is reminiscent of the many inventories of possessions Patrick Bateman provides. Bugzy's house is 'cocaine white' according to the lyrics and as depicted in the video for 'M.E.N', also much like Bateman's New York apartment. However, the biggest likeness between the characters is their lack of belonging and being part of a 'real', tangible world. Similarly to the case of Bateman, in Bugzy's narratives the line between what actually happened and what is fantasy is always blurred, not least because of Bugzy's 'bad boy' persona. Whilst Bugzy professes his love of Manchester, he is, by all accounts, detached from its scene, as Bateman is detached from his reality, so much so that when he speaks, his friends and colleagues often think he is saying something completely different, for example when he is talking to a club patron who asks Bateman what he does for a living and Bateman says, 'murders and executions mostly', but the patron understands it as 'mergers and acquisitions' (*American Psycho* 2000).

In spite of, or perhaps because of, being an abhorrent murderer, Patrick Bateman became the emblem of a generation and Bret Easton Ellis' most notorious character. It is therefore likely that, by possessing so many similar characteristics, Bugzy is destined for comparable longevity in the cultural consciousness.

## Who Run Tingz?

It must be noted that while Bugzy decided to paint himself as Manchester's only credible grime artist, there were several signs of the opposite being true in 2015. Wiley, the 'Godfather of grime', collaborated with Manchester grime artists Wrigz and Trigga as recently as 2014, with Wrigz featuring on 'Bloodtype' on Wiley's *Snakes & Ladders* album. Predictably, Bugzy's conduct did not go unnoticed by these other Manchester musicians and on 3 August 2015 Trigga, Chimpo and Sam Binga released the video to a track entitled 'Who Run Tingz', seemingly a challenge to Bugzy's claim that he is 'Manchester's best' with lyrics like 'What them call me? The Shadow Demon soldier', which draws attention to Bugzy's apparent copying of Trigga with the adoption of this alter ego.

Trigga, a bona fide former gangster from Moss Side, with shots to his head causing him to lose one eye, started his career in the 1980s at the age of seven, as a reggae sound system MC, and went on to become a successful drum and bass artist, but traverses many genres and scenes, collaborating with major grime acts such as Skepta and Wiley (Quinn 2013). The track's lyrics make it clear that it aims to be a much more sincere ode to Manchester than Bugzy's simple '0161 Manny on the map' refrain, with the city's top producers and MCs name-checked, while the bridge's assurance that, 'A we run things, you know' underlines Trigga sees himself and his collaborators, rather than solo star Bugzy, as the musicians defining the Manchester scene. The video also features a blink-and-you'll-miss-it cameo from Manchester singer Bipolar Sunshine, a member of the collective Grey with fellow Manchester artists Jazz Purple, August&Us and GAIKA (Rymajdo 2015). GAIKA, as the opening credits reveal, directed the video, further showing that hailing from Manchester can bring artists as wide ranging as MC Trigga and genre-defying Grey together, thus accenting the unusualness of Bugzy's decision to go it completely alone.

Although Bugzy had a top ten album with *Walk With Me*, chart success is not that important within the grime genre. Indeed, even Bugzy's main opponent Chip ridicules an assumption of success based on numbers sold, rapping on 'Coward' (a diss track aimed at Bugzy's ally and Chip's nemesis, Tinie Tempah): 'Don't give a fuck 'bout millions sold, Whoever's still playing the numbers game, Safe, fuck off, play on your own'. More than ever, reputations can be built as well as destroyed with a few clicks of a mouse. The danger is twofold, as, with grime entering the mainstream, it takes on the characteristics of pop, and the audiences of pop are as fickle as the genre's gatekeepers, as testified by DJ Jukess tweeting a video from inside a Manchester nightclub taken on 25 October 2015, showing a crowd cheering Chip's song 'Run Out The Ends'.

> [While] listening to music has always been a social activity...the 'virtualisation of the living-room bookshelf' radically transforms the communal aspects of a person's listening experience. Sharing this experience is no longer based on *purchase* decisions made over an extended period of time. Rather, it is based on *listening* decisions made in real time (Wikström 2013: 163; original emphasis).

Those real-time listening decisions are ever more visible on social media.

The reception to DJ Jukess' video was likely a result of the two replies that Bugzy released following five consecutive diss tracks from Chip. On 21 and 22 October 2015 Bugzy unleashed 'Wasteman' and 'Zombie Riddim'. According to a *Yahoo* article entitled 'Bugzy Malone has finally replied to Chip and people are not at all impressed' published on 21 October 2015, 'Bugzy flew to the top of the Twitter trending list, but if he was to click on his name, we doubt he'd be pleased with what people are saying' (Anon 2015). Most notably, Bugzy dropped the '0161, Manny on the map' refrain he had become famous for, thus, in one track, destroying the identity he had so carefully built up. Moreover, both tracks' reliance on repetitive hooks suggested that it was himself, rather than Chip, that Bugzy was accusing of selling out, with his club-ready catchy choruses, a stark contrast to Chip's chorus-less disses. But I believe this was a calculated move on Bugzy's part, not only playing to his strength of being able to sing a melody, but being acutely aware that grime was evolving and if he was to be the champion of 'grime 2015' then he would have to play by his own rules. Moreover, as the music industry advances, so must its players. Bugzy recognized the irony required to be a grime star in that climate: one cannot be one hundred percent 'real' when one is 'popular', therefore one must embody the facets with a playfulness. Indeed, in 'Wasteman' Bugzy laughs at himself as he begins by repeating one of his old lines, signalling to his audience that he is in on the joke; that even if he loses the battle with Chip, he is winning anyway by the sheer fact of people knowing who he is and listening to what he has to say.

**Figure 3:** Still from Bugzy's 'Wasteman' video

## Conclusion

In an August 2015 *Guardian* article entitled 'How Bugzy Malone Put Manchester on the Grime Map', Clare Considine name-checks several other Manchester artists, from Trigga to Levelz, a collective that the aforementioned Chimpo is also a part of. Consisting of fourteen members, the supergroup enjoyed steady growth following Bugzy's ascent, with appearances on 1Xtra, Rinse FM and Channel 4's music mag show *Four To The Floor*. Levelz did not engage in Bugzy's beef with Chip, and their approach to music is very different from Bugzy's, perhaps because 'music's adoption by the mainstream is presented as a decline in its social relevance or vigour' (Wall 2003: 13). The group go as far as to say they do not see themselves as a grime act, but are 'pushing towards what comes after grime' (Considine 2015). Still, as their getting booked for shows with artists such as Skepta signified, the collective were seen by promoters as close enough to grime to place them on the same billing as the genre's leading artists. If this recognition was due to Bugzy's achievements or their own hard work is difficult to quantify. The answer most likely lies somewhere in-between. Without Bugzy other Manchester grime artists would have very likely grown in popularity with the expansion of the genre, but the MC will no doubt have speeded up the process.

'Into the devil, I turn', Bugzy raps throughout his musical offerings, a phrase so overused it is one of the features of his output highlighted by Chip in his diss tracks, such as 'Run Out Riddim' where Chip teases, 'You ain't the devil, blud, you're a human being, So you can die like me'. But I believe this ability to mutate has been Bugzy's saving grace as grime continued to enter ever more fickle fan territory with its growth in popularity. However, thanks to being the calculating 'evil genius' of his time, by grabbing his chance in his 'Fire In The Booth' appearance and running with it until the bitter end, Bugzy has shown that he was one of grime's strongest fighters in 2015, and even if not single-handedly, he has certainly played a leading part in putting Manny on the map. For that, Manchester should be thankful to him.

## About the Author

Kamila Rymajdo received a Creative Writing PhD from Kingston University in 2017. Previously she studied English Language and Literature at the University of Manchester, where she also completed an MA. She publishes on music and popular culture in journals such as *Popular Music History* and magazines including *Vice*, *Mixmag*, *The Fader* and *Dazed* and she is music editor at *The Skinny North*.

## References

Anon. 2015. 'Bugzy Malone has finally replied to Chip and people are not at all impressed'. http://www.dailyecho.co.uk/news/13887100.Bugzy_Malone_has_finally_replied_to_Chip_and_people_are_not_at_all_impressed/ (accessed 3 July 2017).

Barfe, Louis. 2005. *Where Have All the Good Times Gone? The Rise and Fall of the Record Industry*. London: Atlantic Books.

Coetzee, J. M., and Arabella Kurtz. 2015. *The Good Story*. London: Harvill Secker.

Considine, Clare. 2015. 'How Bugzy Malone put Manchester on the Grime Map'. *The Guardian*, 14 August. https://www.theguardian.com/music/2015/aug/14/mc-bugzy-and-the-manchester-grime-scene (accessed 28 October 2015).

DJ Jukess. 2015. 'So yesterday we went Manchester and I took it there. The 0161 crew screaming "Run Out The Endz" MAD @OfficialChip'. *Twitter*, https://twitter.com/DJ_Jukess/status/658206436837740544 (accessed 28 October 15).

Fraser, Tomas. 2014. 'How Important are Grime Labels for the Future of the Genre?' *Noisey*, https://noisey.vice.com/en_uk/article/the-label-perspective-on-grimes-revival (accessed 6 October 2015).

Frere-Jones, Sasha. 2005. 'True Grime: A Genre's Magic Moment'. *The New Yorker*, 21 March. http://www.newyorker.com/magazine/2005/03/21/true-grime (accessed 17 October 2015).

Hancox, Dan. 2013. *Stand Up Tall: Dizzee Rascal and the Birth of Grime*. Kindle edition: Kindle Singles.

Haslam, Dave. 2000. *Manchester England: The Story of the Pop Cult City*. London: Fourth Estate Limited.

Hospers, Gert-Jan. 2009. 'What is the City but the People? Creative Cities beyond the Hype'. In *Creative Urban Milieus*, ed. Martina Heßler and Clemens Zimmermann, 353–78. Frankfurt and New York: Campus Verlag.

Kohl, Stephan. 2007. 'The "North" of "England": A Paradox?' In *Thinking Northern: Textures of Identity in the North of England*, ed. Christoph Ehland, 93–116. Amsterdam and New York: Rodopi.

Lee, C. P. 2002. *Shake, Rattle and Rain: Popular Music Making in Manchester 1950–1995*. Devon: Hardinge Simpole Publishing.

Lovering, John. 1998. 'The Global Music Industry: Contradictions in the Commodification of the Sublime'. In *The Place of Music*, ed. Andrew Leyshon, David Matless and George Revill, 31–56. London and New York: Guilford Press.

Quinn, Seamus. 2013. 'Hot Right Now: MC Trigga goes Madd Again'. *Manchester Evening News*, 20 September. https://tinyurl.com/men-6070418 (accessed 17 October 2015).

—2014. 'Hot Right Now: Murkage's French Connection'. *Manchester Evening News*, 16 June. http://preview.tinyurl.com/men-7274627 (accessed 17 October 2015).

Renshaw, David. 2015. 'Bugzy Malone Interviewed: "I'm Trying to Create Art Out of the Pain That I've Experienced"'. *NME*, 28 September. https://tinyurl.com/nme-bugzy (accessed 24 October 2015)

Russell, Dave. 2004. *Looking North: Northern England and the National Imagination*. Manchester and New York: Manchester University Press.

Rymajdo, Kamila. 2015. 'Wot Do U Call It? Manchester's GREY Collective Want to Destroy the Lazy Labels Forced on Black Musicians'. *Noisey*, https://noisey.vice.com/en_us/article/a-deep-conversation-with-manchesters-grey-collective (accessed 28 October 2015).

Shuker, Roy. 2001. *Understanding Popular Music*. London and New York: Routledge.

Thomas, Darcy. 2015. 'A Timeline of Grime from Wiley to Wretch 32 and Skepta to Stormzy'. *BBC Newsbeat*, 12 August. https://tinyurl.com/article-33878212 (accessed 17 October 2015).

Wall, Tim. 2003. *Studying Popular Music Culture*. London: Arnold.

Wikström, Patrik. 2013. *The Music Industry*. Cambridge and Malden, MA: Polity Press.

Zadeh, Joe. 2015. 'Everything We Saw at the Rated Awards, UK Rap and Grime's First Proper Awards Show'. *Noisey*, https://noisey.vice.com/en_uk/article/our-night-at-the-rated-awards-for-uk-grime-and-rap (accessed 21 October 2015).

## Films and documentaries

Harron, Mary. 2000. *American Psycho*. DVD. UK.
Sloth, Charlie. 2011. *It's Grime Up North*. BBC Radio 1Xtra Stories, https://www.youtube.com/watch?v=vhHoJ84Jdqk (accessed 17 October 2015).

## Discography

Bugzy Malone. 2014. *The Journal Of An Evil Genius* mixtape.
—2015. 'Relegation Riddim'. Bugzy Malone.
—2015. *Walk With Me*. Grimey Limey Recordings.
—2015. 'Wasteman'. Rodent Removal Records.
—2015. 'Zombie Riddim'. Rodent Removal Records.
—2016. 'Daily Duppy Pt. 2', *Daily Duppy: Best of Season 4*. GRM Daily.
Chip. 2015. *Believe & Achieve Episode 1*. Cash Motto Limited.
—2015. *Believe & Achieve Episode 2*. Cash Motto Limited.
—2015. *Dickhead*. Cash Motto Limited.
—2015. *Light Work EP*. Cash Motto Limited.
Trigga, Chimpo & Sam Binga. 'Who Run Tingz/MCR'. Girls Music.
Wiley. 2014. *Snakes & Ladders*. Big Dada.

# Index

*24 Hour Party People* 2 *see also* Winterbottom, Michael
808 State 174, 177–78, 186–87 *see also* 'Pacific State'

Aiken, John 18
American Folk Blues Tours 77, 85–89
Animals, the 3, 7
*Architectural Review* 61
Arctic Monkeys 3
Association of Independent Music (AIM) 37
*A Very British Coup* 63

Banham, Reyner 57, 61
Barber, Chris 82
Barker, Andrew 187
Basie, Count 89, *91*
Batley, West Yorkshire 130
BBC blue plaque 2017 110
Beatles, The 3, 7, 17–26, 98, 100–101, 103, 106
    *The Beatles Story* exhibition 24
Beckenham Arts Lab 101
Birmingham 9, 97, 102
Blair, Tony 21
'Blue Monday' 177 *see also* New Order
blues 76–92
blues boom 72, 78, 82, 86–88, 92
*Blues and Gospel Train, The* 86, 88–92, *91*
Bo Diddley 98–99
Bolan, Marc 101
Bolder, Trevor 105
Bourdieu, Pierre 157, 159–61, 165
Bowie, David 10, 97–108
    *Arnold Corns* project 105
    birth, Brixton 98
    brother, Terry Jones 98
    The Buzz (performed with) 99
    childhood in Beckenham and Bromley 98
    *David Bowie* LP (1967) 100–102
    *Hunky Dory* LP (1971) 102–103
    The Hype (performed with) 101
    Jones, David (real name) 98
    Kenneth Pitt (manager) 100
    The King Bees (performed with) 99
    The Kon-Rads (performed with) 98
    The Lower Third (performed with) 99
    *The Man Who Sold the World* LP (1970) 101–102
    The Mannish Boys (performed with) 99
    sexuality 106
    Ziggy Stardust 97–98, 100, 102, 105–109
Bradford 9
Bridgewater Canal 18
Brexit 136, 141
Broken Glass 11–12, 156, 158, 160–61, 171
Broonzy, 'Big' Bill 77, 82–83, 85, 88, 92
Brutalist architecture 57–72
Bugzy Malone 12–13, 190, 196, 204–206
Burawoy, Michael 25–26
Burretti, Freddie 105
Buzzcocks 47

Cabaret Voltaire 120–21, 124
Cambridge, John 101
Chants, The 27
Chester 18
Chimpo 203, 205
Chip 190, 192–93, 197–98, 200–201, 204–206
Chorley 7
Christian, Terry 186
Clapton, Eric 81, 85
Cocker, Jarvis 5, 64–69 *see also* Pulp
Coe, Jonathan 57
Cohen, Sara 24–25
Comsat Angels 63
Cooper-Clarke, John 33
Cotton Famine 78–79
Crass (band) 145
creative industries 39–40, 45–46, 49–50
cultural intermediation 45–46
'Cunard Yanks' 26

*Damage by Stereo* 178
Daniel, Ruth 42
Defoe, Daniel 18
Designers Republic 70
Detroit 182, 185
Dickens, Charles 2
Dixon, Willie 87, 89, *90*
Dizzee Rascal 191–92
*Done and Dusted* 179
Drummond, Bill 31
*Duck Rock* 176

Durutti Column, The 28
Dust Junkys 179

Eagle, Roger 8, 27–28
Echo and the Bunnymen 30–32
electro-funk 158–59
Elgar, Edward 6
Eminem 182, 185, 199
Eno, Brian 176
Eric's club 27–31
Eric's Records 31

Factory Records 24, 28, 31–32, 119, 155, 194
Fall, The 25, 33
Fatboy Slim 180
Fat Northerner 42–43
Fields, Gracie 3
Fisher, Mark 135–36, 150
*Fora do Eixo* (Off-Axis) 37, 51
Frankie Goes to Hollywood 176–77
Free Trade Hall 77, 86–87
Fulwell, Peter 28, 30
Futurama 1 (music festival) 114–15, 123–26
Futurama 2 (music festival) 126
Futurama 3 (music festival) 128
Futurama 4 (music festival) 128
Futurism 176

Gaitskell, Hugh 61
'Gangster Trippin'' 180
Gaskell, Elizabeth 2
Glasgow 9
Glastonbury 10, 179
Glossop 6
goth 127–31
Granada (Television) 77, 86, 88–89
Grandmaster Caz 183
Griffiths brothers, the 8
grime 11–13, 184, 187, 190–201, 203–206

Haçienda, the 17, 24, 27, 30, 33, 155–56, 158, 161, 167, 177, 194–95 *see also* Wilson, Tony
Hamp, Johnny 89, 91
Happy Mondays, the 33, 178 *see also* Ryder, Shaun
Harry, Bill 26
Haslam, Dave 5–6, 24, 174, 182, 195
Hatton, Derek, Cllr. 33
Hebden Bridge 4
Hebdige, Dick 142–43
Herman's Hermits 3
hip hop 11–12, 49, 135, 141, 143, 146, 153, 177–80, 183–88, 191, 195, 197, 199

Hodgson, Nicky (MC Tunes) 12, 174–89
Hooker, John Lee 87
Horn, Trevor 175–77, 189
Hucknall, Mick 30–31 *see also* Simply Red
Hull 4, 7, 10, 97–98, 100–105, 107, 109–10
Hulmes, Helen 87
Human League 62–63, 70
Hutchinson, John 101

'I Am the Resurrection' 177 *see also* Stone Roses
industrial music 120
Inevitable Records 28
Inspiral Carpets 31
International, The, Manchester club 29–30
In the City 41, 43–46
*Invisible Britain* 11, 135–37, 141–43, 146
'It's Grim Up North' 2, 5
*It's Grime Up North* 194

Jackson, Mick (film director) 63
Jagger, Mick 184 *see also* Rolling Stones
Jam, The 137–38, 142–43
Jay, Johnny 175, 179, 184
JME 190–91, 197
Johnson, Lonnie 88–89
Jones, Brian 85, 87 see also Rolling Stones
Joy Division 3, 7, 25n, 28, 31, 115, 118, 121, 124
Justified Ancients of Mu Mu, the 2

Keenan, John F. 112
Keiller, Patrick 137, 140
Kemp, Lindsay 100
Khan, Morgan 157, 160
Korner, Alexis 82, 85, 87
Kraftwerk 64
Kramer, Billy J. and the Dakotas 33

Lancashire 1–2
Lawrence, D. H. 2
Leeds 3, 7, 9–11, 36, 77, 82–83, 85, 88, 92, 112–14, 120–21, 131–32, 194–95
    Queens Hall 112, 115, 123, 125–26, 132
    Town Hall 83
Lennon, John 5
Levelz 205
Lippmann, Horst 86–87
Liverpool 4, 7–8, 11, 120, 195
    Toxteth 27
    UNESCO City of Music 17
Livesey, Yvette 42
Lomax, Alan 82
*Loneliness of the Long Distance Runner, The* 179

Long Blondes 56, 72
Lynn, Jack 58

M1 (motorway) 122
Macmillan, Harold 61
Madchester 4, 11–12, 41, 155–56, 158, 166–67, 170–71, 184, 186
Magic Village, The (Manchester club) 28–29
Mairants, Ivor 81
Major, John 21
Manchester 2, 4–9, 11–13, 77–80, 84–88, *89, 91*, 174–89, 190–91, 193–98, 200, 203–204, 206–207
    football 50
    Northern Quarter 24
    Ship Canal 18
'Mancunian Blues' (MC Tunes) 185
Marcus, George 26
Marinetti, FT 176
Massey, Graham 177, 187
Mayall, John 87
McGhee, Brownie 82, 87
McLaren, Malcolm 117, 176
MC Tunes (Nicky Hodgson) 12, 174–89 *see also* 'Mancunian Blues'; 'My Own Worst Enemy'; 'Primary Rhyming'; 'Tunes Splits the Atom'
Memphis Slim 87–89, *90*
Merseybeat 3, 103
*Mersey Beat* 26
Merseyside 21, 23
Middles, Mick 24
Móran, Raquel 24
Morley, Paul 176
Moroder, Georgio 186
Morrissey 184
Moss Side 174–75, 179–80, 182–87, 196, 203
Muddy Waters 9
Murkage 194–95, 198
Murphy, Matt 'Guitar' 88–89
Music Heritage UK 37
'My Own Worst Enemy' (MC Tunes) 185

Nairn, Ian 61, 69
National Centre for Popular Music, Sheffield 69–70
Newcastle 9, 77, 79, 83, 195
Newley, Anthony 100
New Order 3, 33, 177–78 *see also* 'Blue Monday'
NME 65, 67, 124–26, 128–29, 180, 197
'Northern Powerhouse' 23, 25
northern soul 159

Oasis 3, 7, 24, 31, 197
Off-Axis *see Fora do Eixo* (Off-Axis)
*Only Rhyme That Bites, The* 177
Orchestral Manoeuvres In The Dark 28
Orwell, George 2, 4–5

'Pacific State' (808 State) 177
Partington, Darren 187
Peace, David 122, 130
Perry, Lee 'Scratch' 183
post-punk 3, 10–11, 62–64
Price, Martin 187
'Primary Rhyming' (MC Tunes) 185
Public Image Limited 118
Pulp 3, 9, 64–69 *see also* Cocker, Jarvis
punk 10, 140, 145

'Rapper's Delight' (Sugarhill Gang) 183
Rats, the 101–102, 109
Rau, Franz 86–87
Real People, the 8, 31
Red Hot Chilli Peppers, the 179
Reich, Steve 176
Renbourn, John 81
Reynolds, Simon 62–63, 142, 144–45, 183
Richards, Keith 85, 87 *see also* Rolling Stones
Richardson, Tony 179
Ritz, the (Manchester venue) 29
*Road to Wigan Pier, The* 4
Robeson, Paul 81
Rochdale 3
Rolling Stones, The 88, 92, 99, 101, 103–104, 106 *see also* Jagger, Mick; Jones, Brian; Richards, Keith
Ronson, Mick 101–106
Russell Club (Manchester) 27–28, 30
Russell, Dave 1, 4, 6, 14
Russolo, Luigi 176
Ruthless Rap Assassins 155, 171
Ryan, Tosh 27
Ryder, Shaun 178 *see also* Happy Mondays

Salford 37
Sceaux Gardens, London 68
science fiction 121
Shakey Jake 87
Sheffield 4, 7, 9, 11, 57–72, 88, 120, 195
    Castle Market 70–72
    Gleadless Valley 60
    Hyde Park flats 59–60, *59*, 6–63, 66–67, 69
    Kelvin flats 62, 66, 68
    Park Hill 57–60, 66, 70–71
    *see also* Cocker, Jarvis; National Centre for Popular Music; Pulp

Simply Red 25 *see also* Hucknall, Mick
Skepta 191–92, 200, 203, 206
Sleaford Mods 11, 135, 138–49, 151
    'Giddy on the Ciggies' 142
    'Face to Faces' 143
    'Jobseeker' 151
    'Liveable Shit' 146–47, 151
    'McFlurry' 147
    'Tied Up in Nottz' 138–39
    'Urine Mate' 147
Sloth, Charlie 192, 194, 196, 199
Smith, Ivor 58
Smiths, the 33, 184
Spann, Otis 77, 83, 88
Spence, Basil 63
Spiders from Mars, the 98, 104–106, 110
Spivey, Victoria 88–89
stereotype 42
Stockhausen, Karlheinz 176
Stone Roses, the 33, 177 *see also* 'I Am the Resurrection'
Stormzy 192
Sugarhill Gang, the 179, 183 *see also* 'Rapper's Delight'
Summer, Donna 187
Sykes, Bill 30

Teardrop Explodes, the 30
techno 64, 186
Terry, Sonny 82, 87
Tharpe, Sister Rosetta 82
Thatcher, Margaret 20–21, 33, 158, 163, 175, 182
Thomas, Dan 42
Thompson, Jeff 38
*Threads* (television drama) 63, 122
Trafford Park, Manchester 20
Trident Studio, London 110
Trigga 203–205
'Tunes Splits the Atom' (MC Tunes) 177, 185–86
Twisted Wheel, the (Manchester club) 28–29, 77, 86
Tyler, Imogen 135, 140, 147, 149
    *Revolting Subjects* 135, 147–48

Un-Convention 37–54
    global events 37, 49–50
    internationalization 49–51
    launch 44
    origins of 42
    representing Manchester 38
UNESCO Creative Cities Network 17
United States 8th Airforce 26

Vaughan, Sarah 89
Victoria and Albert Museum 107
    *David Bowie Is* 108
'Video Killed the Radio Star' 176
Visconti, Tony 101

Wah! Heat 30
Wakefield 130
Wakeman, Rick 102
Walker, T-Bone 87
Walmsley, Howard 175, 179
Warp 57, 63–64
Waters, Muddy 77, 82–86, 88–90, *91*
Wayne, Mick 101
Westwood 168–69
White, Josh 77, 80–83, 85, 87–88
Whittaker, John 23
Who, The 104
Wiley 191, 203, 207
Williamson, Big Joe 88
Williamson, Jason 136–37, 139–42, 144, 150
Williamson, Sonny Boy II 88–90
Wilson, Greg 157–58, 160
Wilson, Tony 2–4, 6–7, 12, 25, 27–28, 31, 33, 41, 45, 49, 156, 178 *see also* Haçienda, the
Winterbottom, Michael 2 *see also 24 Hour Party People*
Womersley, J. L 58–60
Woodmansey, 'Woody' 101–103, 105

Yes 176
York 7

*Ziggy Stardust and the Spiders from Mars* 10
Zoo Records 31
ZTT 12, 175–79, 184, 189

www.ingramcontent.com/pod-product-compliance
Lightning Source LLC
Chambersburg PA
CBHW071842230426
43671CB00012B/2038